The Culture
of Bureaucracy

The Culture
of Bureaucracy

Edited by
Charles Peters
and
Michael Nelson

Holt, Rinehart and Winston
*New York   Chicago   San Francisco   Dallas
Montreal   Toronto   London   Sydney*

Library of Congress Cataloging in Publication Data

Main entry under title:

The Culture of bureaucracy.

  Articles from the Washington monthly.
  Includes bibliographical references.
  1. Administrative agencies—United States—Addresses,
essays, lectures. 2. United States—Executive
departments—Addresses, essays, lectures. 3. Bureaucracy—Addresses, essays, lectures. I. Peters,
Charles, 1926–   II. Nelson, Michael.
JK421.C82   320.9'73'092   78-11051

ISBN 0-03-044216-8

Articles on the following pages are reprinted from the *Washington Monthly,* copyright holder: p. 76, © 1969; pp. 8, 37, 146,
181, 217, © 1971; pp. 70, 97, 110, 118, © 1972; p. 79, © 1974;
pp. 4, 140, 251, © 1975; pp. 11, 58, 65, 88, 188, 238, 256, 263,
276, © 1976; pp. 15, 43, 156, 164, 171, 193, 199, © 1977; pp.
268, 271, © 1978. Article on p. 132 © 1977 by Yale University
Press.

Published 1979 by Holt, Rinehart and Winston
All rights reserved
Printed in the United States of America
9 0 1 2   0 9 0   9 8 7 6 5 4 3 2 1

PREFACE

The United States may be the only nation in history whose intended plan of government can be read in the map of its capital city. "The community plan for Washington," writes James Sterling Young in his fascinating study of *The Washington Community, 1800–1828,* "is . . . the most eloquent on record about the kind of government that was envisaged and desired by the pioneer politicians whose job it was to rule the new nation."

Professor Young shows that as one of the purposes of the planners was to express physically the Constitution's separation of powers, the Capitol and the White House were "separated by a considerable distance, and situated as to command different aspects, avoiding mutual confrontation." The idea that Washington's sole reason for being was to represent the rest of the country was displayed in the wide avenues that radiate out from the city in all directions, symbolically inviting citizens to come and be heard. No space was left for the construction of productive enterprises: As constitutional government was to rest in the consent of the governed, so would Washington survive as a city only through the financial contributions of the governed.

Not surprisingly, the plan of the city was somewhat hazy about where the executive departments were to be housed. Vice President John Adams, who served as President of the Senate, had wanted them near Congress; President George Washington argued that they should be close to the White House, where the President could administer them conveniently. (Another reason, Washington explained, was that during the government's residence in Philadelphia, "the universal complaint of [the departmental secretaries was that] while the legislature was in session, they could do little or no business, so much were they interrupted by the individual visits of members" of Congress.) This haziness accurately reflected the Constitution's own failure to specify what the role of bureaucratic agencies in the new government was to be.

A modern map of Washington bears a strong resemblance to the community plan of two centuries ago. But the similarities are largely superficial. In the automotive age, for example, avenues that once seemed wide are now quite congested, and though Washington's matrix of lettered and numbered streets gives the illusion of logical order, it is a rare visitor who does not find himself lost in what seems to be a maze. And while the White House and Capitol still sit prominently at a comfortable distance from each other, the areas between and around them are now dominated by the dozens of massive government buildings that presently house the bureaucracy.

These are subtle changes, not of a kind that maps easily can show. So are the changes in our practice of government that they reflect. Government is more self-contained and immune from popular understanding—as Washington city is—than it ever has been. There are many reasons for this, but the most important is also the most obvious: the rise of bureaucratic size and power in our society. And though civics books and the popular press tell us a great deal about how citizens can and do influence the actions of the 435 representatives, 100 senators, president, and vice-president (the only elected people in Washington), they tell us little or nothing about what the hundreds of thousands of unelected government officials do, or about why they are not responsible to the citizenry.

This is a void *The Washington Monthly* has attempted to fill. We have tried to do so by looking at the bureaucrat the same way an anthropologist would look at the natives of an island in the South Pacific. What kind of people are they? What are their attitudes and values, their customs, their rituals? To what extent does the culture of bureaucracy determine what the government does or does not do? What is life like for the bureaucrat? And, what, consequently is life like for the rest of us?

The most important purpose of *The Washington Monthly* in the decade since its creation has been to "Let the outside in," to show people outside Washington how the bureaucracy really works and how they can make it work for them. We thank the writers represented in this collection who have made it possible for us to do so.

Charles Peters
Michael Nelson
August 1978

CONTENTS

part1
THE NATURE OF BUREAUCRACY

The growth of government bureaucracies both in size and power has been a worldwide phenomenon. Yet, as James Q. Wilson has noted, "the shift of power toward the bureaucracy was not inevitable. . . . Before the second decade of this century, there was no federal bureaucracy wielding substantial discretionary power (in the United States). That we have one now is the result of political decisions made by elected representatives."[1] This draws our attention to the fundamentally *political* roots and nature of bureaucracy.

The articles by Robert Samuelson, James Clark, and Charles Peters make some basic points about the process of bureaucratic ascension in a tongue-in-cheek way. Frequently administrative agencies and policies are created by elected representatives in a hasty and even thoughtless manner. A problem arises, a crisis occurs, a response is demanded. The President goes on television with a plan of action, Congress quickly approves it, perhaps with some alterations, and then political leaders and the public-at-large go back about their business. But the new agency or program is still there, often at a loss as to what comes next. Thus, as Samuelson shows in "A Guaranteed Income for Consultants," did a throwaway line about "inflation impact statements" in a speech that Gerald Ford gave during the height of double-digit inflation in

---

[1]"The Rise of the Bureaucratic State," in Nathan Glazer and Irving Kristol, eds., *The American Commonwealth, 1976* (New York: Basic Books, 1976), pp. 102–103.

1

1974 ripple out through the executive branch in a way that involved bureaucrats' time, consultants' services, and taxpayers' dollars for little or no reason. The various energy agencies, though less frivolous in purpose, were created with similar haste after the Arab oil embargo in 1973.

Once born, bureaucratic agencies and programs are not easily done away with, as Clark learned from his whimsical study of "The International Screw Thread Commission," a "temporary" organization created in 1918 to aid the war effort (The World War *One* effort!). The Screw Thread Commission is hardly atypical. Herbert Kaufman found that of 175 federal organizations that existed in 1923, 148 were still going strong fifty years later—a survival rate of 85 percent. Kaufman describes the consequences of a political system in which government organizations are all but immortal:

> Galvanizing administrative machinery made up of everlasting organizations would be a formidable task. Where time is unlimited, there is no sense of urgency; members of an organization assured of indefinite existence would probably be inclined to move at a much more leisurely pace than the rest of us can afford or tolerate. . . . Moreover, the incessant addition of organizations to the immortal band would surely multiply the interactions and "interfaces" in the system, increasing the number of clearances, reviews, and accommodations required for any action and augmenting the number of potential vetoes throughout the network. . . . Exerting political and managerial influence on such a system would present a staggering challenge.[2]

How do agencies endure? One "offensive" strategy they often use is to see to it that it is in the interests of their relevant publics, especially in Congress and the private sector, to keep them alive. This strategy and its consequences are taken up at length in Part IV. But agencies also develop "defensive" tactics to fend off efforts to eliminate them or even trim their budgets. One such tactic is "The Firemen First Principle." "The very first thing Clever Bureaucrat does when threatened with a budget reduction," writes Peters, "is to translate it into specific bad news for congressmen powerful enough to restore his budget to its usual plenitude." Politics may be the wellspring of bureaucracy, but bureaucracy is the source of a great deal of politics as well.

So far we have been talking only about the growth of government agencies. But once created, these agencies bring the process around full circle by spawning new organizations in the private sector whose purpose is to influence, advise, or interpret the actions of bureaucracy. As

[2]*Are Government Organizations Immortal?* (Washington, D.C.: Brookings Institution, 1976), pp. 1–2.

Nicholas Lemann argues in "The Other Washington: Attorneys, Accountants, and Associations," this spawning process promises not only to alter America's political system, but its social and economic life too.

Bureaucracy, then, is large, powerful, enduring, and pervasive. But what is it like, other than self-interested? Max Weber argued that in theory bureaucracy is technically superior to other forms of organization in modern society because of its "precision, lack of equivocation, knowledge of the documentary record, continuity, sense of discretion, uniformity of operation, system of subordination, and reduction of frictions."[3] Above all, bureaucracy is rational.

But what seems so good in theory has not always worked out that well in practice. For example, William and Elizabeth Paddock ("So Hard to Remember, So Easy to Forget") found *im*precision, *ignorance* of the documentary record, and *dis*continuity in Central American agricultural programs administered by the U.S. Agency for International Development. Though good news from the field traveled quickly up the bureaucratic ladder of authority, they learned, bad news frequently did not. The extent to which the latter—no less necessary for being unpleasant—was suppressed is evident in the fact that the programs the Paddocks chose to study had been recommended to them by government officials, diplomats, and others as AID's *most* successful efforts.

Nor does bureaucracy always act rationally. The idea of the model program, for example, is a sound one—if its lessons are applied when the policy goes full scale. But as Eric Lax shows in "Nothing Fails Like Success," it does not always work out that way. For a prisoner rehabilitation program at New York's Riker's Island, failure became the prerequisite for continued existence; when it succeeded, all was lost.

Finally, bureaucracy does not seem to provide "reduction of friction" to many of the citizens who deal with it. Michael Nelson learned from extensive discussions with citizens from three towns and cities that "people of all classes felt that their treatment (by government agencies) had been bungled, not efficient; unpredictable and bizarre, not rational; discriminatory or idiosyncratic, not uniform; and all too often, insensitive or downright insulting rather than courteous." As indicated by the title of his article, "Bureaucracy: The Biggest Crisis of All," the seriousness of the problems posed by bureaucracy is in direct proportion to its increasing pervasiveness in American society.

[3]Reinhard Bendix, *Max Weber: An Intellectual Portrait* (Garden City, N.Y.: Doubleday Anchor Books, 1962), p. 426.

Guaranteed Annual Income For Consultants

Robert Samuelson

Hereafter, I will require that all major legislative proposals, regulations, and rules emanating from the Executive Branch of the Government will include an Inflation Impact Statement that certifies we have carefully weighed the effect on the nation.
President Ford in his economic speech, October 8, 1974.

In my business—the news business—you either take advantage of other people's problems, or you're finished. You might as well hock your typewriter and hang up your green eyeshade.

That's how I came to hear Max's story. Max drifted into the office late one Thursday afternoon. He was a mess. There were deep trenches under his eyes, his hair had been combed by the wind, and his face bore the scars of a trembling razor. He was 30, but looked 45.

A man in Max's shape needs a drink. I rescued a cup from the trash and poured out the last of my scotch.

"I think I'm just about at the end of the line," Max said in a whisper.

It was late, and I was in no mood for self-indulgent melodrama. But, as I said, we get paid to listen.

"Why don't you tell me about it," I said, mustering what sympathy I could manage.

Max was a government lawyer, a GS-14 or GS-15—I forget which—working in the White House. I knew the type immediately: one of those earnest young men, confident of their own abilities, who had enlisted with Uncle Sam convinced that they could simultaneously satisfy their ambitions and their social conscience.

Max pointed towards his vinyl briefcase. I opened it and on top were two official documents. They had identical headings: "Inflation Impact Statements." The first was an Executive Order from the White House, dated November 27. The second was a memorandum from the Office of Management and Budget, dated January 28.

As I read the documents, their gist became clear. Each department and agency would prepare an "inflation impact statement" for all its major programs. They didn't really have to be followed—only prepared. It was sort of an institutional consciousness-raising exercise. Narrow-minded, agency-oriented bureaucrats would be made to see the wider implications of their actions. Advance public confession would curb sinning.

Max took off his aviator glasses and, with weary resignation, rubbed his eyes.

"There's a scandal here," he said, casually spilling out a phrase that's supposed to make any reporter salivate. I didn't because I figured that Max was either flattering himself or taking me for a sap. I hadn't been born yesterday, and I had seen cases like his before: a bureaucrat with an identity crisis, trying to cleanse his soul by running to the press.

But I let Max trace the dreary chronology. It started back in October when the President asked his speech-writers for some ideas about how to flesh out his anti-inflation address—you know, the one with the WIN buttons. Somebody remembered a memo with the idea for inflation impact statements, like those environmental things. The idea sounded attractive, looked respectable, and blended well with Republican anti-inflationary rhetoric. No one thought much about it. It was just one paragraph in the speech, and the President was scheduled to go on TV in just a few hours.

And these inflation impact statements did have cosmetic appeal. When it came to creating higher prices, I knew the government was a principal sinner. Across the federal landscape, it was a cinch to spot dozens of programs which helped push consumer prices upward. The Interstate Commerce Commission limited truck and railroad competition; that propped up freight rates. The Civil Aeronautics Board made it a crime for airlines to cut fares. The Davis-Bacon Act had the effect of requiring building contractors to use only high-cost union workers. Medicare and Medicaid procedures made Ross Perot a billionaire and contributed to spiraling health costs.

New horrors were being hatched daily, but I wasn't naive enough to think that analysis—no matter how it was labeled—would make much difference. Politics determined the fate of most government programs and regulations. Pieces of paper alone wouldn't change the political situation. Sure, the environmental impact statement said that the Alaska pipeline would make life miserable for the caribou, and that didn't end up preventing the pipeline from being built. Most bureaucrats knew what they were doing. If they went ahead with a controversial program, they usually had compelling reasons: pressure from important interest groups, their own sense of mission, or just an unmistakable mandate from Congress to do something that was blatantly inflationary. Analysis alone wouldn't eliminate these pressures.

I wasn't dismissing all analysis as useless, but my experience was that people only used information when it recommended what they wanted to do anyway. If it didn't, they'd just come up with some conflicting information, making just the opposite points. Such reports weren't hard to find. Somebody—a budget analyst at OMB or a congressional subcommittee or the faceless researchers at the GAO—would be encouraged to produce another study. If a program was popular enough—like the Alaska pipeline—all the analysis in the world was useless.

So, the inflation impact statements were an idea that looked good and sounded nice. But that's all. I didn't need Max to tell me this, especially when I still had hopes of getting out of the office in time to beat the rush-hour traffic. But he did anyway.

"You see this," he said, motioning toward the second of his official-looking documents. It was the one from OMB, and it carried the enticing title of Circular A-107. "It's the rules each governmental department is supposed to follow in drawing up its own rules for writing inflation impact statements. Nothing in government can be done without rules, so we have rules to write rules. The paperwork just expands geometrically. First, the President makes his proposal back in October. It's just one paragraph in a long speech. Then, two months later, the White House gets around to issuing an executive order on how to implement the paragraph. The executive order runs two pages."

He waved the first document at me, and I verified his arithmetic.

"Two months after that, OMB issues its circular explaining the executive order. That's four pages." He was a genius at numbers. "And that's just the beginning. Of the nearly 100 agencies which received Circular A-107, dozens responded by requesting exemptions. Do you have any idea how much paper is involved in the American Battle Monuments Administration requesting an exemption and OMB granting it?"

I didn't, but I was shrewd enough not to let on.

"OMB is still wading through the exemptions. And the departments that don't get them will then have to write up departmental regulations which will probably run 10 to 20 pages each. Multiply that by all the departments and agencies, and we've already got a mountain of pulp. And we haven't even gotten to the statements yet."

It was a familiar tale. Inflation would be forgotten, as everyone worried about coping with the nuisance and the nuances of the inflation impact statements. Most shrewd government lawyers would probably try to limit the number of statements their departments would have to produce by putting a ceiling—say, $50 million—on the kind of actions that required statements. But they had to be careful. The executive order, which didn't expire until the end of 1976, demanded statements, and anybody who didn't like what your agency was doing—for *whatever* reason—could take you to court on the pretext that your impact statement wasn't adequate. Suits meant delays. Like paperwork, they cost money and took time. In the end, the courts would probably support the agencies, but, even if they did, they still couldn't restore all the time and effort that fighting the suit required.

All this was pretty routine to somebody in my business. I didn't need Max in my office, drinking the last of my scotch, as the rush-hour traffic piled up eight floors below my single, sooty window. I had had enough. It was time to get home.

"That's all very interesting, Max," I said, "but what the hell does all that have to do with you?" And by implication—what the hell does all this have to do with me?

It took a while for Max to answer. And before he did, he stared at the scotch bottle a long time, as if somehow that would make it less empty. Finally, he got it out: "The whole thing was my idea, but I didn't realize that it would lead to this." To prove it, he reached into his vinyl briefcase and came out with a dog-eared xerox of a memo on White House stationery.

I didn't know what to say, so I just took the xerox and laid it softly on my desk, next to an empty Coke bottle. I knew what to expect next— a long monologue about guilt and responsibility, the sort of thing that people came to expect from Daniel Ellsberg on Vietnam.

But Max, to his credit, was made of sterner stuff. He came back to the point. "It wouldn't be so bad," he said, "but I know what's going to end up happening. You see, there are limits to honest analysis. You can safely say that something's inflationary, but you don't necessarily put a finger on it. But we demand that everything be precise, so these reports are going to be filled with a lot of dubious statistics."

I could tell that Max had learned a lot since his first days in the White House, when he wrote the memo that set everything in motion.

"What's going to happen," Max said, "is that a lot of the agencies won't be able to handle the extra work load and will have to farm it out. The consultants will have a field day. Each time an agency will have to produce an impact statement it'll mean an $80,000 fee for a consulting firm. Multiply that by a couple of thousand statements a year and you've added a couple of hundred million to the federal budget—all in the name of fighting inflation."

"You know what consultants remind me of?" Max asked suddenly. "Seagulls swarming around a mountain of garbage. Except in government it's all the studies, reports, and evaluations that somebody has said must be done, but nobody really gives a damn about."

Something about the seagulls and the garbage cheered up Max, because suddenly he looked relieved. I was glad, because I couldn't do much for him. "Look," I said, "there's no story here. This kind of stuff goes on everyday in government. But I will give you some free advice. Call in sick tomorrow. Take a few days off. The government won't collapse. Western civilization won't end."

I drove him home. He said he'd think about it.

The International Screw Thread Commission

Jim Clark

On May 31, 1918, the U.S. House of Representatives spent one hour debating the merits of a bill creating the Commission for the Standardization of Screw Threads. The legislation, sponsored by Representative John Tilson of Connecticut, was greeted with general indifference by the members, but there were a few questions. Several congressmen expressed fear that the screw people might be around longer, and cost more, than they were being assured was the case. At that very time, the Congress as a whole was harboring similar fears about World War I. But Tilson promised his colleagues that the commission would need less than one year to reach agreement on screw thread standards, which, he added, urgently required coordination so that the nuts and bolts of our battle weaponry would fit each other. Thus, the commission was designed not only to end itself quickly but also to help end the war. Besides, said Tilson, there would be no cost to the government, "not one red cent."

The Tilson bill received quick House approval and then was guided through the Senate by Senator Warren G. Harding. Harding ran into minor opposition from senators like Hitchcock of Nebraska, who observed, "I think it is very objectionable to create commissions. Congress has already created innumerable commissions, which, like Tennyson's brook, run on forever, even when their authority has ceased." Senator Harding promised his colleague that this commission would not last forever—in fact not for more than 60 days, because the war made hasty resolution of the nut and bolt question mandatory. Senator Harding put teeth into his promise right there on the floor by writing a 60-day limit to the commission's lifespan into the bill.

A House-Senate conference committee worked out the differences between the two versions of the bill and finally created a nine-member commission with authority to work six months.

Although World War I ended without standardized screw threads, or even a report from the commission, Congress gave the group three more years of existence on March 3, 1919. That was a big year, as the members made their first trip to Europe to discuss screw standards with appropriate officials from other countries. Travel and staff expenses were contributed indirectly by the federal agencies which "lent" full time employees to staff the commission. The art of producing the screw thread budget from crisscrossing, countersigned memo-vouchers was so occult as to limit the players in the commission field to skilled bureaucrats. Technically, this particular group received no direct appropriations and therefore no government money, but the bills were paid.

On January 16, 1922, John Tilson reappeared to ask the House to extend the commission for another five years. He announced proudly that the screw thread deliberators had just turned out their first "tentative report." One recalcitrant congressman asked Tilson to "give some good reason why any such extension should be granted to a commission which was organized during the war and which we were told would be able to wind up and standardize most of the matters on which it was working in a very short time." He suggested with sarcasm that perhaps the commission should be appointed for life. Tilson admitted that perhaps it should.

In fact, Tilson did request that the screw thread standardizers be made permanent, in February, 1926. In the debate, Tilson put forth the old enlightened self-denial theory of public finance: "If there is nothing to be done, it will simply sleep."

The commission was perhaps sleeping, but its active metabolism required some sustenance nevertheless. This nourishment was provided according to the first rule of government—that the public employee looks after himself first and his program later, although both concerns are said to serve the public interest (especially in times of high unemployment). The screw thread commission consumed approximately $150,000 during its first eight years of existence, although Tilson, a literalist, repeated that the group had done "great work" at no expense to the taxpayer.

The Congress passed the permanence legislation, and John Tilson left the House in 1932 confident that his commission would live forever. In an Executive Order in 1933, however, President Roosevelt ordered the screw thread body abolished. To anyone not familiar with the U.S. government, this would appear to be the end of the story. Of course, it is not.

Coming out of the throes of the Depression, former screw thread staffers realized that they had never really depended upon Congress for anything other than a kind of official seal of authority. The operating funds had always come from subterranean sources in the form of borrowed employees and miscellaneous contributions from the participating agencies, anyway. Congress was in effect superfluous. So in 1939, the departments represented on the original commission—Commerce, War, Army, and Navy—set up the Interdepartmental Screw Thread Committee, reassembled the staff, and were back in business. Utilizing a boost in prestige during World War II, the committee formed an alliance with screw thread people from about two dozen other countries and created the International Screw Threads Standards Commission.

In 1966, the committee's executive secretary, Irwin Fullmer, retired after 47 years on the job.

In recent years, the government's support for screw thread standardization efforts has fallen from about $500,000 to $250,000 a year. After spending an estimated $5 million wrestling with the problem over the last half century, the screw thread people are definitely cutting back a little. But there are still three international meetings to attend each year. At the latest, the U.S. learned that the Russians had switched to our standards.

On May 31, 1971, 53 years after the House of Representatives gave squeamish birth to the Commission for the Standardization of Screw Threads, Arthur Strang was in Europe for an international meeting of the standard setters. He is chairman of the commission that will not die —one of thousands in the government, which, like crab grass and sewer leaks, spring up irrepressibly everywhere despite efforts to cut off their water. Commissions have the numbers and tenacity that American entrepreneurs once were blessed with—as the old fighting spirit has passed into commissions, which occupy the growing gelatin zone of government. As entrepreneurs of parasitism, the commissions have a bright future, because no one cares as much about cutting each paltry little budget as the members care about seeing them survive. A flowering is therefore assured, and it seems like a good idea for everyone. Although the screw thread committee is a bit crowded, there are still a lot of spots left elsewhere.

Firemen First or How to Beat a Budget Cut

Charles Peters

Since parsimony is becoming almost as fashionable among politicians today as patriotism was in the 1940s, a wave of budget-cutting seems likely at all levels of government. The results could be salutary, but might be disastrous. To avoid the latter possibility, it is essential to understand how the Clever Bureaucrat reacts to the threat of fiscal deprivation.

The very first thing C.B. does, when threatened with a budget reduction, is to translate it into specific bad news for congressmen powerful enough to restore his budget to its usual plenitude.

Thus Amtrak, threatened in early 1976 with a budget cut, immediately announced, according to Stephen Aug of *The Washington Star*, that it would be compelled to drop the following routes:

San Francisco-Bakersfield, running through Stockton, the home town of Rep. John J. McFall, chairman of the House Appropriations transportation subcommittee.

St. Louis-Laredo, running through Little Rock, Arkansas, the home of Senator John McClellan, chairman of the Senate Appropriations Committee.

Chicago-Seattle, running through the homes of Senator Mike Mansfield, Senate Majority Leader, and Senator Warren Magnuson, chairman of the Senate Commerce Committee.

And in a triumphant stroke that netted four birds with one roadbed, Norfolk-Chicago, running through the home states of Senator Birch Bayh, chairman of the Senate Appropriations Transportation subcommittee, Senator Vance Hartke, chairman of the Commerce Surface Transportation Subcommittee, Rep. Harley Staggers, chairman of the House Commerce Committee, and Senator Robert Byrd, Senate Majority Whip.

The effectiveness of this device is suggested by a story that appeared in the *Charleston* (West Virginia) *Gazette* a few days after Amtrak's announcement:

Continued
Rail Service
Byrd's Aim

"Senator Robert C. Byrd, D-WVa, has announced that he intends to make an effort today to assure continued rail passenger service for West Virginia.

"Byrd, a member of the Senate Appropriations Committee, said he will 'either introduce an amendment providing sufficient funds to continue the West Virginia route or try to get language adopted which would guarantee funding for the route of Amtrak.'"

In the Amtrak case, C.B.'s budget-cutting enemy was President Ford. Sometimes it is a frugal superior in his own department. C.B.'s initial response is much the same. If, for example, a Secretary of Defense from Massachusetts insists upon eliminating useless and outmoded bases, the Navy's C.B. will promptly respond with a list of recommended base-closings, led by the Boston Navy Yard.

ANOTHER BAY OF PIGS

An irate constituency is, of course, a threat to all elected officials and to every other official who dreams of converting his appointive status into one blessed by the voting public. Even a small irritation can suffice. Thus, Mike Causey of *The Washington Post* tells of a National Park Service C.B. who, confronted with a budget cut, quickly restored congressmen to their senses by eliminating elevator service to the top of the Washington Monument. Every constituent whose children insisted on his walking all the way up was sure to place an outraged call to his congressman's office. Similarly, a Social Security Administration C.B. faced with a budget cut is certain to announce that the result will be substantial delays in the mailing of social security checks.

Whenever possible, a C.B. will assert that the budget cut is certain to result in the loss of jobs. The threatened employees are sure to write emotional protests to their congressmen. And, as the National Rifle Association has proven, even a tiny minority, if sufficiently vigorous in its expression of opinion—vigorous meaning that they make clear they will vote against you if you fail to help them—can move a legislator to take the desired action in the absence of an equally energetic lobby on the other side.

C.B.'s concern about loss of others' jobs is a deeply personal one. He knows you can't be a commander unless you have troops to command.

Not long ago Jack Anderson discovered that the Navy, trying to adjust to less money than it had requested, was depriving the fleet of essential maintenance, while continuing to waste billions on useless supercarriers and transforming small Polaris submarines into giant Tridents. The reason of course is that the more big ships with big crews we have, the more admirals we need. Rank in the civil service is also determined in part by the number of employees one supervises. Thus a threat to reduce the number of one's employees is a threat not merely to one's ego but to one's income as well.

In its first flush of victory after the 1960 election, the Kennedy Administration embarked on two ill-fated missions. One was the Bay of Pigs. The other was an effort to fire 150 AID employees, all of whom wrote their congressman, as did their fathers, mothers, brothers, sisters, and in all probability their creditors and the creditors' relatives. The 150 were, of course, reinstated.

On the other hand, there are public employees we don't want to fire —teachers in the public schools, for example, where teacher-pupil ratios of 1 to 40 are common. These are the ones C.B. always says he will have to fire when he is menaced with a budget cut. This tactic is based on the principle that the public will support C.B.'s valiant fight against the budget reduction only if essential services are endangered. Thus, C.B. always picks on teachers, policemen, firemen first. In the headquarters bureaucracies of the New York City and the Washington, D.C. school systems there are concentrated some of the most prodigious, do-nothing, time-servers of the modern era. No administrator threatens to fire them. If they are "the fat," and if he is to fight the budget cut, it would of course damage his cause to admit their existence. He must concentrate on threatening a loss of muscle.

Similarly, the Army, when faced with a budget cut, never points the finger at desk-bound lieutenant colonels. The victims are invariably combat troops. This is particularly unfortunate, since in government, as in human beings, fat tends to concentrate at the middle levels, where planning analysts and deputy assistant administrators spend their days attending meetings, writing memoranda, and reading newspapers.

Sometimes, however, the C.B. will be deliberately non-specific about the jobs that might be cut. When the City Council of the District of Columbia recently proposed a $67.2-million cut in the city's budget, Mayor Washington responded with an announcement that he would have to fire 4,000 city employees, but with no indication of exactly where the axe would fall. This tactic is designed to arouse all city employees who don't want to be among the 4,000—which of course means *all* city employees—to write the City Council protesting the outrageous cuts.

Another approach, which might be called "How Can You Guys Be Such Scrooges," was tried on the Council by Joseph Yeldell, the director of the city's Human Resources Administration, who proclaimed that yes, he knew exactly what the budget cut would do to his department, it would mean the cancellation of the foster parents program for 2,000 orphans.

But such appeals are guaranteed to work only during the Christmas season. The more reliable year-round tactic is to threaten the loss of essential services that affect almost all voters.

John Lindsay was a master of this technique. Confronted, for example, with a 1971-72 budget of only $8.6 billion, he said he would have to fire 10,000 policemen, 2,500 firemen, 3,600 garbage workers, 12,000 hospital workers, and 10,800 teachers.

In the end, he didn't have to fire anyone. Abe Beame was not so lucky. He threatened to fire 67,000 similarly essential employees, and—when the bastards actually cut his budget—found that he really had to drop 35,000.

There's the rub. If we really cut the budget of the C.B. who has bluffed by saying that he will have to fire essential employees, he may —to preserve his credibility—actually have to fire them, instead of the middle-level newspaper-readers who are the real fat. Consider what happened to the New York City Parks Department after it was forced to cut back. According to Donald Singleton of the *New York Daily News*, it became "so short of basic manpower, so top-heavy with supervisory and administrative officials . . . that it all but abandoned most of the city's 1,400 public parks to armies of drunks, junkies, and juvenile delinquents." Singleton compared the vacancy rates for supervisors and workers: For five categories of supervisory positions paying from $17,-000 to $25,000, the vacancy rates were, respectively, 22, 15, 13, 12, and 0 per cent (the 0 was for the $25,000-a-year jobs). For the workers, the attendants, the laborers, the gardeners, the pruners and cutters, and the custodians, the vacancy rates were 92, 57, 53, 31, and 93 per cent.

If we continue to let the Clever Bureaucrats of this world take charge, we could end up with a government of planning analysts, friends of congressmen, and trains running to Bakersfield via Stockton.

The Other Washington: Attorneys, Accountants, and Associations

Nicholas Lemann

Living in Washington, D.C. today, there is an exhilarating sense of being at a crucial juncture of history, one of those points where various factors can combine to push a city over the line of greatness. San Francisco must have been like this in 1849, and Chicago in 1880—there's a feeling of limitless possibility, of gold lying in the streets, of fortunes to be made by one and all. Historical moments like this come about when a city's economic potential expands dramatically as some great resource is discovered, like gold in San Francisco or railroads in Chicago. Usually these resources bring about a tremendous stimulation of the capitalist process as it's usually defined—goods or services are made available for which there's considerable public demand—but in Washington it's different, and even better as far as the city is concerned. The root of the boom is the federal government, which, because it's not subject to the usual dictates of supply and demand, may never stop growing. The autumnal air of faded grandeur that eventually settles over most cities may never come to Washington.

Half of this boom—the growth of the government itself, and the enrichment of its own employees—is fairly well known, but the other half isn't. The federal government has also done wonders for its state and local sisters and, most importantly, for private enterprise. During the 1960s, as the government's money, scope, and power grew, a mistrust of the bureaucracy by liberals and conservatives alike led to more and more work being farmed out to smaller jurisdictions and to experts. Thus while in the last 20 years the federal budget has more than quintupled, the number of civil servants has remained relatively constant; the increase has been in what is contracted out. The federal government now pays $60 billion a year to private contractors of one kind or another and another $50 billion to state and local governments and non-profit institutions.

Perhaps even more important, the growth of the government's regulatory power has so excited and alarmed the general populace that vast and increasing sums are being spent to fight, wheedle, cajole, and observe various federal agencies. The government doesn't pay for this secondary growth, but it is certainly the cause of it. The consulting firm that tells corporations how to avoid new regulations is no less a beneficiary of big government than the consulting firm that tells agencies what regulations to draw up in the first place—in fact, most consulting firms do both.

There's no more visible sign of the government-spinoff boom than the architecture of downtown Washington. The southern end of Washington is full of mammoth government office buildings that house the various departments and agencies. Directly north of them is an old downtown area that, like downtowns in most eastern seaboard cities, is dominated by large retail establishments and has seen better days. Thirty years ago, when this retail area was in its prime, most of Washington (besides it and the government buildings) was just houses.

In the last 20 years, however, the area immediately west of the old downtown, comprising about 25 good-sized city blocks, has been completely transformed, its houses torn down and office buildings erected in their place. Because of zoning laws that place an absolute limit on height but allow a generous ratio of building size to lot size, these buildings all look the same—big and box-like, 11 or 12 stories high. Because they were all built over a fairly short span of time, they're all in the same concrete-and-glass architectural style.

A newcomer to Washington might assume that these buildings house various parts of the ever-expanding government, but in fact that's not the case. The government occupies some space in the new downtown, but the great majority of its expansion has been in the suburbs, because the new downtown is too expensive. The General Services Administration, which rents the government's office space, has a rent ceiling of about $7.50 per square foot; in the new downtown it's hard to find anything for less than $8 per square foot, and the newer buildings go as high as $12.75. Nobody but private enterprises can afford the space, but the occupancy rate would make a real estate developer in New York or Atlanta seethe with envy.

Ever since about 1960 these buildings have gone up at a rapid pace, interrupted only by the recession of the early 70s, when Washington's builders found that in a surge of optimism they had overbuilt and were stuck with empty office space. However, while in most cities the real estate market is only just starting to recover from that crushing blow, Washington has righted itself quickly. By 1975 the building boom had resumed with a renewed fervor; in that year, developers put on the market three million square feet of new downtown office space, which by past standards would have been considered a four-year supply of space. That much building was a risk, but the developers (and their investors) had good reason to be confident and were prepared to take it.

A SINGLE HUGE STRUCTURE

Of the ten big office buildings going up in downtown Washington that year, the biggest was 1800 M Street, which at 500,000 square feet was more than twice the size of its closest competitor. Its developer, the Oliver T. Carr Company, originally intended to put up two buildings on the lot instead of one, but the Equitable Life Assurance Society, which financed the project and owns the building today, suggested that there might be more long-term profit in a single huge structure.

Construction of the building began in June of 1973, and four months later Carr put up a temporary two-story leasing office on the site in order to begin selling space. It also printed up a glossy brochure and took out some newspaper ads. The brochure, which was written in free verse and had on its cover the building's semi-abstract logo, which looked like a Franz Kline painting, began like this:

"We would like to tell you about an office that we're planning for you.
It is not what you are expecting.
It is quite a bit more.
Quite a bit different.
Quite exciting.
'Office' probably isn't even an adequate description.
Let us explain."

What "quite a bit more" meant was that one didn't make a buck in downtown Washington real estate by aiming at economy-minded clients. It's a class market, so 1800 M was to be a class building. The architect was Byron Black of Weihe, Black, Jeffries, and Strassman, which along with Vlastimil Koubek is one of the Big Two firms for Washington office building design. Black designed the building to look like two buildings separated by an interior courtyard. At the corner of 18th and M the building notches inward, creating a second open space. Inside, there are six high-speed elevators in each half of the building, near-invisible air-conditioning vents, recessed lighting, and wall-to-wall carpeting and modern art lithographs in the hallways. As the brochure pointed out, the building is in close proximity to "luncheons at the finest restaurants" and has three levels of interior parking. Major tenants could design their own interiors. At $9 a square foot, it was one of the best deals around. Although the Carr Company feared that the building's size would scare tenants off—everybody likes to look like he occupies major space in his building to impress clients—by the end of 1976 1800 M was 98 per cent full. The leasing took 18 months, three times longer than is usual for an office building, but it will be worth it in the long run.

THE THREE A'S

The chief market for Washington office space is what's known as the three As—accountants, associations, and attorneys. Sure enough, 1800 M's first tenant (and, at 56,000 square feet, its largest) was an accounting firm, Coopers and Lybrand, which in February 1974 signed a ten-year lease with Carr. Coopers and Lybrand is the world's largest accountant, with 300 offices and 19,000 employees, 7,000 of whom work in the company's 80 United States offices. Annual revenues are $450 million. In the general Coopers and Lybrand scheme, the Washington office is not a big deal.

But it's becoming bigger. Construction crews are encamped in Coopers and Lybrand's hallway, spoiling the view of the long leather couches and white rugs in the reception area; they're renovating some additional office space to house Norman Auerbach, the company's New York managing partner, who's found he has to spend a couple of days a week in Washington. The Washington managing partner, John Silton, has just signed on for some additional space in the building, and says he thinks Washington will be one of the company's big offices in a few years.

Like everybody else in 1800 M, Coopers and Lybrand is a beneficiary of the Washington boom; like all the other tenants, 15 years ago it wouldn't have thought about occupying the kind of space it now occupies. From the 1920s to the early 60s, the office had four or five employees and was essentially an adjunct to Coopers and Lybrand's Baltimore office that dealt with the Internal Revenue Service. It did no actual accounting work. In 1964 the Washington office split from Baltimore and grew to 12 people. By the early 70s its quarters in a building at 1100 Connecticut Avenue were getting awfully cramped and it hired a real estate consultant who led it to 1800 M Street. Two hundred and forty people work in the office now, not counting the people who are moving in from New York.

The office has grown nearly 5,000 per cent in 15 years chiefly because of the government. The IRS kept amending the tax code, and the Securities and Exchange Commission made *its* regulations vastly more complex, and Coopers and Lybrand realized that it needed a staff of people to monitor and interpret changes in the law that would affect its clients' bookkeeping. The same complexity that caused that growth also gave rise to research firms and trade associations that interpreted regulations for their own clients, and these firms needed accounting services—so Coopers and Lybrand expanded its services again. Pretty soon the government's regulations began to get so complicated that *it* couldn't understand what was going on in the tax, securities, and bookkeeping fields—so it started to hire consultants who did understand, Coopers and Lybrand among them. Half the firm's Washington business is now for the government. Other companies began to contract with the government too, and soon government contracting got so complicated that Coopers and Lybrand set up a branch to advise companies on the accounting aspects of that.

Then, seeing what a tangled web it was creating in the accounting field, the government started to think about regulating accountants, so Coopers and Lybrand had to worry about keeping an eye on those regulations and trying to influence them in a favorable direction (through testimony, not lobbying), which is why its New York managing partner is going to be spending time at 1800 M Street. "We get a lot of business from the vastness and complexity of government regulations," says Silton. "Every time the government redoes the tax code, in effect it increases our revenues, although as professionals we abhor the law." The company's Washington business, Silton says, can only increase as more kinds of financial reporting are required of business. The American Institute of Certified Public Accountants opened a growing Washington office four years ago. Arthur Andersen's president, Marvin Kapnik, is spending time in Washington regularly. Peat, Marwick, and Mitchell is moving next year to an expanded Washington office.

ELABORATE CLOAKS OF ANONYMITY

The second A, attorneys, provided 1800 M's second big tenant, the firm of Morgan, Lewis, and Bockius, which in July 1975 signed a five-year lease. Morgan, Lewis takes up two floors of the north half of the building, and its dark, lush, woody decor is in marked contrast to the white-carpet-and-chrome offices of the building's second-largest law firm, Shaw, Pittman, Potts, and Trowbridge, which has a ten-year lease on two floors over on the south side of the building. There are 13 law firms in all in 1800 M Street and about 160 lawyers working in them, which makes them the building's biggest genre of tenant. All the firms list themselves in the *Martindale-Hubbell* law directory as being specialists in practice before government agencies.

Most of the firms are hidden behind elaborate lawyerly cloaks of anonymity: they don't list their clients in *Martindale-Hubbell,* and they don't give interviews for fear of appearing to advertise. About a third are the Washington branches of big firms in Los Angeles, Chicago, Philadelphia, and other big cities, and handle the ever-growing government work of their clients back home. Some, like the Atlanta firm of Alston, Miller, and Gaines, which has a new office in 1800 M and just lost two partners to the new administration, may be trying to take advantage of a particularly favorable political climate. But most are Washington-based. Some are registered lobbyists. The dizzying range of a Washington law firm's activities is suggested, if only barely, by the building directory's listings of the organizations headquartered at one of 1800 M's firms:

Lane & Edson PC (for professional corporation, as opposed to partnership)

L & E, Inc.

National Association of Housing Managers and Owners

National Housing Rehabilitation Association

National Leased Housing Association

Potomac Institute Metropolitan Housing Program

Council of State Housing Agencies

The Institute for Professional and Executive Development Inc.

Committee for National Museum of the Building Arts

City of Baltimore Washington Office

"Clients use us as an address," says Bruce Lane, the firm's senior partner. "They're not big enough to maintain separate offices." The firm is seven years old and has a growing practice, largely in housing matters that involve the government—real estate law, tax law, securities law, federal housing law. Lane is a registered lobbyist who tries to influence legislation on tax breaks and other subsidies affecting the housing industry. Just a couple of months ago, Lane got his picture in *Fortune* for heading a coalition of low-cost housing lobbyists that got some tax shelters written into last year's tax reform act.

The law firms have their own association, of course—the American Bar Association, which has its Washington office at 1800 M Street. The ABA has been growing as fast as everybody else in the building. Fifteen years ago its Washington office handled only government relations and employed three or four people; now it rents 42,000 square feet for more than 100 employees, who cover a wide range of issues: one recent ABA newsletter discussed legal developments affecting judgeships, the criminal code, campaign reform, grand jury reform, consumer protection, and direct election of the President, among other things.

The growth, says Herbert Hoffman, director of the office, has come about because the ABA decided to cover a broader range of governmental issues, and because the government started doing more things that affect lawyers. Hoffman says the ABA does some things that affect lawyers' pocketbooks, but that it's mostly a public-interest organization, involved in making America "a better place to live, a better place to raise your kids." In the Washington office, he says, "I can't think of any purely trade issues. I can think of some that those who want to malign the legal profession say are trade issues. Take attorneys' fees. You could say lawyers want to be paid more—but lawyers have to eat too, and low pay can discourage people from taking on certain kinds of practice."

Indeed, Hoffman is right: on the ABA's terms, what it does is in the public interest. Its studies and its lobbying are built around the general goal of extending legal services to more people in America, which theoretically would be doing them a great favor. Thus the ABA is opposed to federal no-fault laws on the grounds that they deprive people of the right to representation. The ABA's stand on public-interest lawyers is pay them more so the public can have quality representation too. Mental health? The ABA wants to give the mentally ill the right to hire lawyers. Judicial salaries? Higher ones will improve the quality of American justice. If you believe that the more lawyers (and the better paid) the better, it's logic you can't argue with. And the ABA's public-interest aura is infinitely helpful in achieving its goals, now that lobbyists and special interests are in disrepute.

All the lawyers at 1800 M Street were an important factor in attracting another major tenant, National Economic Research Associates, a consulting firm that moved there, its office manager says, because "this is a prestige building, and there are people in this building like Morgan, Lewis and Shaw, Pittman who we're associated with and who we want to be associated with." NERA, as it's called, does a good deal of consulting for law firms, preparing supplementary studies for use in antitrust cases. NERA was founded 15 years ago in New York, but its Washington office has been growing by leaps and bounds. Ten years ago it employed three people, but now there are 56.

AN AWESOME RANGE

The third A, trade associations, is well represented in 1800 M Street, most prominently by the ABA, but by several others as well. Particularly intriguing is an organization called Hauck and Associates, which is in association *management* without being an association itself. Its potential range of activities is wide—it can serve as the office of a trade association and handle all its activities; it can be the Washington office for a trade association headquartered elsewhere; it can do one specific thing for an association, like monitor government regulations or publish a newsletter; or, in the case of an association that already has a Washington office, it can act as a consultant in association management, providing studies and advice. The awesome range of Hauck's potential activities has not yet been achieved because it's a new firm, founded in 1974. It moved to 1800 M in 1975 because its president, Sheldon Hauck, says the location was good and "this is a first-class office building. It helps attract employees. Clients like to come here—it sets a tone for their organizations."

Hauck started the firm after ten years in the association business and three years as a lawyer. After passing through the Pet Food Institute and the National Broom Council, among others, he decided to go into business for himself. So far he has four clients: three associations connected with the food business, and the brand-new International Discotheque Association. Hauck doesn't lobby, but he and his staff do keep up on and write up all federal regulations affecting their clients, which is a major task. They organize industry-wide conferences in the United States and abroad, and publish a vast array of public-relations documents. The future for Hauck Associates, again, looks bright. In the company's brochure, it lists the major trends in the association business over the next 25 years. Number one is this: "More regulation by the Federal Government seems inescapable."

Wandering through the well-appointed halls of 1800 M Street, a sameness sets in: dozens of blond-wood doors emblazoned with the names of firms and associations, which open to reveal deep-pile-carpeted reception areas. A few prints here, some potted plants there. In every office there seem to be bound copies of the federal code somewhere, and fresh copies of the *Congressional Record* and *Federal Register,* which someone is reading in order to keep up on the regulations affecting whoever the client happens to be. Back in a corner office is the boss, in a meeting or talking on the phone; in smaller offices flanking his there are younger people doing research and writing it up into reports. The dozens of associations, consultants, corporate lobbyists, and so on that fill up the rest of the building all fit this general pattern; listing them all would put you to sleep, but some of the noteworthy ones are these:

1) An organization called UBA, which used to stand for Unemployment Benefit Advisors but now doesn't stand for anything. UBA lobbies the government to keep down the degree of federal influence on unemployment benefits and workmen's compensation, preferring to leave them under the states' jurisdiction. Although UBA is a non-profit corporation that subsists on voluntary contributions, these contributions all appear to come from businesses that fear federal control over benefits programs will mean higher taxes for them.

2) The Washington office of American Medical International Inc., which defines itself as "an international health care services company." So far its office, which opened this year, has a staff of only six, but it's likely to do well: its field is "international government health care consulting," and it is headed by a former deputy assistant secretary of Defense for health, who ought to know his way around the government contracting offices.

3) The International Snowmobile Industry Association, which lobbies the government on issues affecting snowmobile manufacturers, of which there are plenty. The association, which was founded in 1965, wants safety standards its members can live with; land-use laws that allow snowmobiling on other people's property and on government parkland; fairly lax noise restrictions; and quite a few other things. In addition, it sets up industry-wide training programs and the like.

4) The Washington offices of a number of major corporations, including Union Camp, Burlington Industries, Dow Chemical, Marathon Oil, and A&P. These offices handle lobbying, monitoring of the government, and some polishing up of the company image—all, from the companies' standpoint, with good reason. Burlington expects to spend $25 million this year complying with government plant regulations. Union Camp has produced an elaborate Bicentennial message about "freedom," that is, the free enterprise system, which is fighting off the encroachments of "the central government." Anybody who reads business publications, or even the oil companies' newspaper ads, can see that the government is an obsession with every major corporation in America, and that obsession, whether or not it's justified, gives rise to amply budgeted Washington offices.

5) Golembe and Associates, a ten-year-old, $1.2-million-a-year con-
sulting firm that primarily advises banks and financial houses on internal fiscal planning. It emphasizes, its brochure says, "relationships with
legislative or regulatory bodies," particularly by monitoring legislation
and giving expert testimony before the government. Golembe also
publishes several periodicals and sponsors seminars for executives.

6) The Washington office of Barton-Marsteller, which calls itself "a
public relations/public affairs organization operating on a world-wide
scale." In its reception room, a UPI machine softly ticks out the news
of the world, while inside a dozen "government relations specialists"
work on "resolving problems at the national level." This apparently
means that they lobby or advise corporate executives about how to
lobby or testify themselves.

That seems vague, but vagueness is in long supply at 1800 M Street.
People are loath to say exactly what they do, in the way that a car
manufacturer might say, "I make cars"; they prefer to speak in broad
generalities about ranges of services. In going from office to office, I
could find only one small place that was involved in actually producing
some sort of goods for the consumption of the general public—a magazine called *Ladycom* that goes out to wives on military bases. Otherwise, everyone seemed to deal in expertise, advice, meetings, reports,
access. It occurred to me that it would be possible for a single company
to hire half the building simultaneously to provide one service or another—an oil company in Los Angeles, say, could have its government
relations office at 1800 M, its association, its association's consultant, its
L.A. lawyer's Washington office, its Washington lawyer, its Washington
lawyer's antitrust consultant, its public relations office, its own economic consultant, and so on. In all these offices people would be poring
through government regulations and then explaining them.

The standard moral judgment that is passed on this great web of
explainers that fills up 1800 M Street and the buildings like it is that they
may not be doing anything productive, but that's all the fault of big
government. If the government would mind its own business and not
make so many regulations, there would be no need for every productive
company to hire an array of unprotective companies for protection.

But, that is, at best, about half true. For one thing, the effects of the
government's power flow two ways: if regulations are costing some
companies money, other companies exist on subcontracted government business or on particularly favorable regulations. If the private
companies themselves are models of tough, streamlined efficiency, it's
curious that they spend so much of their money on soft services from
Washington, often supporting their various consultants in a manner far
grander than most of their own executives.

Judging from what's happening in downtown Washington, the traditional economic order is changing. It used to be assumed that the key to an economic system was production: those who owned property and controlled the means of production were the ones who got rich, and everybody else worked for them for somewhat less than the value they added to what was produced. While this makes perfect sense, it does seem now that the fastest growing sector of the economy is what might be called the non-productive sector, and that this sector, instead of being a mere adjunct to the process of producing goods, has enormous power itself. For all the flaws of old-fashioned capitalism, it's worth doffing our hats a moment at its passing, if only because it was centered around the late concept of productivity. Now, with the nation so vastly complex and so minutely regulated, the torch is passing from those who make things and sell them to those who can explain how it all works. The need for them appears to be limitless. Simply understanding our society has become the most valuable economic commodity.

Unlike raw materials, expertise is not something that gets depleted, and unlike consumer products it is not something for which demand dries up. Its future as an economic commodity in America is bright and secure—and by extension, the Washington building boom is continuing apace. I asked Philip Carr whether all the talk of cutting down and simplifying big government scared him, and he said, "This government's not going to get smaller. Jimmy's got a great idea, but you're not going to cut heads. This is a federal city. It's not going to get smaller. Tucson can get smaller. We can't. It might change, sure. We may be sitting here in five years and it won't be the three A's any more. It'll be the three B's or something."

The Carr Company is now building a complex of three buildings in downtown Washington, called International Square. Each of the three will be 400,000 square feet. Rents will start at $10.75 and go as high as $12.75. The complex will open in June, and it is already 65-per-cent leased. And downtown being about filled up by now, the company is further broadening its horizons. Philip Carr is very excited right now about an old, run-down area just west of downtown called the West End, where the company has been buying up acres of land. Like a frontiersman, which, in a way, he is, he gets a gleam in his eye when he talks about the West End. "That's virgin land out there," he says.

So Hard to Remember, So Easy to Forget

William and Elizabeth Paddock

In the 1940s the American people began a long journey that was to take them to the hungry nations of Asia, Africa, and Latin America. It became an emotional crusade involving the government, national foundations, church groups, universities, and scientists. Other "developed" countries one by one joined us in this crusade. The United Nations took up the cause, declaring the 1960s to be the "Decade of Development." The total cost to the American people to the beginning of 1971 was 100 billion tax dollars plus the money and energies of the many nongovernment organizations.

This enormous expenditure has been justified for many reasons, but the dominating motive has been the conviction that we "cannot live as an island of affluence in a sea of poverty," that if the world is to have peace it must be stable, and for the poor nations to achieve stability they must be "developed."

In the last few years enthusiasm for the crusade has flagged as the development of the poor nations seems, somehow, always to recede, no matter how much money is spent, no matter how many new ideas are put into operation. In fact, by now, the only people who remain enthusiastic seem to be those of the receiving countries (provided they get to spend the money, themselves, without strings), and the staffs of the massive (and firmly entrenched) development bureaucracies inside and outside the government. As for the stability of the world, seldom has it seemed more elusive. Fighting for it with the sword of development has come to seem rather futile and out of date.

Reprinted from *We Don't Know How* by William and Elizabeth Paddock © 1973 by The Iowa State University Press, Ames, Iowa 50010.

The authors, firm believers in the doctrines of development and long involved in the struggle, believed now was the right time for a report about foreign aid which would be not only optimistic but useful as a guide showing how a variety of development projects had indeed succeeded. We were thinking of more than a glorification of all those thousands of people who have given up the amenities of their homes and gone out to strike development sparks in the suffering areas of the world's hungry nations. We wanted to give an account of a dozen or more effective development programs in the hope that the lessons learned from them could be applied elsewhere.

With nothing more definite than this in mind we set out to find the most promising region (not a single country) in the world to study. We began by talking to government officials, businessmen, diplomats, foundation officers, directors of international agencies, missionary groups, and the like. We asked, "What area in the whole world of development can we visit in order to see the most optimistic case for foreign assistance, an optimistic case based on valid accomplishments already achieved, not on blueprints or future hopes?"

The almost universal consensus, at the end of 1967, was that we should go to Mexico and Central America. This was the area with the most promising growth statistics, the experts said, and the cause for this was largely aid from a number of different development organizations.

We asked key officials with both private and government development organizations to recommend their most effective programs in Mexico and Central America. We asked that they name programs that were at least three years old so we could see progress already accomplished, rather than progress hoped for. We wanted to visit and examine those specific programs which the administrators of development organizations themselves assured us were especially effective. It was important that the praise for the projects come from the men responsible for the planning and financing of them, rather than from the press or the people carrying out the work in the field.

We organized a list of "effective development projects" and traveled some 25,000 miles to inspect them. We not only held more than 200 prearranged interviews but talked with everybody in sight—government officials, scientists, merchants, peasants, laborers, doctors, and lawyers. Upon arrival at a project, our usual procedure was to be briefed by the officials in charge, who then would arrange our tour and go with us or send an aide to answer our questions in the field. Whenever possible, we returned alone to the project, so we could study it without official guidance. We wanted our study to be a genuinely independent audit.

The oddest thing came out of this research.

When we examined these projects in the field, we found they were not at all as described by the high officials back home (Peace Corps, AID, Inter-American Development Bank, and the rest). The projects were not necessarily ineffective; they were just different, sometimes unrecognizably so.

We do not question the sincerity of the officials who gave the recommendations, but certainly we now question the accuracy of the information fed back to them from the field. Always it is biased in favor of their programs. Always the reports are favorable. Journalists somehow never seem to write critical records of specific projects; perhaps it is because their studies are so often made on grants from the organizations being studied—or else they are hoping for grants for future studies. For the record, we financed this research trip ourselves, and thus were beholden to no organization.

CHOCOLA TREAT

An agricultural experiment station operated by the Guatemalan government is located at a town on the Pacific Coast called Chocola. This station was once the focus of a major U.S. effort to assist agriculture throughout this coastal area of Central America, and a lot of U.S. money went into it.

I had last visited Chocola in 1958 with Louis Franke, then head of the U.S. program for agriculture in Guatemala. He was about to be transferred to Argentina and was anxious to show me what he had accomplished before leaving Guatemala. "This is my major contribution," Franke said. He was rightly proud, for it was a beautiful experiment station.

Unlike most foreign aid administrators, Franke had brought to his job a good technical background and a lively interest in tropical farming. He knew that Guatemala's future depends on agriculture and he was able to convert this knowledge into action by getting the United States to put money into this station at Chocola and another at Barcenas.

At Chocola, a laboratory was built, followed by classrooms, dormitories, offices, a cafeteria, and so on—all with U.S. funds. Guest houses were constructed, and the station soon became a favorite spot for U.S. government personnel to visit.

Chocola was designed to become a major agricultural research center, concentrating on the problems of principal tropical commercial crops like coffee. It was also to be a training center offering short, practical courses to farmers and agricultural extension agents from all of Central America, so they could carry home with them updated knowledge of improved farming practices.

This preface will help explain why I was so pleased when Covey Oliver, assistant secretary for Inter-American Affairs in the Department of State, told me that one of the projects I should visit was an experiment station established with AID support at Los Brillantes, located near Chocola. I was doubly pleased because back in 1956 I had had a small hand in selecting Los Brillantes, from several possible sites, for a substation to augment the work at Chocola. Thus by visiting Los Brillantes, a project which Oliver indicated already shows "evidence of success or which [is] sufficiently well established so that a significant effect on development can be confidently predicted," I could also stop by and see Chocola.

Now, on this revisit to Guatemala's south coast, I could see at once a definite increase in cattle production. This seemed to jibe with a current policy in economic planning—namely, encouraging the developing countries to diversify their agriculture in order to alleviate dependence on a single crop—in the case of Guatemala, coffee. The planners say that such dependence makes a nation highly vulnerable to the vagaries of the international market and most governments have long tried to encourage the production of more kinds of crops.

But how to effect the diversification? That was the specific task assigned to Los Brillantes—a difficult one because theory and practice unfortunately are at odds.

CASHEWS AND ORANGES

Assistant Secretary Oliver had urged me to visit the experiment station at Los Brillantes precisely because it was effectively solving this difficult, complex problem; that is, it was finding crops into which Guatemalan farmers could diversify and still make money. With half of Guatemala's export earnings coming from one crop, he said, AID is keenly interested in helping Guatemala break the shackles of coffee dependency.

Oliver told me a great deal of progress had been made at Los Brillantes through the introduction of rubber and citrus as new crops. The station was supplying seedlings and advice on how to plant them, and AID was providing the loans needed to support this diversification. In addition, he said, research was moving ahead on other crops, such as black pepper, vanilla, cashews, allspice, mangos, tea and achiote.

At Los Brillantes, the first person I met was Raymond Stadelman, a man whose writings I have admired for so long I thought he must be dead. His *Maize Cultivation in Northwestern Guatemala* remains the classic background study on the agriculture of the highland Indians of Guatemala. Stadelman was now working here on rubber, and AID, according to Oliver, was greatly pleased with his progress.

Earlier, I knew, Los Brillantes had been kept busy for at least five years supplying rubber seedlings to Guatemalan farmers who had planted some 27,000 acres of rubber. Now, to my amazement, the place seemed dead. The reason, Stadelman explained, was that Guatemalan farmers were interested in planting rubber only as long as AID provided money on easy terms (such as a seven-year grace period before repayment begins).

When the loan money was used up (some loans were sizable: one farmer received $884,000) the station, once a beehive of projects, fell into the doldrums. With prices as low as they were, neither rubber nor citrus was sufficiently attractive to the farmer without the easy loan money.

Now Stadelman was working alone. Support from AID to the research station had been reduced solely to providing his salary. No one could have been less optimistic about the future of rubber cultivation in Guatemala than Stadelman himself. He was even less optimistic about the possibility of receiving the additional support needed to change the direction of this work or to revive it. I commiserated with him and left as he was preparing for a visit by Congressman Clarence Long of Maryland and Nathaniel Davis, the new U.S. ambassador to Guatemala. They would be arriving the next day for the same reason I had come—American officialdom had told them it considered this to be a good and thriving development project.

Why were the embassy and Washington continuing to send such visitors to see the "successful" AID program at Los Brillantes? Was it that they had not yet heard that the program had dried up?

BACK TO THE GRAVEYARD

From Los Brillantes I drove, for old times' sake, 30 minutes down the road to the station at Chocola. Superficially, it looked much as it had in 1958, except that the beautiful buildings were empty.

A second glance showed it to be a disaster area. Its staff consisted of a single agronomist, a Guatemalan, Efrain Humberto Reyna, who had the equivalent of a high school education in agriculture. With the help of only two field hands, he was trying desperately to manage this huge station. Never have I seen a harder working, more dedicated, or more lost soul. Poor fellow, he had literally nothing with which to work—no equipment, no help, and obviously, only hand-to-mouth money. He was puppy-dog happy to see me, as if I were the first visitor in 10 years. The whole station is presently funded, all from the Guatemalan government, the equivalent of $3,500 per year. Occasionally, Reyna is able to scrounge a little fertilizer from manufacturers. And that is his support.

And yet at the time of my visit, this was the one and only coffee research station in operation in all of Guatemala, a nation that still relies on coffee to pay for 36 percent of all its imports. The total effort of government research to find more economical ways to produce this crop, to combat diseases and pests, to solve harvest and processing problems rested on the shoulders of this one man.

The dormitories, which U.S. tax money had built, had last been used six months earlier when they housed eight students for six days. The last course prior to that had been held nine years ago.

It is painful to go on. The Chocola station is today a graveyard where the forgotten bones of this carefully planned major aid program have been left to rot. The chairs, typewriters, desks, furniture—even the microscopes and pH meters—are still there, stenciled with the letters S.C.I.D.A., the long-forgotten alphabet soup designation for the cooperative program that operated for a few years as a joint venture of AID's predecessor, the U.S. International Cooperation Administration (ICA), and the Guatemalan Ministry of Agriculture.

Incredibly, I found there was no cooperation, nor had there been for years, between Chocola and Los Brillantes a few miles away. These two agricultural stations were separated as if by the Great Wall of China. The reason for this, I learned, was that there had been some jurisdictional scuffling between the Guatemalan Ministry of Agriculture and AID. The result: neither worked with the other.

Chocola is an illustration of one tragic aspect of our development work: *AID has no memory.*

AID programs are constantly scrapped, abandoned, or started anew —or forgotten. Budgets are cut and then, as an alibi, Washington primly says it is time for the local government to "take over." The local government, however, usually has neither the money nor the talent (nor, sometimes, the interest) to take over. Thus another orphan program joins the graveyard.

New foreign aid directors arrive in the capital, sweep the decks clean, and begin anew. Back home a President is elected and his new foreign aid administrator also sweeps clean. No one takes the time to learn. What preceded? Did it fail? Did it succeed? Why?

A long-time AID friend says, "Every morning we wake up and laboriously reinvent the wheel."

COWS AND BUNNY RABBITS

Wherever the United States has a foreign aid program it has a staff that supervises the spending of its money, plans its use, and cajoles the local government into actions intended to make the money effective. The staff is called a "mission" and the man in charge is the "mission director."

Deane Hinton, U.S. AID mission director in Guatemala, was fresh from the National War College and recently decorated with a Superior Honor Award. Undoubtedly Hinton, whom I found to be a likable man, was highly regarded as an administrator at AID's Washington head-quarters.

Like AID mission directors around the globe, Hinton was filling an important post within the embassy structure. The AID director is generally the principal economic counselor to the ambassador. Although this was Hinton's first assignment in Latin America, he had served at several embassies in Europe and elsewhere, mainly as a political affairs officer. As is true of nearly all other AID mission directors, he had had no experience as a technician. Thus I was not surprised to learn that he knew little about agriculture even though this is the major economic business in Guatemala. But I was startled by the way he expressed it, although it was refreshingly honest.

"I don't know a cow from a bunny rabbit," he told me. "I'm a political economist."

I asked Hinton about how AID was performing in Guatemala. The answers he gave could have come from any of several other highly-regarded AID mission directors whom I have known.

> Paddock: What is the most effective AID program in Guatemala?
> Hinton: The agricultural school at Barcenas. We were able to convince the minister of agriculture that this agricultural school is important.
> Paddock: The director said he was having a problem placing some of the graduates. Of the 26 new graduates in forestry, not one of them has a job in sight.
> Hinton: I don't know about that.
> Paddock: I understand Barcenas includes the forestry school the U.S. government helped establish 10 years ago and later helped merge with the agricultural school there.
> Hinton: I don't know anything about that. You must remember that I have only been here 15 months. There is a lot about previous programs I don't know.
> Paddock: Is any money going into the experiment station at Barcenas?
> Hinton: What experiment station? There is no experiment station there in the sense any of us would think of one. It's a work farm for the Barcenas students. The farm is terribly run down, stupidly managed, and the United States has never helped it with funds.

Paddock: I don't mean the school's farm, I mean the experiment station. When I worked here in the 1950s this and the station at Chocola formed a major U.S. government effort. . . .

Hinton: I know nothing about it. I'm still learning. I have my hands full trying to keep track of what is going on today. I don't have the time to go through all the past records.

Paddock: What U.S.-supported project are Guatemala's officials most enthusiastic about?

Hinton: None. There is probably no one in the Guatemalan government who would be sorry about our leaving or even notice if we left tomorrow. I'm talking about projects. Loans are another matter. Everybody wants loans.

Paddock: I'm interested to know why you chose the Los Brillantes coastal experiment station and the nearby agricultural school at Barcenas as projects for the new ambassador to see on his first trip into the country last week, and also why you considered them worthy of inspection by Congressman Clarence Long, who went with him.

Hinton: The trip was planned for the Congressman and he didn't want any briefings. He wanted to get out into the country and these fit his two-day itinerary nicely.

Paddock: What is the most important thing AID can do in Guatemala?

Hinton: Be smart enough to operate as a catalyst for change. We should emphasize the training of people and the need for changes in their fundamental attitudes. In addition to giving them new technical skills, we should expose them to new ideas.

Paddock: How would you do this?

Hinton: We are doing it in a training program in social sciences at the local university.

Paddock: How did you happen to choose social sciences?

Hinton: We had a study made of the university, and the study showed this was the area of greatest need.

Paddock: Who made the study?

Hinton: Gene Martin.

Paddock: What is his specialty?

Hinton: He is a social scientist.

This is an old story. In 1963 AID hired the Center of International Studies at the Massachusetts Institute of Technology to find an answer to the agricultural dilemma of the world's hungry nations. The center assembled a group of experts who set about interviewing agriculturalists and scientists from such other fields as anthropology, sociology, and psychology. The $100,000 study, published in book form, showed that each specialist finds solutions in terms of his own discipline. If you hire a social scientist to study the university, you end up with a solution that involves social science.

I myself am no different. Being a former corn breeder, I lose few opportunities to emphasize that corn is of major importance in Central America and Mexico. That I know this about myself makes me wary of the same bias in others.

Paddock: What do you consider Guatemala's most serious problem?
Hinton (after a discussion of some political dilemmas): Agriculture. And for the first time we are going to take a serious look at the Guatemalan farm picture.

He went on to explain that through his efforts, a contract had been arranged with Iowa State University to send a team of agricultural economists to Guatemala to make an analysis of the role of agriculture in the development of the Guatemalan economy.

Paddock: Why are you using Iowa State University?
Hinton: Because it's a good agricultural school.
Paddock: Are you familiar with the Iowa State-Guatemala Tropical Research Center, operated here by Iowa State from 1945 to 1955? That was the program which brought me to Guatemala originally.
Hinton: I've never heard of it.
Paddock: That program emphasized agriculture. It was then taken over by the International Cooperation Administration which, as you know, was the predecessor agency of your own AID. At one time the annual U.S. budget for Guatemalan agriculture was nearly $1 million. That certainly represented a major interest in those days.
Hinton: I've been here too short a time to know the details of previous programs. However, I know Iowa State is a good university and they have good men.

Of the four authors of the study for which Hinton had contracted Iowa State, only one was then in Guatemala. He was a young graduate student named Eric Graber, and I sensed he was doing most of the field work for the study. Our conversation went like this:

Paddock: Are you familiar with an earlier Iowa State agricultural program in Guatemala?
Graber: I have heard there was some kind of program but that's all I know about it.
Paddock: I am interested in what you think has been the most effective U.S. effort in Guatemala.
Graber: The Peace Corps. Of course I'm prejudiced because I was once with the Peace Corps.
Paddock: What do you consider to be the most effective AID program in Guatemala?
Graber: I haven't found one.
Paddock: What will your current study indicate?
Graber: We would like to determine the priorities for investment in agriculture.
Paddock: Do you know what use will be made of the report for which you are collecting data?
Graber: I really have no idea.

EVEN IOWA FORGETS

In April, 1969, Iowa State University published the report, a full two inches thick, titled: *Agricultural Development and Policy in Guatemala.* When I read that its purpose was to review the extent "to which the agricultural sector has changed since 1950," I realized it covered part of the 1945–55 period when Iowa State had operated its own agricultural experiment station in Guatemala. Writing Graber, I asked if his group had consulted any of the reports published during the course of that earlier program. He replied: "I don't remember those specific reports." Thus, like AID, Iowa State, too, has no memory.

I wrote to Hinton some nine months after the report had been released, asking two questions: How has the report been used? Which of its recommendations have been acted upon? He replied that the report had been circulated widely but had "encountered a fairly general lack of interest."

Not surprising! The report begins with these deadly naive and patronizing sentences about a nation which, it would seem, no one at Iowa State had ever heard of before (in fact, they might have been written in 1852 by John L. Stephens, the first U.S. envoy to Guatemala):

> Guatemala lies just south of the Yucatan peninsula in Central America. It is bounded on the north and west by Mexico, on the east by Belice, to the south and east by Honduras and El Salvador, and on the southwest by the Pacific Coast. Although Guatemala contains only 108,889 square kilometers, approximately the size of the state of Louisiana, it has a very wide geographical diversity.

This study, remember, was intended primarily for Guatemalan officials and Americans stationed there. I wonder how many bothered to read through this two-inch rehash of all the appallingly familiar data which had been kicking around the back offices for years. Fifty officials? Twenty? Five? No one?

In his letter, Hinton commented that it was "still too early" to say which of the Iowa State recommendations would actually be put into practice, but "I am happy to tell you . . . the Government of Guatemala seems to have accepted . . . one of the recommendations, the idea of placing more emphasis on basic grain cereals, particularly corn."

Hinton's letter was postmarked Santiago, Chile. He had been transferred there to head up another program where, in the deeply entrenched tradition of AID, he doubtless was again starting from scratch.

When I wrote to the new U.S. mission director in Guatemala, his assistant answered, "I can assure you that the report has had a major impact. . . ." The result: another U.S. loan to Guatemala, this time for $23 million.

I did not have the heart to write to Hinton that the corn seed stock from the old Iowa State College-Guatemala Tropical Research Center is sitting in a storeroom at the experiment station at Barcenas. It was put in storage 10 years ago when ICA stopped funding the program. A faithful Guatemalan there is keeping the seed collection in what he believes is good order, just in case someday someone wants to use it.

How could this have happened? Former Secretary of State Dean Acheson, from his years of experience, pointed at the answer when, after a highly optimistic White House briefing about Vietnam by the Joint Chiefs of Staff, he said President Johnson had been "led down a garden path. . . ." Actually, Acheson is more exactly reported to have said, "With all due respect, Mr. President, the Joint Chiefs of Staff don't know what they're talking about." He claimed that field reports written near the scene of combat in Vietnam were rewritten as they passed through each higher echelon. With each rewriting the reports reflected less and less the pessimism at the front and more and more the optimism that prevailed in the Pentagon.

The same reporting situation occurs with development projects in the "third world," and with the same result. Gunnar Myrdal, writing about South Asia, said, "Optimism, and therefore approaches that make optimism seem more realistic, is itself a natural urge for intellectuals. . . . All [economic] planning . . . tends to err on the side of optimism. . . ." This can similarly be found in Latin America and, I am sure, in Africa as well. (In virtually every interview for this book which involved an unfavorable view of a development project, I was told, "Don't quote me." But no one ever said that when their remarks were favorable. Thus the syndrome feeds upon itself.)

The most easily understood examples of this are the numerous congressional fact-finding missions where congressmen travel abroad to evaluate foreign aid projects. The congressman arrives at the foreign capital; he is met by the ambassador and the AID mission director. Off they all go to see the mission's best project, and at its best appearance. You remember, like Sunday dinner for the preacher or parents' day at school. Who shows the failures? Who would be so naive as to suggest showing them? Who even wants to see them?

Nothing Fails Like Success

Eric Lax

As a governmental technique, the model program is doomed from the start. For one thing, it must show results by a specified time. The model may be granted a temporary extension, but must ultimately face an up-or-down judgment. This contradicts the good sense of any self-respecting agency, which lives on perpetual expectations. For another thing, model programs always attract adverse publicity because they are limited attacks on widespread problems.

Nonetheless, once in a while you find a model that is a genuine success. Take the job training program for convicts on Rikers Island in New York. After three years of federal seed money, the training center was thriving, and its record was so exemplary that everybody wanted to adopt it. Several agencies across the federal, state, and local spectrum clamored for the Rikers center. The shops and tools and teachers were already operating and ready to continue. It was only a matter of continuing the money, and choosing the victorious sponsor.

The Rikers program may merit only one line on somebody's budget, but it is a good example of what happens to a successful experiment once it loses the privileged status of being a model and has to stand in line with the rest. The fate of the training center may not be enough to prove a bureaucratic law, but it should help any model program manager avoid the perils of unmitigated success.

Rikers Island is a dot of land surrounded by barbed wire that practically adjoins the runway at New York City's LaGuardia Airport. On Rikers are housed the inmates of the New York City Reformatory, the Adolescent Remand Shelter, the New York City Correctional Institution for Women, and the New York City Correctional Institution for Men. There are about 5,000 men and women incarcerated on the island. About 2,000 of them, of which approximately 90 per cent are Puerto Rican or Black, have been sent there for as long as a year, awaiting trial because they could not raise bail money. The remaining 3,000 are serving sentences of up to five years in cramped, overcrowded cells and dormitories (two people in a six-by-eight-foot cell, for instance).

Because Rikers Island is a reformatory and correctional institution, we should expect that there should be a lot of reforming and correcting going on. There isn't. What there is a lot of, according to one guard, is "enforced idleness instead of rehabilitation." Inmates have nothing to do but march from one area to another, wait to be marched somewhere else, and stare at those bits of wall that aren't lined with other inmates. This may provide some inkling as to why they riot now and again, as they did in August, 1970. Because they have unlimited time to talk with each other about their criminal specialities, Rikers inmates become (or, rather, think they become, judging from the high recidivism rate) better car thieves, better robbers, and better muggers by the time they leave.

In October, 1965, in an effort to provide rehabilitative training for at least a few of the convicted male inmates (there are no programs for those awaiting trial), the Departments of Labor and HEW funded a pilot Manpower Development Training (MDT) program at Rikers to be administered through the New York City Board of Education. A $2.3-million classroom and shop facility was built and stocked with machinery. In the following three years, 1,200 inmates, most of them adolescents, were given basic education courses and trained in such skills as printing, woodworking, machine shop, furniture-finishing and repair, and metal-working—the job areas most open according to the New York State Employment Service. Programs concluded coincidentally with trainees' release dates, and once they were free, all trainees were able to take up jobs, often for the first time in their lives.

In an attempt to evaluate the Rikers program, Benjamin Malcolm, Deputy Commissioner of Corrections for New York City, wrote his master's thesis on it for New York University. Part of his thesis was a study of recidivism among a group of regular inmates. Although there are no definite figures available for the reconviction rate of all ex-Rikers inmates, or for those at other prisons, Malcolm's study showed that the recidivism rate for MDT graduates was only one-third as high as that for regular inmates.

SEARCHING FOR SUGAR DADDY

On August 22, 1969, the funding authorization for the model MDT program expired, and the facility was closed. But because the program's record was outstanding, and because a request for additional funds had been submitted, there was every expectation of reopening it within a month.

Eight months passed, and nothing happened. Evidently, any concern felt by the Board of Education over the delay in funding the program was at best half-hearted. They apparently made little or no effort to find out what was causing the holdup, and since the money was not immediately forthcoming, the program staff was assigned to other schools.

Continued funding often becomes a bigger problem with models than with regular programs. Much like a Peace Corps volunteer, the federal government is supposed to support its models only until the locals can run them and fund them. The early assurance of support on the part of the locals, however, is often superseded by a nostalgia for the federal benefits, and a search for some way to get them back. Cities and states tend to view models as short-term gifts with the potential of being long-term gifts. Once the original grant is given, nobody can abandon the idea that somehow the big donor will come through for more. Thus, in the Rikers case, to get the money the agencies first had to convince Washington that they were healthy enough to someday take over the program. For the second installment, however, they had to evidence enough helplessness to justify more of the same. None thought that they should pay.

Notwithstanding the money problems, in April, 1970, in what can only be called a flash of optimism, the Board of Education appointed Mrs. Alice Reed to be teacher-in-charge for the new program, then expected to begin in June. Mrs. Reed—a very competent and determined lady who is a trained social worker and experienced teacher—was also involved with the first programs. When the money did not arrive, Mrs. Reed set out to discover both why her program was not yet going and what it would take to get it going. What it took was 23 months. (It should be pointed out that although Mrs. Reed had the title of teacher-in-charge, she was not paid for that position until the program began. Her real job was as coordinator of the Concentrated Employment Project in East and Central Harlem and South Bronx. All her effort on behalf of the MDT program was strictly a matter of her own time and money.)

She first learned that because the first New York MDT programs had been such successes there were several agencies that wanted to administer subsequent ones. Among them were the Board of Education, which submitted the proposal for the program Mrs. Reed was to head, the New York City Department of Corrections, several private trade schools, the New York State Employment Service, and a private organization which administers federal grants through a program called Group Relations Ongoing Workshops, Inc. (GROW). She also learned that every proposal has an identification number while it is processed through the various agencies. According to the Board of Education, the number for their Rikers Proposal was MTI-5157. All she had to do was follow her number to the money.

CHASING MT1-5157

Armed with this information, Mrs. Reed called several people whom she thought would either know, or be in a position to find out, what had become of the Board's proposal. Each of them did, in fact, tell her what the status was of proposal of MT1-5157. Unfortunately, each gave her a different answer.

Her first call was to the office of Senator Jacob Javits. One of his aides checked and reported that the proposal had passed through the New York State Education Office, Manpower Division, and had been forwarded with a low-priority rating to the New York Employment Service. Before Mrs. Reed could express surprise at the low-priority rating, the aide told her that according to his information, proposal MT1-5157 was GROW's and not the Board's. Mrs. Reed called the assistant director of the New York City MDT office to check on the number of her proposal. It was, he assured her, MT1-5157. She then called the director of the fiscal office at the Board. He told her the same thing, adding that the program had been budgeted for $399,000 for 360 inmates for 44 weeks. The next call was to someone else in the New York City MDT office, who told her that proposal MT1-5157 had been submitted for MDT in conjunction with GROW, but that the two had different proposal numbers, and that the MDT program would follow the GROW program, with a budget of $367,000, not $399,000. All that didn't really matter anyway, since he added that the proposal had been rejected by HEW and Labor and was undergoing revision. With the revision, came a new identification number, MT17148-7153. It is unclear whether anyone except the phantom who numbers things was aware of the change.

A few weeks after this incident, Mrs. Reed still had made no progress, and the inmates rioted. Congressman Biaggi visited Rikers and was quoted as being "shocked" to find the training facility closed. (Before running for Congress, Biaggi was a police detective lieutenant and was once Policeman of the Year, he still has an active interest in the rehabilitation of convicts.) Mrs. Reed immediately called him, and his staff began their own investigation.

Shortly after she called Biaggi, an aide to Governor Rockefeller told Mrs. Reed that, according to a letter he had from the New York State Employment Service, proposal MT1-5157 was truly from GROW, not MDT. But the people at the City Board of Education, being educators and therefore of the conviction that numbers are absolute, were not to be dissuaded and stoutly maintained that MT1-5157 was, and always would be, their number.

Soon after that, Javits' office called with the news that the New York State Employment Service had rejected the MDT proposal and that the GROW proposal had been rejected in Washington because 1) it was too expensive and 2) the New York City Department of Corrections had not approved it.

Biaggi's office also tried to trace the budget cuts, but made no progress. Finally, on December 15, 1970, he telegrammed Secretary of Labor James Hodgson, urging immediate approval of the Board of Education's Rikers MDT proposal. On December 17, a letter signed by Biaggi and 17 other New York City Congressmen was sent to Hodgson urging his support. On January 12, 1971, Hodgson wrote to Biaggi and said that the proposal would not be approved because of insufficient funds.

BOBBLING THE BUCK

Biaggi then did a very clever thing. He called Hodgson's office and asked for an appointment for the entire New York City delegation to meet with him regarding the Rikers program. Rather than have a congressional sit-in, Hodgson suddenly allowed that he could release $100,-000 immediately and an additional $100,000 in July.

In mid-April, 1971, however, 20 months after the facility was closed, and almost a year after the new program was to have begun, the funds still had not been released. This prompted a telegram from Biaggi to Hodgson, saying, "It certainly appears that your department is trying to frustrate this project for fiscal 1971." Two weeks later, Hodgson advised Biaggi that the funds would be released within two weeks.

In fact, on May 3 they were forwarded to the New York State Vocational Office in Albany, where they were promptly "administratively lost." A call from Biaggi on May 26 to see what had happened to them produced a two-day flurry of activity culminating in the funds' discovery. On May 28, the Rikers Island Manpower Development Training Program was almost funded for $258,932. It turned out, however, that the print shop appropriation was deleted in Washington but the funds to staff it remained intact. Instead of letting Mrs. Reed try to apply the money to approved sections of the program, the State of New York demanded that the authorization be returned to Washington so the proper cuts could be made. This, mind you, is the same New York State that constantly complains of near-bankruptcy and cries for additional revenue sharing.

Finally, Alice Reed and her 11 teachers and counselors were able to begin their program at the end of July with a budget of $213,000. Their efforts were impaired by the fact that the shop machines, being federal property, and therefore unusable without proper authorization, had been sitting as idle as the Rikers inmates for two years. Many of the machines were rusty and unusable, but only $1,000 was allotted for machine repair.

Now, 78 inmates are receiving basic education classes, as well as training in wood shop, metal fabrication, or machine shop. Such items as a $35,000 offset camera are going unused because, among others, the print shop was not refunded, and more than a third of the classrooms and shops are not being used because there is no money to staff them. Because the typing classes were not refunded, Mrs. Reed spent $350 of her own money to buy a self-teaching typing course.

Mrs. Reed is already pushing to get the program funded for next year, but after all this, who knows? What can you say about a model program that was just that, and then for two years was nonexistent? The ironic thing is that about halfway through her bureaucratic ordeal, Mrs. Reed was talking with one of Javits' staff. What would have happened, she asked, if we had lied about our success and shown that the model program had actually failed in many ways? "Well," the man replied ruefully, "since model programs remain model programs until they work well, you would have been told to change a few things around, to try harder, and then been refunded for another three years."

Bureaucracy:
The Biggest Crisis of All

Michael Nelson

The hallmark of the company town is that it provides its people with not just jobs, but everything else, including entertainment. In Washington, of course, the bureaucracy is the company, and not surprisingly Washingtonians find its foibles to be an endless source of merriment. *The Washington Star* daily runs a "great moments in bureaucratese" feature called Gobbledygook; *The Washington Monthly* has its "Memo of the Month"; and Senator Proxmire grabs headlines with his monthly Golden Fleece Award, uncovering government-funded studies on "the sex life of the fern" and the like.

Washingtonians also seem to assume that if they are laughing at bureaucracy, the whole world must be laughing with them—when it's time for Americans to get serious about politics, they, like their brethren in Washington, surely must drop bureaucracy and start talking about "issues." But to the rest of the country, bureaucracy really isn't the least bit funny. It *is* the issue.

In fact it is not too much to say that out where the services of the government are delivered, the performance of the bureaucracy constitutes the biggest crisis facing our country today. It grows in each of the millions of direct, "routine" contacts that take place every day between citizens and the agencies of their government, many of which are supposed to be helping them. In contrast to Watergate and Vietnam, this crisis is neither readily identified nor easily cured; it is insidious, the more so because it manifests itself in such ordinary ways.

Bureaucracy isn't limited to government, of course, or to the United States. In China, it concerned Chairman Mao more than any other problem, enough so that he plunged his country into near-chaos in an attempt to deal with it. In this country we haven't had a Mao, and with any luck we will never need one, but we do have to recognize that the problem is as serious here as it was in China.

I began to find this out a couple of years ago, after I decided to try to learn what politics and government look like from a citizen's-eye view—what people think about when they think about the political system. I did so by going to three towns to talk with three classes of people—poor whites in Augusta, Georgia, professionals and business-men in Towson, Maryland, and blue-collar workers in New Milford, New Jersey. I drew people's names randomly from the phone book, wrote to tell them I was interested in finding out what was on their minds concerning politics, and asked to come visit for a couple of eve-nings with them and a few of their friends and families. I didn't bring in a long list of questions; instead, when I got to their homes, I repeated my interest in hearing about their concerns, then sat back and listened as they talked, partly to me, but mostly with each other. Unlike a pollster, I was as interested in what people chose to talk about when they talked politics as in the specific opinions they expressed.

As the conversations rambled along, these people began to paint a verbal picture of the political world as they saw it. To my surprise, what loomed largest in that portrait was not presidents or elections or issues or the rest of the stuff we usually think of as "politics." In fact, when people spoke of current affairs and the like (mostly, I suspect, because they thought it would please me), they did so stiffly, with uncomfortable pauses and lags in the conversation. The subject they warmed to with raised-voice, table-thumping intensity was the bureaucracy—not the anonymous, bloated, big-B Bureaucracy of Chamber of Commerce af-ter-dinner speeches, but rather the specific agencies of government they felt intruding into their personal lives.

As one might expect, each class of people dealt with somewhat differ-ent groups of agencies—the well-off with, for example, the IRS, the blue-collar families with the unemployment office, the poor with the Social Security Administration. But regardless of their class, almost all saw little connection between political issues and their own lives. They saw a great deal of connection, however, between bureaucracy and their daily concerns.

Further, they didn't like that intimacy, those intrusions. It meant dealing with organizations that were not only large and impersonal, but whose actions sometimes seemed to defy all reason. For example, Frank, a prosperous middle-aged lawyer, told of trying to find out from the IRS how his purchase of a condominium would bear on his taxes. "I went all the way to the IRS district director before I could get anybody to listen to what I was saying. The district director finally says,

'Well, I can't help you; you have to talk to the agent of the day'—you know, call a number and agent so-and-so answers. So when I finally reach him, he says, 'Does your company subscribe to Prentice-Hall and Commerce Clearinghouse and different tax services?' I said yeah. He says, 'Well, you better look it up there because that's more help than we can give you.'"

Martha, a retired spinster, had been supporting herself with a small social security check. Ordinarily, that would have entitled her to get additional Supplemental Security Income (SSI) benefits. But because she had saved over the years for her burial, she told me, she had accumulated more in the bank than SSI recipients were allowed to have. Thus, the local office turned down her application, though a sympathetic caseworker advised her that if she went out and spent her savings, she would become eligible.

RANDOM AND ARBITRARY

Bureaucrats' behavior also seemed random and arbitrary, though for those who were shrewd enough, it could be gotten around. A real estate dealer explained that "It's very difficult to get the right information out of the government in my business. Trying to get a decent appraisal out of a government official—the VA or the FHA—is unbelievable. The red tape. If he appraised it, that's the last word—that's it. And the only way we could rectify two of the things that came in grossly underappraised was to go to our congressman, who used to be a neighbor. He helped us out."

All too often, though, an inept agency action gave the appearance of being malicious. Curiously, many of the poor whites were certain that the government now discriminated against them, using evidence like Homer and Viola's. "I know a black man who used to work at the truckstop," complained Homer, a young part-time school janitor. "His wife went down there and said him and her was separated and had two young 'uns. And at that time she's been drawing welfare and food stamps for two years and she said they never had so much as come to her house." "And that woman came down here and went through every cabinet I got, that welfare woman," added Viola.

'IN 30 DAYS I'D BE STARVING'

For some, the inherently complicated nature of bureaucratic procedures was a source of anger and confusion. After Willie's husband Fred, a mechanic, broke his arm, she went down to the food stamp office. "I had a note from the doctor saying he'd have to stay out of work for ten months. They told me I could get the stamps but I'd have to wait 30 days. I told her that in 30 days I'd be starving and she could forget about it." Ron, an unemployed landscaper, dreaded going down to the unemployment office. "You have to get on one line for this and another line for that, and the people behind the counter—they're busy, I know—but they treat you like you're probably a rip-off artist or something. You know, guilty until proven innocent."

The impersonal nature of agency contacts further incensed people. Diana, a university press editor, complained about "the computerized courtesy" of form letters from the IRS: "We got a letter saying come down to the IRS at such-and-such a time, blah, blah, blah, and bring all your papers—very impersonal.

"So we go down and it turns out that nothing is wrong. Well, Good Lord, I've been paying taxes for 30 years and nothing's ever been wrong. Why do they need to call me now? Just more big brother."

Even worse was having to rely on a large, anonymous, and hence unpredictable organization for basic sustenance. Gene and Ella, who live off his VA disability payments, got very upset when some bureaucrat waited too long to get the checks out. "If a man is depending on that check," said Gene, "he could be sitting out in the street with his family maybe for ten days if his landlord wants his rent on the first. You can get pretty hungry from the first to the tenth waiting for that check, and they should take that into consideration. Some of them wait until the last minute and foul everybody up, and it can be real costly to people."

What is striking about these complaints, and the scores of similar ones I heard, is not that people don't like bureaucracy. After all, who does? I once taught a course in public administration to a class of government employees, and even they couldn't muster up a kind word for it.

THE NATURE OF THE COMPLAINTS

What is striking is the nature of the complaints. As every scholarly treatise on the subject will tell you, the great advantage bureaucracy is supposed to offer to complex, modern society is efficient, rational, uniform, and courteous treatment for the citizens it deals with. Yet not only did these qualities manage to conceal themselves from the people I talked with, it was their very opposites that seemed more characteristic. People of all classes felt that their treatment had been bungled, not efficient; unpredictable and bizarre, not rational; discriminatory or idiosyncratic, not uniform; and all too often, insensitive or downright insulting rather than courteous. It was as if they had gotten stuck with a new car that not only did not run when they wanted it to, but that periodically started itself up and drove all around their lawn.

Equally curious, the agencies that drew the most fire were, on the whole, those whose business is supposedly providing benefits to people —social security, food stamps, welfare, tax counseling, and so on. It is not surprising, of course, that people grumble when the government exacts taxes and other burdens from them. But when in the process of supposedly doing something for them it makes them hopping mad, then we have a problem.

SPANNING PARTY LINES

This last point is underscored in a recent report to Jimmy Carter from Richard Pettigrew, a presidential assistant working on reorganization. Pettigrew sent out a letter to every representative and senator asking them which federal programs their constituents thought were "administered least efficiently," "most confusing," "least successful in achieving their stated objectives," involved the most "excessive paperwork," and, finally, were "most responsive." Though congressmen, who are at the receiving end of almost all citizen complaints against the government, were the logical ones to ask, evidently no one ever had before. More than 200 of them replied, often in great detail. Their answers, interestingly enough, were quite uniform, spanning party and ideological lines. (The author of a call for "less government involvement in the 'daily lives' of individuals and businesses," for example, was George McGovern.)

Two agencies ranked high in all four "bad" categories: The Department of Labor's Office of Workers' Compensation Programs, which administers the black lung program and workmen's compensation for federal employees, and the Social Security Administration. (It is worth remembering here that the agency's old age insurance program seemed to work fine; it was the disability insurance, Medicare, and Aid for Families with Dependent Children that drew all the flak.)

The Veterans' Administration was next on the list; it scored badly in three categories. The IRS, Immigration and Naturalization Service, and Small Business Administration showed up in two. Among the others that were singled out frequently: the Occupational Safety and Health Administration, the Department of Housing and Urban Development, the Civil Service Commission, the Farmers Home Administration, the Postal Service, the Economic Development Administration, and the Employment Retirement Income Security Administration.

Aside from the IRS and, perhaps, OSHA, all of these are, supposedly, benefits agencies. The patterns of complaints Pettigrew found—unnecessary delays in processing cases, agencies' failure to provide people with information, and "outright rudeness"—were very similar to the ones I heard.

Clearly, then, the message Americans are sending—that they feel and resent the weight of government agencies pressing in on their personal lives—is an urgent one; with the benefit of hindsight, it becomes obvious that they have been trying to get it through for some time. It was expressed at Jimmy Carter's town meetings and phone-ins, for example (not to mention his election itself)—in the plea for help from a Cleveland woman who couldn't get her mother's GI Bill benefits straightened out, the complaint of a Lanham, Maryland job-seeker that she had been frozen out of civil service employment, the California man's protest about letters the Post Office takes forever to deliver, and so on. And, most obvious, there is all that congressional mail.

'DEAR ABBY'

Unfortunately, the message generally has been ignored. Though Carter described his town meetings as "a learning process rather than a teaching process," the White House seemed more excited about the public relations benefits of being seen listening to people than the listening itself. The press was alternately miffed and condescending. *Time,* for example, thought the questions asked at the televised phone-in in Los Angeles were "either soft or silly"; columnist Joseph Kraft said the radio program that started it all was "a set of 'Dear Abby' phone calls to the President."

Similarly, though congressmen respond vigorously to the specific complaints of their constituents, they rarely dig deeper to discover the patterns of agency practice that underlie them. In most congressional offices, the legislative staff almost never tries to learn anything from the casework staff, which handles complaints (in fact, there's a powerful status difference between the two, and snobbery often keeps the high-status legislative assistants from even talking to the lowly caseworkers). Putting out fires as they occur translates into votes; finding out why so many fires take place, though, would be not only long and tedious, but difficult to dramatize to the folks back home as well.

Thus, Pettigrew blandly reports, "even the offices of those senators and congressmen with legislative responsibilities for various programs acknowledge the acute need for administrative reform. The office of Senator Harrison Williams, for example, was extremely critical of the

Department of Labor's Office of Workers' Compensation Programs, calling the program 'unresponsive, unorganized, and insensitive.' " Representatives John Dent, Phillip Burton, and William Ford were among those equally critical. As all four gentlemen are, and have been for some time, influential members of the congressional committees that are responsible for the OWCP (Williams is chairman of the Senate Labor Committee; Dent, Burton, and Ford are senior Democrats on House Education and Labor), they obviously bear some of the responsibility for the OWCP's shortcomings. Yet, like most of their colleagues, they have found it easier just to slam away at an agency than to do whatever is necessary to improve it.

'NO JOBS'

Congress not only fails to correct a lot of the problems citizens have with government; it creates a good many of them by writing bad laws. Senator Lawton Chiles's complaint to Pettigrew that many people's SSI payments go down dramatically whenever their VA benefits go up can be traced to a problem in the law, not the agencies. As a VISTA volunteer representing people at social security hearings, I frequently heard vocational experts testify that my clients should be turned down for disability benefits because they were healthy enough to do sit-down jobs like those at a local Borden's plant. The fact that Borden's had had a "no jobs" sign in the window for as long as anyone could remember was irrelevant; the fact that it was irrelevant was due to the way Congress had written the law.

None of this should be taken to mean that agencies are blameless or that there is nothing they could do to make things more pleasant for the people they deal with. For example, the IRS set up a toll-free number that citizens could call for help with their taxes. Fine. But according to Senator William Proxmire, the line is almost always busy during tax season, for 23 consecutive days in one case. Why offer a service and not deliver it? OSHA made it a practice to concentrate its fire on small businesses rather than large ones; where is the sense in that? And what is the justification for outright rudeness in any situation?

Social Security disability hearings again provide an extraordinary case in point. The agency is notorious for having more than half its determinations that applicants are ineligible for disability benefits or SSI overturned if appealed—usually by its own administrative law judges. What is worse, many congressmen reported, in the four to eight months it takes to get a favorable decision, people have lost their homes, spent hundreds of dollars on lawyers, even died. When I asked Michael

Naver at Social Security why local bureaucrats made so many wrong determinations in the first place, he pointed out that "the hearing is the first time anyone in the Administration actually sees the applicant—physically sees how he moves, how he talks, how he copes, and so on. Until then, we're just looking at a file." Again, common sense—never mind human decency and courtesy—would seem to cry out for a change in administrative practice here.

As with poor congressional law drafting, obvious deficiencies like these could be remedied with a little more care and concern; for that reason alone they are probably worth reforming. But if bad guys and bad practices were all that there was to the problem, such tinkering with the machinery—the usual activity of reformers—would be all it would take to solve it.

Unfortunately, the problem is far more fundamental than that. It is basic to bureaucracy, built into the relationship between citizens and government in a democratic welfare state. It lies in the simple difference in perspective between agency and citizen, a difference that makes it difficult if not impossible for the two to deal in a mutually satisfactory way. Perhaps it can be best understood by starting with the desk that lies between them.

OF COURSE

On one side of the desk is the citizen, a unique individual with a unique set of circumstances. Think of Martha, the woman who, because she had saved for so many years for her burial, had more money in the bank than the SSI law allowed its beneficiaries to have. She is, of course, a whole person, and wanted to be treated as a whole person. Special consideration? Of course. Bend the rules a little? Certainly; I'm different. And she is different, as is every other person who sits on her side of the desk.

Across from her is the bureaucrat. He is there not as a friend or neighbor, but purely as the hired representative of his agency. As much as possible, that agency is supposed to execute the law as written, that is, to function as an efficient machine. It's not supposed to do whatever it—or one of its employees—wants, or feels is right. That means the bureaucrat, sitting as he does at the bottom of the agency ladder, must function as a cog in that machine. He is empowered only to do certain limited things, and only for those clients who are eligible. By definition, he must not look at the whole person, but only those features that enable him to transform her into a "case," a "file." His first job, then, is to fit this woman before him into a category: eligible or not; if so, for what and on what terms. Once classified, she becomes subject to the same treatment as all the others in her category.

CONSIDER THE ALTERNATIVE

So Martha did not get her SSI check. The fact that her savings are for burial purposes, not high living, could not even be considered. If that sounds horrible, consider the alternative: bureaucrats with the discretion to waive the law at their option. One would like to think they would do so for good-hearted purposes, but our experience with government is that agencies that are free to exercise the most discretion in applying the law—the regulatory boards, contracting agencies, even judges sentencing criminals—tend to use that discretion in ways that harm, not help, the average man. As bad as machine bureaucracy is, the obvious alternative is worse.

Even good intentions can't do very much about this fundamental problem of perspective, as I learned from my experience in a legal aid office in Augusta. Everyone who worked there was zealously dedicated to "serving the people;" their long hours at low pay proved that. We thought of ourselves as the anti-bureaucracy agency, tilting against the local welfare, food stamp, social security, and VA offices on behalf of our clients.

THE GOOD GUYS AND THE BAD GUYS

Thus, I was amazed to learn that many poor people regarded us as just another bureaucracy—couldn't they tell the good guys from the bad guys? But they were right. We, too, had our eligibility requirements, kept them waiting in the outer office, got impatient when they didn't keep to our schedules or rambled off the subject. We didn't look at them as whole people any more than our fellow federal employees in the other agencies did.

So what is to be done?

First, although there are limits to what we can do to change bureaucracy, there are ways we can cut it down to size, minimizing the number and complexity of contacts between citizens and agencies. For instance, the vast array of government programs designed to give people sustenance (welfare, disability, social security, unemployment, veterans pensions, workmen's compensation, food stamps, Medicare, Medicaid) really are addressed only to two simple needs: the need for money to live on, and the need to pay for health care. A guaranteed annual wage (with poverty the only measure of eligibility) and a national health care system would take care of those needs far more simply than the present system, and because of the simplicity, at a reduced cost. Caring for people through outright handouts would also vastly reduce that grating citizen-bureaucrat contact. The advantage of this shines through in the experience of the Social Security Administration. The administration of the old-age pension, whatever you might say about its conception, is simple and popular—I heard almost no complaints about it and neither did the congressmen who reported to Pettigrew. It was the highly complicated SSI, disability, and welfare programs that spawned all sorts of problems.

One reason this kind of simplicity isn't more widespread is that the government's intentions are, in a way, too good—we can't bear to give away money without making sure it's well deserved. Any small-town mayor can tell you that if he wants federal money for some well-deserved project, he has to put up with reams and reams of forms and meetings designed to insure that the construction company doesn't discriminate in its hiring, that the plans are perfectly sound, that the environmental impact of the project won't be adverse, and so on. These are all worthy goals, but they create a lot of bitterness and kill a lot of projects. Sometimes it's better for the government just to take a deep breath and *give* away the money, trusting its recipient to spend it in reasonable ways and accepting that there will be some who won't.

WHAT CANNOT BE ELIMINATED

Of course, any simplification will still leave a lot of bureaucracy standing, so it's important to try to reform what bureaucracy cannot be eliminated. The press can play a large role in this, by giving its audience a running commentary on what parts of the government work, what parts don't, and why, so that we can apply the lessons elsewhere. It certainly doesn't do that now—at the Office of Workers' Compensation Programs, they kept waiting for the flock of reporters to descend when Pettigrew's report came out, but nobody called. Exposing Watergates is fine, but these days lawbreaking is the least of the government's problems.

But most of the burden of dealing with these problems should be shouldered by the government itself. For one thing, we need to teach as well as learn about how bureaucracy works in this country. Our present system of civics education in the public schools, sticking as it does to explications of a constitution that doesn't even mention the bureaucracy, tells people almost nothing about how to make agencies work for them. I would bet that for every thousand people in this country who could list the Bill of Rights and name all nine Supreme Court justices, you would be lucky to find one who could explain his rights against federal agencies and name the members of even one regulatory commission. Because we don't teach these things, we shouldn't be surprised that people feel ignorant and overwhelmed when they have to deal with as many agencies as they do.

GROWING MEANS LISTENING

Elected officials also need to learn more than they do, and in a democracy learning means listening. Most politicians do this chiefly by taking polls, but pollsters get their answers by asking people questions about the things the pollsters (or more precisely, the people who hire them) think are important. As a result, we end up with reams and reams of data about what grandma thinks about the Panama Canal, assuming she cares enough to have an opinion, and nothing at all about what is on *her* mind. Forums like Jimmy Carter's phone-ins, where the citizens themselves decide what to talk about, would be far more educational for Washingtonians who venture out into the bush than the latest Caddell poll.

Listening, learning, and reading are only the first steps, of course; the government has also to act to make itself work better. Now and then proposals for accomplishing this come forth, usually involving some sort of "ombudsman" agency. But a new spirit is at least as important as a new agency; in fact, the Office of Management and Budget in the executive branch and the General Accounting Office in the legislative could, under their charters, do as much investigating of the government as anyone could want, but they don't. The point is to care enough about the government's grating inefficiencies to attack them with passion.

MOSTLY ABSENT

That passion is mostly absent today because criticism of big government is the exclusive province of the right, which doesn't want social welfare programs in the first place. So proposals to meet the bureaucratic problem head-on usually involve throwing out the baby with the bath—getting rid not only of the bad apparatus but also of the good program it's supposed to implement.

In fact, the bureaucracy crisis is an ideal issue for liberals, who *want*

the government to meet the major problems of the nation. As Pettigrew's study showed, popular dissatisfaction with government stems
from its failure to deliver on promised services, not from the regulatory
ills you see detailed in the Mobil Oil ads. A 1976 survey by Potomac
Associates found that Americans—even self-described conservatives—
want the government to do more to help the elderly, make college
available to young people, reduce air pollution, improve health care,
and so on. Liberals need not worry that any concession to critics of
bureaucracy is an invitation to reaction—the New Deal has already
been ratified.

If anything does set off a wave of right-wing, anti-government fervor,
it will be the failure of liberals to see to it that the government Americans want need not be gargantuan or staggeringly complex, and must
be delivered efficiently and courteously. Over the years, liberals have
responded to popular demands with an impressive set of promises; now
they must be willing to deliver on them. It will be a huge effort—Mao,
after all, started a "cultural" revolution toward that end, and even that
was only partially successful. But if the effort isn't made, the mood of
sullen resentment I found in people I talked with eventually will turn
to angry action. And when it does, expect the worst.

part 2

(MIS)MANAGING BUREAUCRACY: LEADERSHIP, BUDGETING, AND ORGANIZATION

The Constitutional Convention of 1787 was concerned about how the executive branch of the new national government would be managed. One of the main problems the Framers saw in the old Articles of Confederation was that the executive departments were administered haphazardly, by legislative committees on a part–time basis; not surprisingly, the resulting inefficiency had cost the colonies dearly in the Revolutionary War. The Framers' solution was to vest responsibility for running the executive branch in the President by giving him the power to appoint (with the Senate's advice and consent) full–time secretaries to manage the departments. Their assumption—that if clear lines of responsibility and command were established, presidential management of bureaucracy would be a fairly simple task—seemed appropriate at the time. The original State Department, after all, had only nine employees; the Justice Department, as it is now called, consisted of the Attorney General and his secretary.

But in the almost two centuries since, the size and powers of bureaucracy have grown enormously, and with them the obstacles to effective management. One such obstacle is the power of the federal employees themselves. As Walter Shapiro found in "The Intractables," Presidents discover upon taking office that it is all but impossible to overhaul bureaucracy substantially against civil servants' wishes. Even as Jimmy Carter was campaigning in 1976 on the promise to reduce the number of federal agencies from 1900 to 200, federal employee unions and their allies in Congress were circling the wagons to protect their present powers and perquisites.

Presidents also find that the budgetary process is a less effective management tool in practice than it is in theory. For example, in planning the $500 billion budget for Fiscal Year 1979, President Carter found that more than 95 percent of it was, for all intents and purposes, money that had to be spent whether he liked it or not; it was already mandated by existing law or practice. Part of the problem can be traced to the kind of open-ended appropriations described by Shapiro in "Wildly Out of Control."

One of the grim consequences of bureaucracy's near-immunity to presidential control in domestic affairs is that most Presidents grow weary and give up the fight. In 1967, for example, Lyndon Johnson launched a simple program to build public housing on federal land in the inner cities. The Department of Housing and Urban Development, which had not been involved in the planning, reacted sullenly at first, then tried to make the program its own by adding in all sorts of auxiliary goals. As a result, the "new towns in-town" proposal sank under its own weight. That, James Fallows argues, is "Why Presidents Like To Play with Planes Instead of Houses"—why they frequently turn to foreign affairs, where their power is less fettered, and neglect the more complex world of domestic bureaucracy.

Removed from the active support and attention of the Presidents who appointed them, agency heads often end up "going native," becoming "prisoners of their agencies." Instead of trying to manage, they work to advance their agencies' interests and enlarge their budgets and responsibilities. (This is never so clear as at the end of the fiscal year, when agencies go on what Charles Peters calls their "Spring Spending Spree." Because of changes in budgeting procedure, what Peters describes as happening in June now happens in September. Otherwise, everything he says is still true.

A great deal of the agency head's time gets channeled into apparently meaningless "housekeeping" details, a point which comes through unwittingly in an article about Social Security Administration Commissioner James Cardwell that first appeared in an SSA publication called *OASIS. OASIS* titled it "A Day in the Life of a Government Executive;"

The Washington Monthly reprinted it with an added subtitle: "Where Did You Go? Out. What Did You Do? Nothing."

Even more disturbing is that at the same time Commissioner Cardwell was fiddling, his agency was burning. The SSA had been assigned the task of implementing a new program of Supplemental Security Income for the aged, blind, and disabled. The result: a "Battle of the Barons" within SSA for control of the new program. John Fialka's article is a grim reminder that when in-fighting becomes more important to managers than fulfilling their agency's purposes, it can cause great distress to the citizens whom the agency is supposed to be helping. Another example is Michael Aron's chronicle of what "Dumping $2.6 Million on Bakersfield" did to that California town. Every concerned agency and organization, it seems, agreed that migrant workers needed a government-supported health center. Every agency and organization also felt that it and it alone should be in charge. The consequences of this particular bureaucratic territorial war were as unfortunate as they were predictable.

Some executive officials, however, never give up the fight to make bureaucracy accountable. The key elements to successful management seem to be: accurate information about what is going on at all levels of the agency, extraordinary persistence, and a solid feel for politics. Many "scientific management" strategies omit the latter, but as Steven Weisman explains in "Why Lindsay Failed as Mayor," this is a fatal error—politics and administration are synonymous. A more successful model of executive control is described by Jack Gonzales and John Rothchild in "The Shriver Prescription: How the Government Can Find Out What It's Doing."

The Intractables

Walter Shapiro

Presidential campaigns are designed to breed illusions. Every four years the country goes off on a bender of positive thinking. Candidates criss-cross the nation stressing what they are going to do in office, ignoring the obstacles they will have to surmount in order to do it. In 1976, both parties had candidates who promised to deflate the "bloated" federal bureaucracy. Anti-government rhetoric has always been a staple of the Republican right, but now it has become an article of faith for many Democrats as well. Jimmy Carter won the Presidency by telling voters, "Don't vote for me if you don't want the government bureaucracy reorganized." His main challenge for the nomination came from California Governor Jerry Brown, who is even more of an anti-bureaucratic hardliner than Carter.

If a presidential campaign is a period of raised expectations, then the victor's term of office is often a time of dashed hopes. In 1960, Senator John Kennedy promised to "get America moving again." In 1961, President Kennedy discovered that all movement was blocked by the conservative coalition in Congress. Jimmy Carter—the man who promised voters to never tell a lie—assured them that "when I get to Washington, I'm going to change the federal government drastically." One assumes Carter was sincere. But so far, at least, not much of real substance has happened.

To get a sense of where some of the opposition might come from, I talked to the leaders of several important federal employee unions about what they thought of Jimmy Carter—several months *before* the election. The results were near unanimous. James Rademacher of the National Association of Letter Carriers was scathing in his criticism of Carter. The officials of the National Federation of Federal Employees were equally hostile. Frank Taylor, the union's public relations director, said, "We object to politicians lying. Carter knows he can't cut the bureaucracy from 2,000 agencies to 200. He couldn't find the bathroom if he did." The union's president, Nathan Wolkomir, chimed in with this familiar critique of Carter: "He never speaks on the issues. All we know is that he's for God and against sin." Clyde Webber, the rotund president of the American Federation of Government Employees, was somewhat more cautious. He admitted that he was "very much concerned" about Carter's anti-government rhetoric, but added, "I'd be reluctant to out-and-out condemn Carter. After all, we have to live with whoever is President."

The other group that had legitimate grounds to fear Carter is what might be called the poverty-industrial complex. This is the broad array of groups whose basic industry is ministering to the psycho-social problems of poverty. These are the service-deliverers, the social workers, the mental health professionals, and the storefront lawyers who depend on a steady flow of funds from labor-intensive federal programs designed to help the poor. Any President who wants to find money for new domestic initiatives recognizes that he must cash in some of these expensive residues of the poverty program and replace them with some variant of a guaranteed annual income. Carter alludes to this strategy when he talks about "one nationwide payment to meet the basic necessities of life." Back in 1971 when the unlikely duo of Richard Nixon and Pat Moynihan tried to enact a guaranteed annual income under the label of the Family Assistance Plan, some of the most devastating opposition came from social welfare organizations.

It is difficult to accurately reflect the viewpoint of the entire poverty-industrial complex because it has no central headquarters. Instead, it is made up of hundreds of little baronies concerned about specific pieces of social pork-barrel legislation. Most of these groups are not easily identified as lobbies. Non-profit organizations like the American Psychological Association and the National Association for Mental Health take a proprietary interest in community mental health legislation. The National Association of Social Workers has a more than casual interest in the fate of Title XX—the social services component of the welfare program. Because most of these "white hat" groups enjoy tax-exempt status (and are theoretically barred from devoting more than a minute proportion of their energies to lobbying), few of their Washington representatives are willing to talk for quotation about politics. But chatting with a number of them did produce a series of bitter attacks on Carter. These comments rarely involved substantive criticisms of Carter's social welfare policies. Instead, they concerned Carter's religion. One Washington lobbyist, who also fancies himself a civil libertarian, said, "I distrust all Southern Baptists, they just don't understand the pluralism of American life." A key figure in the mental health field complained about Carter's "evangelical dimensions" and diagnosed him as suffering from a messiah complex. A round-table discussion with staff members of one of the more important groups in the poverty-industrial complex produced vigorous nods of agreement when the senior official present commented unfavorably on Carter's evangelicalism.

An anti-government Democrat like Carter could win the nomination and the general election without the support of these social welfare groups and federal employee unions. But forces like these already have shown their capacity to make life miserable for him once in office.

Recent political history provides a few sobering lessons about how resistant the federal government is to change. Carter promised to "reorganize the executive branch of the government to make it efficient, economical, functional, and manageable for a change." He was not the first President to make this bold pledge. Another recent President called for "a complete reform of the federal government itself" because the executive branch "has become a hopeless confusion of form and function. . . ." It was only a few years ago that Richard Nixon said these words in his 1971 State of the Union Message. Government reform was Nixon's "sixth great goal." What Nixon proposed was the creation of four super-agencies to take the place of all existing Cabinet departments except for State, Treasury, Justice, and Defense. The idea was never even seriously discussed. No one—neither congressional committees nor important lobbies—wanted to jeopardize their existing relationships with Cabinet agencies. It was clear that the AFL-CIO would fight as hard for the Labor Department as the farmers would for Agriculture. Even the environmentalists did not want to risk their fragile pipeline to the Interior Department. *Lesson—everyone prefers known bureaucracies to the unknown consequences of reform.*

It is equally instructive to take a look at the last serious effort to trim the size of the federal work force. Back in 1968, when Lyndon Johnson was fighting for a 10-percent surtax to finance the Vietnam War, he reluctantly agreed to support an amendment by Senator John Williams of Delaware in exchange for that influential Republican's sponsorship of the surtax proposal. The Williams amendment was simple: For every four federal workers who left the government through normal attrition, only three would be replaced. Once passed, the Williams amendment provided Congress with splendid opportunities for high farce. Each time Congress passed an appropriations bill, it included a rider that exempted the specific agency from the provisions of the Williams amendment provided of 1968, one third of all federal employees had been excluded from the coverage of the Williams amendment. Before the amendment was mercifully repealed in 1969, it appeared that the American Battle Monuments Commission would be the only agency to actually be forced to reduce the size of its workforce. *Lesson—there is no structural reform so ingenious that it cannot be thwarted by Congress on a piecemeal basis.*

IN UNION THERE IS STRENGTH

The Congressional Budget Office has estimated that federal salaries are expected to rise by $25 billion to $74.3 billon annually in 1981. Increases in the cost of retirement and fringe benefits are expected to be equally precipitous. Any presidential effort to reduce these costs will face bitter resistance. Federal unions, particularly the three postal unions, are renowned for their ability to organize letter-writing campaigns to Congress when they fear that any of their perquisites are threatened by legislative action.

A close working relationship with Congress is not the only weapon in the arsenal of the government unions. Few outside of government recall that the country faced an illegal postal strike back in 1970. That strike ended only when Richard Nixon called out the National Guard to deliver the mail. It is less likely that a Democratic President, elected with labor support, could get away with such a hard-line response. Talking with James Rademacher of the letter carriers indicated that the postal workers have not lost their affection for this tactic. Even Clyde Webber, the cautious president of the largest union representing white-collar government employees, also obliquely referred to the possibility of a federal employee strike. He noticed with obvious glee that "a few weeks ago our people stopped working down there in Panama on the canal.... You couldn't get ships through the canal for a week...."

The government unions would not stand alone in any of these battles. The mail-handlers, the postal workers, and the American Federation of Government Employees (AFGE) are all important members of the public service department of the AFL-CIO. And there is little doubt that the AFL-CIO is prepared to make a determined stand against any effort to adjust federal salaries or benefits. A visit to John McCart, the executive director of the AFL-CIO's public service department, was enough to dispel any doubts on this point. McCart, a small, thin man with a soft voice, all but said that anti-government rhetoric reflects "anti-union attitudes." It's a strange viewpoint that equates the problems of steelworkers and machinists with those of GS-11 program analysts in the Commerce Department. But such are the demands of coalition politics within the AFL-CIO. McCart admitted that blue-collar unionists sometimes displayed the same attitudes toward government workers as their fellow taxpayers. "The obligation we have in the public service trade unions," McCart said, "is to make our brothers and sisters, our confreres, aware" of our viewpoints and concerns.

HERE'S THE KICKER

The pension issue provides the clearest example that federal workers have little in common with other AFL-CIO members. The federal pension system is unlike anything in private industry. Between fiscal years 1974 and 1976, the cost to the government of federal pensions jumped 53.2 per cent. It is easy to understand why. Not only are federal pensions tied to the Consumer Price Index, but government retirees get an additional one-percent bonus (or "kicker" as it is called in government circles) each time the CPI rises by three per cent. In a time of rampant inflation, federal pensioners can see their real income rise by more than four per cent annually. It's like continuing to get seniority raises long after retirement. What accentuates the problem is that this "kicker" works like compound interest—each one-percent pension bonus becomes part of the base used to calculate the next cost of living adjustment. The Congressional Budget Office has estimated that elimination of the "kicker" would save the government $2.81 billion by 1981.

It is not surprising to hear Clyde Webber of the AFGE defend the pension "kicker." He claims that the public outcry over this quaint practice "just goes to show you that a person who retires is just put on the shelf." It is a little more disheartening to hear the same rhetoric from John McCart of the AFL-CIO, who might be expected to reflect a slightly less parochial viewpoint. But, like Webber, he described it as "an issue that is receiving an awful lot of uninformed publicity."

The stubborn opposition that a President like Carter would face from the AFL-CIO is not limited to basic issues like salaries, benefits, and the size of the work force. John McCart made abundantly clear that the AFL-CIO would cast an equally jaundiced eye at efforts to restructure the federal government. The following exchange illustrates the extent of the AFL-CIO's tunnel vision all too clearly:

Q: How involved would the AFL-CIO be in any reorganization efforts under a President like, say, Carter?

A: Any reorganization is invariably accompanied by some kind of adverse effects on some workers. People are transferred, offices are abolished, and positions are downgraded. Sometimes we've objected to government reorganization in total, other times we've offered constructive alternatives. I guess you'd have to call us skeptical on the whole subject.

John McCart's comments suggest that any government reorganization plan developed by Carter would have to be negotiated with the AFL-CIO. It is not a cheering prospect. An administrative genius could not develop an effective method of bureaucratic reform that did not adversely affect some of the federal government's vast army of planners, coordinators, facilitators, and analysts. There is even some doubt that a President like Carter could reduce the size of the federal work force by placing restrictions on new hiring. The sorry history of the Williams amendment suggests how strongly government agencies will resist cutbacks in the size of their staffs, even if it is carried out through normal attrition. A federal job freeze would also place a President in sharp conflict with the demands of black and women's groups for continued hiring to meet the goals of affirmative action within the federal work force. After his "ethnic purity" remark, Jimmy Carter would be particularly vulnerable to pressure from the Congressional Black Caucus and similar groups.

It is easy to picture the conflict over any presidential effort to reorganize the federal bureaucracy or to limit increases in governmental salaries and benefits. In the end, it would boil down to a simple power struggle—the President versus the AFL-CIO and the federal unions.

BATTLING THE 'WHITE HATS'

The action becomes much more complicated if a new President tries to reorganize domestic social welfare, educational and health legislation. Each piece of legislation that comprises the social pork-barrel has its own configuration of powerful supporters. These groups, likely to emerge as the implacable opponents of any change in the status quo, range from tax-exempt national associations to friendly congressional committees to bipartisan political lobbies like the National Governors Conference and the big-city mayors. Add to this alliance such important voices as the editorial pages of *The New York Times* and *The Washington Post*, which generally reflect the attitudes of the social welfare establishment. Groups like these never allude to their own self-interest. Instead, they present their heavily emotional arguments as the self-appointed spokesmen of the nation's children, elderly and welfare recipients.

The power of these ad hoc coalitions is illustrated by the failure of White House efforts since 1969 to abolish, or even significantly trim, the $633 million in educational funds appropriated annually for "impacted" areas. These school districts are not "impacted" by poverty or severe educational problems. All they suffer from is a higher than average concentration of federal workers. It is one of the more ludicrous income transfer programs ever devised by the federal government, since many of these districts, such as the Washington suburbs, are among the richest areas of the country. No one any longer attempts to defend this program on grounds of logic or equity. But school districts have come to consider this federal subsidy as their due and the money flows to far too many congressional districts for a President to ever assemble a majority to curtail this mindless federal program.

Another example of a federal program that refuses to die is the Hill-Burton Act which funds hospital construction. Although the rapid increase in hospital costs is directly attributed to an over-supply of hospital beds, the federal government continues to spend more than $200 million annually to add to this surplus. The school lunch program is another social welfare program that has such sentimental appeal that it never would be cashed in to pay for a guaranteed annual income. In fact, a new President may have his hands full preventing the Democratic Congress from providing subsidized lunches for all school children, regardless of family income. When Jerry Ford vetoed an expansion of the school lunch program, *The New York Times* thundered back with an editorial entitled "Vetoing Children."

DOWN HOME PRESSURE

Richard Nixon fancied himself as the President who halted more than 40 years of the overcentralization of federal authority in Washington. To some degree that self-assessment is justified. In 1966 state and local governments received $13 billion from the federal treasury. By 1976 that figure had grown to $63 billion annually, thanks largely to such Nixon-era reforms as revenue-sharing and the expansion of few-strings-attached grants to the states. In a period when a number of states and cities are teetering on the brink of financial ruin, federal grants now comprise 25 percent of the budgets of state and local governments. Any effort to alter the status quo virtually ensures the spirited opposition of the nation's governors and mayors. Congress would be hard pressed not to be swayed by this type of lobbying. An individual legislator is almost inevitably going to oppose cutbacks in federal grants if his home-town mayor tells him that any reduction in federal funding will threaten the solvency of his city.

ANOTHER IKE?

The prospects for reform are not totally bleak, however. For one thing, it is at least theoretically possible that a Democratic President could do to the poverty-industrial complex what Eisenhower did to its military counterpart when he ended the Korean War. For another, a President who reorganized domestic social welfare programs would have a few allies in Congress. The Budget committees of both the House and Senate are sensitive to the need to spend the government's limited social dollars as efficiently as possible. Perhaps the most dramatic conversion experience was that of Edmund Muskie, the chairman of the Senate Budget Committee. In a well-publicized speech in October 1975, Muskie asked, "Why can't liberals start raising hell about a government so big, so complex, so expensive, and so unresponsive that it's dragging down every good program we've worked for?" Between the lines of that Muskie speech was the message that liberals had better consider cashing in some of the outmoded social programs if the government was ever going to generate enough new revenue to pay for national health insurance.

Despite this base of potential congressional support, any President trying to reform the bureaucracy and abolish ineffective social programs is likely to be beaten by the intractable opposition of those who continue to derive small benefits from the current system. Federal workers are unwilling to forego any of their fringe benefits, even if they know that their intransigence is merely postponing an inevitable day of fiscal reckoning. The social welfare establishment has become so wedded to existing social programs that they, rather than the remaining handful of congressional troglodytes, have become the most powerful obstacles to fundamental change. Albert Quie, the ranking Republican on the House Education and Labor Committee, and one of the most respected critics of current social welfare programs, is very pessimistic about the chances of cashing in labor-intensive social programs and replacing them with some form of a guaranteed annual income. He sees the social workers as the primary villains because they refuse to recognize that their salaries are draining off money that could otherwise go directly to the poor. He fears that it will take a federal financial crisis on the order of New York City's to bring about reform. In short, things must get a lot worse before they can get better.

These arguments are not designed to dissuade Presidents from taking on the federal bureaucracy. What is needed, however, is a realistic appreciation of the magnitude of the task. The election of a new anti-government President would, in itself, change little. The opposition to change is far too well-entrenched to be dislodged by a few Presidential speeches and the appointment of a government reform commission. To have any lasting impact, a new President must see government reform as his major domestic priority. He must subordinate virtually all other political considerations to the need to assemble a coalition to battle the federal unions and the social welfare establishment. Even then, it will be one hell of a fight.

Wildly Out of Control

Walter Shapiro

There is a certain look and feel to the books which bear the imprimatur of the Brookings Institution, Washington's most prestigious research center. Their unadorned covers and their unwieldy titles presage a terribly detailed analysis of a narrow aspect of economics or public policy. Despite Charles Colson's alleged interest in bombing the building, Brookings seems the least likely place in Washington to arouse a passionate response.

That's why it is so surprising to discover that the best political book of 1975 was a Brookings study. With its plain brown cover and off-putting title, Martha Derthick's *Uncontrollable Spending for Social Services Grants* appears to be the kind of Brookings report which will be little noticed by anyone but graduate students in public administration. Such are the dangers of deceptive packaging. In 115 tightly written pages, Martha Derthick has managed to produce the most lucid analysis of the internal workings of the Department of Health, Education and Welfare since the publication of Daniel Moynihan's *The Politics of a Guaranteed Income* in 1972. Such a detailed account of the inner-workings of a federal program is a rare accomplishment. But if we are going to reform government, we will need more analyses like Derthick's which tell us what government is actually doing.

Derthick tells the story of an expensive HEW program gone wildly out of control. Given the complexity of the subject, it is difficult to convey all the details without resorting to oversimplification. Yet the story should be disseminated as widely as possible because it illustrates the difficulties that the President—no matter who he is—will face in attempting to tame the HEW bureaucracy.

Uncontrollable Spending is a history of the social services component of the welfare program, with a particular emphasis on the critical period between 1969 and 1972. The program in question had its genesis in 1962, during the optimistic days of the Kennedy Administration, when it was a cardinal principle of liberal faith that if you hired enough social workers to provide services to the poor, it would somehow reduce the size of the welfare rolls. The program was vague to begin with— "social services" were never adequately defined—but by 1969 state governments began to realize that there were virtually no federal controls on the program. Put bluntly, HEW had obligated itself to reimburse the states for 75 percent of the cost of virtually all social services to current, former, *and* potential welfare recipients. (When Congress finally caught on to what was happening in 1972, Rep. Martha Griffiths angrily noted, "Under a potential receiver you can pick up Christina Ford and John D. Rockefeller.") To make matters worse, Congress had neglected to place a ceiling on how much could be spent under this program.

A large portion of Derthick's monograph describes the process by which various states caught on to the potential of these social services grants. California was the first to recognize that the benefits were virtually unlimited: between 1967 and 1972 California received 25 to 36 per cent of all federal funds spent on social services grants. Originally, the legislation, like most federal matching grants, had been designed to stimulate the states to provide new social services. California skirted this requirement through shrewd bureaucratic maneuvers: "Activities that were already being performed . . . were now provided in a way to maximize federal money." California officials had recognized that when grantsmanship is played with enough sophistication, it is virtually impossible for officials in Washington to distinguish between a new program and an old program with new, brightly colored packaging.

Unlike the authors of most Brookings studies, Derthick recognizes that the history of government programs depends as much on human beings as it does on policy parameters and bureaucratic organizational charts; she was willing to conduct interviews as well as sift documents. The nuances provided by the interviews enhance the entire manuscript. Although character development is hampered by the rigidity of the genre, *Uncontrollable Spending* is sprinkled with little human vignettes. There were the middle-level HEW officials who were so delighted to have a functioning program of their own that they were out promoting the matching grants at a time when they should have been trying to put a damper on state claims for reimbursement. Their philosophy was—according to an aphorism which spread through HEW in 1971—"You hatch it, we match it." Then there were private consultants like William Copeland, who, for an appropriate fee, went like a Pied Piper from state to state explaining the intricacies of federal reimbursement for social services.

The situation came to a head in the fall of 1971, when Illinois, faced with a politically unmanageable budget deficit, tried to pass on to HEW some of the costs of "state programs dealing with drug abuse, alcoholism, mental illness, mental retardation, and juvenile and adult corrections." The boldness of the Illinois gambit was impressive. Upkeep costs for the state's prison system were passed on to HEW under the rationale that the jailing of the inmates was "responsible for family breakup which results in the family remaining outside needing to go on the AFDC [Aid for Dependent Children] rolls." Such bureaucratic imagination was the contribution of William Copeland, who had added Illinois to his list of clients. As one state official put it, "We really do have to thank him. We would never have tried anything so outlandish except for him."

The outcome? Thanks to a complicated legislative maneuver by Illinois Senator Charles Percy and the high-priced legal help provided by Covington and Burling, in early 1972 HEW approved the Illinois plan. New York promptly submitted a similar proposal. New York's success triggered a front-page article in *The New York Times,* implicitly extolling the virtues of what some had begun to call "back-door revenue-sharing." The *Times* article sparked the interest of Senator Russell Long, who quickly recognized something was amiss. Congressional rumblings began to register on the Richter scale of the Washington press corps, and "this government blunder, hitherto obscure, suddenly became news." By the end of 1972, Congress had enacted into law a $2.5-billion ceiling on the entire program, and each state's share of the kitty was allocated on the basis of population, rather than on the number of reimbursement vouchers sent to Washington. Once Congress had seemingly reformed the program, the whole issue disappeared from the news as rapidly as it had become a national concern.

But this congressional crackdown was an isolated victory. HEW efforts to belatedly police the administration of the program were entirely thwarted by the political clout of the social welfare establishment. In late 1972 HEW published proposed new regulations tightening the operations of the social services program. Within two months the Department had received 200,000 letters of protest. A coalition of 16 national welfare organizations joined forces to battle the new regulations. Private charities, which had received only a small portion of the funds under purchase-of-services agreements with state governments, were particularly energetic in their lobbying efforts. Even a conservative Republican congressman like Robert Michel of Illinois "had to backtrack a bit" when he learned "that a number of my friends who are involved in all this volunteer work are going to be shut out from doing their thing for the community." Small wonder Congress postponed the effective date of the new HEW regulations until 1975. They were never applied. In 1974 Congress had passed an entirely new law (known as Title XX). Rather than finally bringing this $2.5-billion social pork-barrel program under tight administrative control, Title XX gave the states unprecedented latitude in spending their social services allotment. And that's where the matter stands today.

Uncontrollable Spending is not a brief against federal grants for social services. Nor is Derthick interested in illustrating the shoddiness of most HEW conceptual thinking about strategies to aid the poor. Both points, however, are implicit in the material she has assembled to document her case of the lack of administrative control over a major HEW program. Derthick's focus—and here Brookings takes its toll—is on the much narrower question: Where were the HEW comptrollers and the Office of Management and Budget (OMB) while the states were looting the federal treasury with matching grants for social services? Her analysis of the failure of OMB is particularly striking: the President's budget analysts were so taken with the concept of purchase-of-services, an integral part of the federal matching grants, that they were blinded to the flagrant abuses inherent in the program.

Derthick's primary interest is the administration of HEW, not the goals of HEW programs—a subject which would provide enough grist for a score of other authors. Like others in the Brookings mold, Derthick sees herself as a professional writing for other professionals and therefore doesn't waste time answering open-ended conceptual questions. That's why her conclusion, while unobjectionable, is not apt to become a rousing battle cry: "Strengthening the executive agencies of control may slightly reduce the chances that something like it will happen again, but the procedural and organizational constraints that can be introduced through budget and financial management offices . . . can neither alter the fundamental forces of political life nor forestall human error." In an era when reforming the federal bureaucracy is every politician's favorite campaign promise, it is important to maintain a grudging appreciation for the magnitude of the task.

Why Presidents Like to Play with Planes Instead of Houses

James Fallows

In 1934, when Congress was giving him everything he asked for, Franklin Roosevelt agreed to his wife's plea to take on one New Deal project as his own, without congressional help. The project was the rehabilitation of Arthurdale, a community of starving miners in West Virginia, and Eleanor saw it as the showpiece of a new America, the model of how rural virtues and urban wealth could be combined. Over the next five years, Arthurdale never moved much further than the Roosevelts' requests to private philanthropists. By wartime, the plan had been abandoned, and after the war the few relics were sold off.

Some parts of the President's job had changed by the time Lyndon Johnson took office—such as his freedom to conduct war without consulting Congress—but not the frustrations of domestic projects. Martha Derthick's book, *New Towns In-Town,** part of the Urban Institute's studies of why government doesn't work, examines a particularly dismal failure. The book tells why the President who could send half a million men to war and drop all the bombs he wanted could not get a few creative, hopeful pilot housing projects built.

The book's doomed hero, the "New Towns" program, was one of the bright spots of Johnson's last year in office. By mid-1967, Derthick says, "Housing for the poor had been much on the President's mind." Well it might have been, since the ill-housed poor of Watts and Newark were

New Towns In-Town. Martha Derthick. Urban Institute, $2.95.

70

calling it to his attention. At the same time, unpleasant publicity about Vietnam was beginning to tarnish Johnson's record as America's domestic reformer. An ambitious housing program might be just the thing to set the record right once more. But, as Johnson knew, housing was also the notorious quagmire of domestic politics. The main obstacles to urban housing were cost and protests: the costs were mostly for land and the loudest protests came from those who lived on the land before the bulldozers and construction crews moved in. Johnson thought of an inspired solution:

> One morning in August, 1967, as he was sitting in his bedroom at the White House and talking to Special Assistant Joseph A. Califano, Jr., it occurred to the President that federally-owned land in the cities could be used for housing. Within hours, his staff had assembled a working group . . . to figure out how this could be done.

If the federal government could turn over its land to the cities, Johnson reasoned, it could beat both problems at once: the land would be free or cheap, and the tenants could not possibly complain. It would be the ideal guns-into-butter trick: converting air bases and prison sites into new housing projects.

Less than a week after his talk with Califano, Johnson's staff had drawn up the first New Towns plan. Although Johnson saw these federal cities as a blessing spreading over the entire country, he intended to start in one special area: his own federally-controlled city of Washington, D.C. "We wanted to do it all over the country," Derthick quotes an aide as saying. "We wanted to do it well in Washington first, so that every mayor and congressman could see it done."

A perfect tract was available—335 acres of rolling, wooded land near the Fort Lincoln district in northeast Washington. The National Training School for Boys was on the site, but it was planning to move to West Virginia. Jumping ahead of the other agencies which had been queuing up to take the land when the training school moved out, Johnson imposed his New Town project. On August 30, 1967, Johnson announced plans for "a new, attractive, and well-balanced community at a major gateway to the nation's capital . . . this new development can be the best of communities."

While Johnson's staff was working out the legal and financial details for this 5,000-unit beginning, teams of special agents began tours of other cities to find suitable tracts of federal land. After screening for obvious problems—racial tensions, for example, which eliminated Milwaukee; or federal installations which were likely to swell and need more land rather than surrender any—the teams trimmed the original list of 48 cities to six. One, like Washington, was especially close to

Johnson's affections: San Antonio, Texas, became the President's second-favorite project. The others were Atlanta, with extra land near a prison; San Francisco, with two spare military forts; Louisville, with an unused area near a V. A. hospital; Clinton Township, near Detroit, with free air base land; and New Bedford, Massachusetts, with a soon-to-be-closed Job Corps center.

But as the list of New Towns was prepared, the New Town idea was undergoing fundamental alterations. In the most absorbing part of her book, Derthick explains the crucial change that occurred when the New Towns went through the bureaucracy of the two-year-old Department of Housing and Urban Development. Starting out as a simple plan for quick, cheap housing for the poor, the New Towns emerged as a more sweeping, more ambitious, and eventually more vulnerable proposal for urban development.

At first, HUD resented the plan that Johnson handed down to them. Even the least perceptive administrators could see that it was at least an implicit criticism of the job they had done. Quickly, however, HUD warmed to the plan, realizing that it could be a vehicle for the Department's own advanced theories of urban planning. Where Johnson had seen a way to get roofs over poor heads, HUD envisioned communities "new" in every sense—technically, socially, racially.

The most controversial of these goals—most of which were missing from Johnson's first plan—was racial and social balance. While normal housing projects were mono-racial encampments of the poor, HUD wanted to see whether families of different races and incomes could be attracted to the same community. Doing so meant, among other things, keeping the proportion of poor and black residents below the critical mass that would drive the middle-class families back to the suburbs.

Johnson's staff knew what HUD was doing, and they apparently approved. If the President's social proposal became even more creative and exciting, so much the better. The difficulty, however, was that the very changes which turned New Towns from a construction project to an idealized model, minimized its chances of ever being built. A prophetic memo, sent by Abner Silverman of HUD, pointed out the problem: "In one sense, the report suggests that each of these new areas be given a 'model city' treatment without providing the financial incentives inherent in that program."

This, as it turned out, was the central theme as one New Town after another bit the dust. The rewards Johnson and HUD had to offer might have been enough to get a normal housing project started, but were not big enough to lure the cities toward New Towns. The one weakness of her book is that Derthick never quite explains just why the New Towns were so much more repugnant to the cities than more conventional projects would have been; the general impression is that the resistance grew from roots deep in custom, bias, and small-town thinking. The results were unmistakable.

A SUDDEN GROUNDBREAKING

The gradual disintegration of the Washington project set the pattern. The first objections came from middle-class blacks, who did not like the idea of a nearby poverty-housing project. Trying to counter that by consultation and "community participation," HUD soon found several groups squabbling over who really represented the local people.

The project's several goals—quick results, social engineering, technical innovation—began to appear contradictory. The parts of the project that could be built most quickly—cheap, plain housing for the poorest people—were dangerous to build first if the project ever wanted to lure suburbanites. The more creative types of housing were also dangerous, often because they had never been tested and might collapse. In other cities, HUD later showed that it was willing to barter away its airy goals in order to win local support, but in Washington, with idealism pumping from director Edward Logue on down, the planners persisted. None of the basic problems—cost, design, pacifying the neighbors—had been solved when, a few months before leaving office, Johnson insisted that the project break ground, while he could still claim credit. Barely making the deadline, the token groundbreaking ceremony took place on January 15, 1969. The only houses uncontroversial enough to build then were 120 units for the elderly, people who would not strain the schools nor antagonize the neighbors. With Johnson out of office, the project was turned back to local authorities; the presidential push which alone had held it together was gone. In 1970, HUD turned the project over to Westinghouse for further development, sometime.

In other cities, where Johnson could not glower at tardy builders, the objections came more quickly and the New Town deaths were more sudden. In San Antonio, Congressman Henry Gonzalez initially welcomed the plan to turn part of Fort Sam Houston into a housing site, but after the fort's commander reminded him of the jobs which a strong air base brought to the district, Gonzalez turned against the New Towns. Even before the Fort Lincoln groundbreaking in Washington, San Antonio's plans had been canceled. In San Francisco, plans had barely been announced to turn Fort Funston and Fort Miley into New Towns when local conservation groups erupted in outrage. Bristling as ever with civic pride, they urged that the forts be made into parks. Briefly victorious, they got the New Town plans killed—only to find, several months later, that a military office center would be built instead.

Louisville proved that the screening for racial tensions had not been thorough enough. When the New Town was first announced, Louisville officials were busy protecting themselves from attacks on the segregated housing they had built. New Towns seemed like the answer, until aldermen decided that the project was "so racially sensitive" it would have to be abandoned. Confirming Silverman's prediction, they hinted that they would go ahead with a normal housing project, if only they didn't have to push this balanced-community goal.

New Bedford's problems were less racial than suburban. Even though the city's mayor had asked for the program, rather than watching it descend from the inscrutable HUD, the families who lived in cozy bungalows did not want a New Town in their midst.

The two cities where New Towns survived this initial-catastrophe stage had such favorable circumstances to start with that anything less than success would have demanded explanation. Atlanta was already in the middle of its own low-cost housing campaign when its New Towns project was announced. Unlike other cities, Atlanta knew that neighbors to the New Town site would not complain: one was a giant prison, the others were railroads and highways. And, in the face of likely objection, HUD dropped some of its racial goals. But before the project could begin, an unexpected citizens' suit froze it.

In Clinton Township, HUD found the ally it lacked everywhere else —a local group ready to build its own momentum for New Towns. If partial construction of 160 units, a fraction of the original plans, can be counted success, then Clinton was successful. Even those meager results, Derthick says, are due more to the Clinton group's ingenuity than energy from HUD.

THE INDEFINITE LIMBO

Toting up the results—three projects canceled, the rest in indefinite limbo, 120 houses built, 160 more underway—Derthick concludes that the New Towns were a disaster, and asks what went wrong. The answer points at the heart of the way the federal government works.

The first premise of the New Town syllogism is that housing, like education, has always been done by local governments. If Johnson could have ordered 5,000 houses built as easily he ordered 5,000 bombs dropped, then the New Towns would be built today. But, since mayors and city councils must approve the plans, the federal government must convince them that its projects are all right. If the cities are already convinced—as they clearly have been about law-enforcement grants—then money or free land is all the incentive needed. If the cities resist, the federal government must find sweet, alluring veils to throw over its programs. (Derthick spends an awkward few pages on this point, concluding: "These cases taken together suggest the proposition: the greater the local support for a project, the greater the likelihood of success.")

The second New Town premise is that the cities were not happy about the program. New Towns was not the first project to meet this response: Model Cities, school integration plans, and certain welfare proposals have been much less popular. The common explanation for them, Derthick says, is that only the federal government is far enough removed from local biases and interests to propose truly innovative social changes. Those being changed often resist.

But if Model Cities could get started, why not New Towns? The reason is that the federal government had far fewer rewards to offer. From the beginning, Johnson decided that New Towns would be *his* program; he would not go to Congress for a new law. This may have been the only way to start the project at all; it gave New Towns what Derthick calls the "executive virtues" of "energy, speed, and flexibility," and it kept the program from the petty complaining, pork-barreling distortion, and probable death it would have faced in Congress. Still, without special legislation, New Towns was equally doomed. Johnson wanted, in effect, to give the federal land away; the General Services Administration refused to do so without legislative authority. So, cities chosen for New Towns were offered land at hardly-bargain rates for projects they didn't want. The failures cannot be too surprising. Similarly, Johnson's attempts to declare military land "surplus" without consulting the sacred armed services committees in Congress left him, New Towns, and HUD in such a weak position that small-time soldiers like those at Fort Sam Houston could kill the project by complaining to their congressmen.

Derthick never makes the comparison, but it is difficult to read these stories of presidential failure without remembering what Johnson was doing at the same time. The same bedside confession that produced New Towns may also have led to a new search-and-destroy policy. While petty obstacles frustrated his plan to build a few harmless houses, Johnson found no obstacle at all to his plans for Vietnam. The disproportion is too obvious to need explanation. It may help explain why Presidents besides Johnson are also more engrossed with land-clearance in the Mekong or special deals in Moscow than with urban renewal in St. Louis or conferences with mayors.

Spring Spending Spree

Charles Peters

For Washington's contract hustlers—the defeated Congressmen, retired military officers, and assorted confidence men who live by procuring government contracts for their employers in the hinterlands—April is not the cruellest month. They have learned that in spring the bureaucrat's fancy turns to spending.

Like so many of the real scandals of the federal bureaucracy, this annual flowering of the Washington money tree occurs without even slightly intruding upon the awareness of the average citizen. His ignorance merely reflects that of the journalists and political scientists who are supposed to monitor the government and whose performance over the years has brought us all to our present pass.

The crucial fact behind the spring spending spree is that the money Congress appropriates to a federal agency for one fiscal year, July 1–June 30, cannot be spent by the agency in the next fiscal year. If the Department of Labor has $23 million of its budget left on the morning of June 30, for example, and manages to spend only $1 million by midnight, it forfeits the other $22 million. This is stimulus enough to get the check writers busy, but there is another incentive: the agency director's fear of looking bad on Capitol Hill.

Every agency director must appear before the Congress to defend his budget request for the next fiscal year. The director whose agency is spending less money this fiscal year than Congress gave it to spend is certain that Representative Sadistic Lee Vicious (D-Ohio) of the House Appropriations Committee can hardly wait to ask, "Well, Mr. Director, if you overestimated your costs for this year, why in heaven's name shouldn't we assume you're presenting us with another inflated budget for next year?" Of course, the agency director could protect himself by requesting a lower appropriation for next year. But this, needless to say, is unlikely.

The director's terror of Congressman Vicious is passed on to all of the subordinate administrators in the agency: the boss's budget is the sum of their budgets, and now they fear the boss will do unto them exactly what he fears Congressman Vicious will do unto him.

The plot is complicated by the tendency of Congress to sit later and later into the calendar year, which means the agency may not receive its appropriation until well after the start of the fiscal year in which the money is to be spent. The later Congress sits, the longer it can deliberate. The longer it deliberates, the later the appropriations are likely to be. The later the appropriations, the more likely that money will pile up; the more money left, the more frantic the spring spending spree will be.

So the stage is set for a bureaucratic bacchanal that exceeds the taxpayers' worst nightmares of Washington extravagance. Word goes out to all hands to spend and spend and fill every slot. People who hadn't a prayer of being hired yesterday practically have their applications filled out for them by eager administrators. Projects which even the stenographers knew should never see the light of day are exhumed and given life, provided only that they cost money. Contractors whose goods and services were scorned last month now find themselves offered another cigar and asked if they shouldn't, in all justice to themselves, raise their prices.

Innocents think that government enters into contracts with private industry and universities out of belief in the efficiency of free enterprise and confidence in the expertise of academia. The real reason is that agencies can spend money faster with the device of the contract than without it. Goods and services can be paid for with this year's money —even though they may not be delivered until next fiscal year—so long as the contract is signed on or before June 30. This process is called "obligating" money, which in the bureaucratic thesaurus means the same as spending it.

For example, the Peace Corps on June 30 has $5 million unobligated funds for the training of Volunteers. It can spend only one day's worth of that money if it does its own training. If it contracts with several universities to do the training, however, it can sign contracts for $5 million on June 30 obligating funds that can be paid to and spent by the universities throughout the next year.

Those who picture federal employees living a life of perpetual coffee break should visit a government contracting office on June 30. The furor may be equalled by what happens on the floor of the New York Stock Exchange on a record trading day, but the Wall Streeters at least stop at 3:00 P.M. The June 30th contract binge goes on until midnight.

Next morning, however, everything changes. Now, suddenly, we are in the new fiscal year and Congress has not passed the appropriation. Word goes out that we must be very careful about spending until we find out how much money we are going to get. Administrators, who were reprimanded for their sluggishness in staffing up, now find that they cannot hire men infinitely more qualified than the characters Personnel was waylaying out in the streets last month. Often a complete "freeze" on new employment is ordered. A rare idea for a really good project is put in cold storage with the lament, "What a shame we don't have the money for it." Yesterday's heroes, the contract hustlers, find the cigar box snapped shut and themselves subjected to endless cross-examination and caustic comment on the quality and cost of their companies' work.

Finally, sometimes as late as November, the agency receives its new appropriation. Its spending machinery, rusting since July 1, may not return to maximum efficiency for several months. Even if it gets in gear immediately—even, indeed, if the appropriation was passed on time—there is the unhappy probability that Congressman Vicious was right in suspecting inflation in the agency's estimates. Thus, for one reason or another, the money piles up, virtually guaranteeing a repetition of the rites of spring.

Spring's one consolation is the possibility that the good men or the good projects rejected last July may be remembered and hired or implemented before midnight on June 30, when the gravy train once again turns into a pumpkin.

Since this article appeared in 1969, nothing has changed but the season—the "spring spending spree" is now a "fall spending spree." (Congress changed the dates of the fiscal year; it now ends on September 30 instead of June 30.) Thus, the General Accounting Office reports that 65 per cent of all federal research and development contracts get approved in September, the Federal Railroad Administration issued 42 per cent of its contracts in the last 10 days of Fiscal Year 1976, and so on.

A Day in the Life of a Government Executive

"A Day in the Life of a Government Executive" was written for OASIS, *a publication of the Social Security Administration. Its ironies may be unconscious, but they are devastating nonetheless—and provide the truest picture of life in the upper levels of bureaucracy we have ever encountered.*

As Commissioner of Social Security, James Bruce Cardwell administers a program that touches the life of virtually every American and handles one out of every $4 spent in the government.

What follows is a typical day.

Rockville, Maryland

The Commissioner's day begins at 5:45 A.M., more than an hour before his chauffeur will arrive to take him into the District. In suburban Maryland there is near-quiet at this time of day. The Commissioner takes advantage of the silence to enjoy a leisurely cup of coffee with his wife and to scan the morning papers.

At 6:50 the Commissioner's chauffeur, Willie Falcon, arrives in a small government sedan. Commissioner Cardwell climbs into the car with a pair of worn leather briefcases at his side. Each briefcase is stuffed with the inevitable governmental memoranda which have been a part of his life for the last 30 years.

As the sedan edges onto Interstate 70 and heads toward the Washington Beltway, Commissioner Cardwell's workday has already begun. He uses the half- to three-quarter-hour travel time for reading Social Security Administration staff reports and memoranda submitted the previous day.

7:30 a.m.

The Commissioner arrives at HEW, North. He will spend the morning here before going on to the Woodlawn Social Security complex near Baltimore. The Washington office maintains liaison with other HEW components and congressional committees. While Woodlawn is only 30-some miles distant, it is nevertheless too far from the seat of government.

He takes the elevator to his fourth floor space and greets Mary Grabarek, the office secretary.

The Commissioner's private office at HEW is attractive but utilitarian —a massive walnut desk, beige carpet, a few pieces of darkwood furniture with vinyl upholstery. Opening off the Commissioner's office is a small library. Handsomely bound government volumes line bookshelves along the wall, and a conference table sits in the center of the room.

In his office, Commissioner Cardwell begins work by scanning press reports on items of interest to Social Security. He then turns his attention to the more time-consuming task of reading and signing correspondence prepared by his staff.

8:00 a.m.

Deputy Commissioner Arthur Hess arrives. The previous day was the Deputy Commissioner's birthday and the Commissioner asks about his evening dinner party in Annapolis. They then turn their attention to an item in the morning press reports about a Dartmouth University student who has had his social security benefits terminated on a legal technicality. It is decided that the Office of the General Counsel should look into the case. Another item discussed is a call the Commissioner made to the Office of Management and Budget to check on the status of SSA's request to build two new headquarters buildings—one at the present complex in Woodlawn and the other in downtown Baltimore.

8:15 a.m.

Commissioner Cardwell briefly outlined for *OASIS* an upcoming presentation in the Secretary's Chart Room. "Usually, I'll meet with the Secretary . . . well, every morning that he's in town. His staff and the agency heads are always present at those sessions. Wednesdays are a little different, however. These meetings are opened up—more staffers —and there is usually a presentation of some sort. For instance, the HEW Comptroller recently gave a presentation on cash flow analysis.

Today, the Secretary has requested that we give a general presentation on the status of the social security program."

8:20 a.m.

Commissioner Cardwell and Deputy Commissioner Hess leave the Commissioner's office for the Secretary's Chart Room. They meet SSA's Deputy Chief Actuary, Francisco Bayo, on the way. Bayo has just arrived at HEW, North, and will be available for long-range actuarial projections, if needed, during the morning's presentation.

8:30 a.m.

Secretary Caspar Weinberger, Under Secretary Frank Carlucci, and 20 to 25 other top Department executives enter the Chart Room and take designated seats around the room's long oval table. Five minutes elapse while coffee is served from an adjoining anteroom and materials related to the SSA presentation are sent around the table.

Secretary Weinberger then opens the meeting and immediately gives the floor to Commissioner Cardwell. The Commissioner outlines the morning's program, saying that the presentation would be in three parts: 1) a review of basic social security program data; 2) a report on current problems confronting Social Security; and 3) a period for questions and answers.

Deputy Commissioner Hess gives a comprehensive, 20-minute chart presentation of basic social security data—extent of coverage, number of people receiving benefits, benefit amounts related to average monthly earnings, etc.

Commissioner Cardwell then outlines the problem areas. He says throughout its history there has been tugging and pulling about the basic purpose of social security. Originally designed as a means of replacing part of family income lost due to age or death, social security has grown to include other programs, other benefits. That growth has been accompanied by a public uncertainty about what social security now promises—and about its ability to deliver on those promises.

The Commissioner cited a series of articles on social security which were reprinted in *Chicago Today* and distributed nationwide via the *New York Times* News Service. The articles are very critical; they charge that social security is a rip-off and assert that retirement plans available through private companies would yield bigger dividends for smaller investments.

"The press tends to focus on sensational aspects of the program," the

Commissioner says. "And while there are legitimate issues raised in these articles there are also serious misstatements."

The Commissioner then reviews what he considers legitimate issues regarding social security. Is social security adequate? Are social security contributions regressive? Does social security treat men and women, rich and poor, minority and majority, equally? Will low population growth and an increasing number of retirees mean an unfair financial burden for future workers? Is there a necessity for the social security retirement test?

The Commissioner says these questions, together with proposals for general fund financing and negative income tax, are being studied by the Social Security Board of Trustees and the Advisory Council on Social Security.

"The Advisory Council began work on May 3 and will finish by the end of the year. The Council seems especially capable of dealing with these issues," the Commissioner says, "and we can expect some proposals from them deserving of consideration."

During the question-and-answer period, the Secretary focuses on what is being done—on what can be done—about the bad publicity.

Commissioner Cardwell replies that a response to the *Chicago Today* series has been written by Professor Richard E. Johnson of the University of Georgia. Dr. Johnson is a nationally recognized authority on insurance and is a former executive of two leading private insurance firms. SSA's Office of Public Affairs is negotiating with the *New York Times* News Service, the Commissioner says, to distribute the Johnson article. The Commissioner also notes that former HEW Secretary Wilbur Cohen is writing a rebuttal which will be available later in the month.

9:40 a.m.

Meeting adjourned, Commissioner Cardwell speaks privately with the Secretary for a few minutes before leaving the Chart Room.

9:45 a.m.

Commissioner Cardwell and Deputy Commissioner Hess meet briefly in the hallway outside the Chart Room with Lew Helm, Assistant Secretary for Public Affairs. Helm tells the Commissioner that his office would be available to lend assistance to SSA in rebutting the *Chicago Today* series of articles criticizing the Social Security program.

9:50 a.m.

Stanley Thomas, Assistant Secretary for Human Development, catches the Commissioner just as he is preparing to leave the building and requests a brief meeting. Commissioner Cardwell, Deputy Commissioner Hess, and Thomas duck into a small anteroom nearby. Thomas says he met the day before with the National Council on Children and Youth and that this organization would like SSA to undertake a program to locate an estimated 200,000 to 400,000 disabled children who are eligible for, but not enrolled in, the SSI program.

"You're saying a . . . well, a sort of SSI alert for children. Right?" the Commissioner asks Thomas.

"Yeah, it would be something like that."

Commissioner Cardwell asks how they want to proceed. Thomas replies that, tentatively, a feasibility study for a pilot program would be conducted first. Maybe five states. The Commissioner says he will have his people look into it and get back to Thomas.

"They want a rush on this," Thomas says.

"So what else is new?"

10:05 a.m.

Commissioner Cardwell and Deputy Commissioner Hess leave HEW, North, for SSA headquarters in suburban Baltimore. During the hour-long journey, the discussion covers the morning's session with the Secretary, the remainder of the day's agenda, and an upcoming meeting with Mayor Donald Schaefer of Baltimore on the new downtown building.

11:20 a.m.

Arrival at SSA headquarters.

The Commissioner's Woodlawn office on the ninth floor of the Altmeyer Building is a near replica of the one he has just left in Washington but has a few more personal touches.

11:30 a.m.

A closed luncheon meeting with several members of the executive staff is held and runs until 12:50.

Doris Conley, the Commissioner's secretary at Woodlawn, told *OASIS* that working luncheons are more often the rule than the exception. "The travel time between Washington and Baltimore breaks up the rhythm of the work day," Doris explained. "With the Commissioner's tight schedule, that hour lost in travel is very important. We often find it necessary to schedule meetings through the lunch hour."

1:00 p.m.

This is the Commissioner's regular Wednesday meeting with all bureau directors and assistant commissioners.

Commissioner Cardwell opens the meeting by briefly reporting items of interest discussed in his meetings with Secretary Weinberger and other HEW officials during the past week.

One item the Commissioner talks about is a growing consensus among HEW staffers to lobby for restricting the use of the social security number as a general identification number. Their thinking, the Commissioner reports, is that such restriction would protect public privacy and prevent a monolithic computer filing of citizens' records and activities.

"I think the privacy issue is one of legitimate concern," the Commissioner says, "but I'm not sure we want to support this particular move. I think the emphasis is wrong. It should be on the proliferation of the data itself—on the actual need of this or that institution to have information and not on their means of . . . well, filing or classifying it. They can always adopt their own numbering systems.

"What I'm saying is this. By concentrating on restricting the use of a social security number as an identification number, we sidestep more basic issues of individual privacy. [Pause] Am I right on this?"

After a brief discussion, the bureau and office heads are asked to prepare memos on their positions.

The Commissioner also reports Secretary Weinberger's concern about the recent "bad press" given social security and outlines the steps taken to rebut printed misstatements.

Another item reported is an agreement reached with the Treasury Department to issue SSI replacement checks without waiting to see if the original check was negotiated.

"A small victory—but a victory," the Commissioner says.

He then turns the discussion to the new Federal Labor Standards Act and its effect on SSA operations. The new Act *requires* that clerical and many technical employees be paid for any overtime work rather than be given the option of compensatory time off. There is a general consensus that the Act could detrimentally affect SSA operations.

A quick around-the-table check with each bureau and office follows. Are there any problems? Is there anything to report? Any comments?

Input is sparse this week. Within 10 minutes, everyone present has either spoken or declined to speak and the last half hour is turned over to an Office of Research and Statistics committee studying proposed changes in the disability program.

2:45 p.m.

Bureau of District Office Operations Director Robert Bynum has asked for a brief meeting with the Commissioner. The schedule does not indicate what will be discussed.

Commissioner Cardwell and Bynum seat themselves at a small office sidetable over coffee. After a few comments on the weather, the Commissioner says he is planning a meeting sometime later with bureau directors and assistant commissioners to frankly discuss problems and accomplishments of the past year. The meeting, like an earlier one in May, would be held informally, outside SSA, and probably last two days.

"I think that's a good idea," Bynum says. "It's . . . it's a good way to open communications channels among our offices."

"Yes, we can look at what we've done thus far, look at any problems, look at any mistakes we've made," the Commissioner said. "The kind of organizations which worry me the most are those that close ranks and are not ready to admit mistakes."

Bynum and the Commissioner then turn to a discussion of administrative entanglements plaguing the SSI leads program and to the rationale for a zero-base analysis of BDOO operations.

The latter topic is of special concern. It involves a far-reaching analysis of the present work force and operating systems within BDOO. Such an analysis begins at a "zero-base" with no assumptions and proceeds to evaluate what resources and operations are necessary to achieve organizational goals. Bynum expresses concern that the analysis will interfere with processing of field office workloads. The Commissioner says the task force for the analysis will be as unobtrusive as possible and that other bureaus are also slated to undergo the same thing.

They then discuss an invitation from the National Council of Social Security Management Associations to speak at their convention in San Francisco this October. Bynum says he will accept the invitation to speak and Commissioner Cardwell says he can make no commitment at this time but will note it on his calendar as a possibility.

3:30 p.m.

A meeting with Texas business executive Mitchell Hart has been scheduled and *OASIS* given permission to sit in. However, Hart requests a private session with Commissioner Cardwell to talk about his data processing firm's problems in obtaining subcontracts from carriers which process Medicare claims.

4:30 p.m.

Commissioner Cardwell is slated to meet with BHI Director Thomas Tierney and Tierney's committee on National Health Insurance. However, the meeting with Hart runs longer than expected. At 5 o'clock, with the Hart meeting still in session, Commissioner Cardwell asks Deputy Commissioner Hess to chair the National Health Insurance meeting.

"It isn't uncommon for the Deputy Commissioner to take over for me when there are schedule conflicts," Commissioner Cardwell says. "He is an exceptional administrator . . . a fine person. I believe Art Hess reflects the kind of leadership we want to develop here."

Hess apologizes to the committee for the delay, says he realizes the time is inadequate but that another meeting can be arranged later. He then asks for a report on committee problem areas and asks if any assistance from the Commissioner's office is needed.

Deputy Commissioner Hess has the same directness, the same decisiveness in these sessions as the Commissioner. Yet there is a difference in their manner, which may be traced to their professional backgrounds. Hess approaches a problem with the probing exactness of a lawyer (which he is), and the Commissioner brings to a problem the analytical detachment of an ex-budget officer (which he is).

5:10 p.m.

The Commissioner's meeting with Mitchell Hart ends; since Deputy Commissioner Hess has taken the meeting with the NHI committee, the Commissioner decides to squeeze another meeting into the day's calendar.

On any given day, there are more people waiting to see the Commissioner than can be scheduled. Many appointments must be postponed or fitted into breaks in the schedule. Doris Conley earlier notified an inter-bureau committee studying SSI provisions for drug addicts and alcoholics that they would be "on hold" that afternoon. She now calls them in.

During the few minutes it takes the committee members to make their way through the maze of corridors and up the elevator to the ninth floor of the Altmeyer Building, Commissioner Cardwell calls his wife. He assures her that he will be on time for his son's birthday celebration at seven.

The major thrust of the discussion with the new committee is toward resolution of a misunderstanding between SSA and New York City officials. NYC officials erroneously believed that SSI would pick up drug addicts and alcoholics disabled by their addiction alone.

Deputy Commissioner Art Hess spoke with *OASIS* earlier about the demands made upon the Commissioner by the schedule he keeps. "As you can see, one meeting often runs into another. And the day's itinerary is subject to change at a moment's notice. Handling this sort of workload calls for a quick transition of thought and a refocusing of attention upon a completely different—but equally complex—set of data. It's a helluva job."

6:10 p.m.

Meeting ends; Commissioner Cardwell asks that Doris have Willie bring the car around to begin the 45-mile drive home.

Because today is his son's birthday, he is able to gracefully bow out of a Washington engagement he would otherwise be expected to attend. The missed engagement is a dinner at the Washington Sheraton-Carlton Hotel where Wilbur Cohen, former HEW Secretary and an old friend of the Commissioner's, will be the evening speaker.

"I do regret not attending the dinner this evening. But not that much, I guess. One of the toughest parts of this job is separating family obligations from work obligations. I don't like to take the work home . . . to have it intrude on all facets of my life. I like a few hours of leisure away from it all."

At home, the Commissioner usually sequesters himself in his den with a new best-seller or joins Mary Louise for a few hands of bridge with neighborhood friends. During the fall and winter months, he follows the fate of the Capital city's football team, the Washington Redskins.

Much of his free time is spent with his family. Two of his four sons —David Bryan, 18, and John Richard, 10—live at home and the two elder sons, James, Jr., 26, and Mark Edward, 24, are married and live in other areas. Vacations for the Commissioner and his family are rare and therefore highly valued. Recently the Cardwell family managed to break away for a four-day vacation.

Battle of the Barons

John J. Fialka

Reformers who believe that a federal takeover is the solution to the welfare mess will be interested in the following story about the Supplemental Security Income program.

SSI (and get your initials straight as we go along, because there's lots more to come) is the part of Pat Moynihan's Family Assistance Plan (FAP) that made it. Rather than federalize the entire welfare system through a negative income tax, as Moynihan (and others, such as candidate George McGovern) proposed, Congress voted in October 1972 to take over and administer directly only those programs providing extra money to the elderly, blind, and disabled.

The federal takeover was scheduled to begin on January 1, 1974. Giving away billions of dollars a year is not an easy job. Because it had a reputation as the most efficient agency in the government for this sort of thing, with the largest computer system ever devised for peacetime use, the job of writing the checks for the new program was given to the Social Security Administration (in recent years, a division of the Department of Health, Education and Welfare).

Social Security, which had expected the assignment and was proud of its reputation, had been preparing since 1971 to undertake this new task. The "can do" spirit was nourished with substantial amounts of overtime, some $60-million worth a year. Training programs and other nonessential activities were curtailed throughout the agency as the SSI crunch approached. According to James B. Cardwell, the commissioner of Social Security, at one point 70 per cent of the agency's 86,600 employees were working on SSI.

Ed Cramer, public affairs officer for Social Security's San Francisco region, remembers standing in the Treasury Department's payment office in San Francisco on December 30, 1973. It was one of those moments that bureaucrats take pride in. The stacks of freshly printed gold checks (to distinguish them from the regular Social Security checks, which are green), were ready to go, arranged by zip codes. He passed his hands idly over the stacks of checks. Then he pulled out a few at random to see what they looked like. He was horrified. Under the new law, the maximum amount of an SSI check was supposed to be $235.

"These checks were for between $600 and $800," Cramer later recalled. "We tried to stop the run."

John A. McConnachie, commissioner for the region, decided that would be impossible. There would be hell to pay if those checks didn't go out on time.

Early the following morning, New Year's Eve, McConnachie and a platoon of his office workers arrived at the payment center, determined to do what they could. Because there were millions of dollars' worth of checks stacked in there, Treasury officials were reluctant to let them in. McConnachie had to convince them that he was there to try to save federal money, not to steal it.

There wasn't time to go over all the checks by hand, so the team selected certain zip codes that appeared to have the most flagrant overpayments. By the end of the day, they had plucked out 3,000 checks, most of them sizable overpayments headed for Ventura County.

McConnachie thought he had pretty much cleaned up the problem. But he had barely scratched the surface. According to a team of state auditors who have examined a sample of the 540,693 California SSI cases, 55 per cent of the checks were wrong. A total of $49,652,000 was overspent in California by SSI during the program's first six months of operation.

Six months later the scene was repeated in Vermont. A quarter of a million dollars in overpayments went out to 2,366 recipients. Social Security chased those checks with mailgrams, notifying Vermont recipients that a mistake had been made and the federal government wanted the money back.

In October the people who had received the mailgrams got another batch of inflated checks. Within the SSI system, there was frenzy. The final blow came in November when, somehow, the system selected about 220 Vermonters who had dutifully returned their earlier overpayments and stopped their November checks entirely.

Nine months later, early last August, there was still another variation on the theme. Programmers discovered that a crossed signal had mistakenly told the computer that 15,000 SSI clients had been underpaid for about a year. In the twinkling of an eye, $10,516,000 had gone out in overpayments.

At that time, government had paid out $8 billion in the first year and a half of the new program. Over $400 million of it was *known* to have been paid out by mistake. By 1976, this figure was up to $547 million. Middle-level Social Security bureaucrats believe that when all the returns are in, the government will find that it paid out over $1 billion too much during the beginning months of the SSI program.

But only part of the damage caused by SSI's problems can be measured in numbers; the rest is measured in grief. *The Washington Star* has printed dozens of stories about people caught in the grip of this maladministered computer payment system. Social Security, having misspent the money, is bound to try to get back as much as it can. SSI clients, because they are the nation's blind, disabled, and elderly, are, by definition, the least likely to be able to pay it back.

A CASE STUDY

Consider the case of Mrs. Frances Blakeney, 62, a widow who lives in a small cottage in the Watts section of Los Angeles. She has heart trouble and diabetes. She has no outside income and—like many people on SSI—measures her life by the checks that appear in her mailbox once a month.

Her case should not be very complicated. She is entitled to $195 a month in normal Social Security widow's benefits, benefits paid for by the payroll deductions taken from her late husband. This comes in the form of a monthly green check.

She also is entitled to a gold check for $85 a month from SSI because she is disabled and cannot work.

During the spring and summer of 1974, Mrs. Blakeney found herself receiving checks made out to two different names. One was for "Francis C. Blackeney," and one had the proper spelling of her name on it.

The widow says she called her local Social Security office right away and was told not to worry because they were probably retroactive checks that she was entitled to because of her disability claim. A case worker, she said, explained how she could cash them by signing them Francis C. Blackeney and then signing her right name underneath.

There were six or seven of the Blackeney checks; Mrs. Blakeney is not quite sure. She remembers spending them, though.

"I stocked up quite a bit on staples. I must have a lot of sugar-free, low-salt food and that's pretty expensive," she explained. "I bought some clothes, some underclothes, and a new black-and-white television. That's all the recreation I have, you know," she said.

Then the computer caught up with her. Computer-written form letters began arriving in her mailbox in August. The first one said her payment would be cut because "you and your spouse are now living together in your own household."

Now that *was* disturbing, because Mrs. Blakeney's husband died in 1970. She complained to her local office and they apologized for the error.

About a week later another computer letter arrived. This one said, "we made an error," and promised that one of her two monthly SSI checks would stop.

In September, the Blackeney checks stopped, and Mrs. Blakeney thought little about the matter until seven months later, in April 1975, when Social Security summoned her to her local office for an interview and presented her with a bill for $2,099.

The agency, she was told, was preparing to subtract $50 a month from her SSI check for 80 months. That was a considerable blow to the widow who, in good months, may build up as much as $20 in her savings account.

Mrs. Blakeney appealed her case to a Social Security administrative law judge, who admitted he could not figure out from the records just how much the widow had received in overpayments. He decided that it would be "prohibitive" to take $50 a month, so he ruled the agency should deduct $25 a month for the next 80 months.

FIGHTING TOOTH AND NAIL

At this point the average recipient might have given up, but Mrs. Blakeney was angry. She took her case to the Appeals Council in Washington, which functions as Social Security's administrative version of the Supreme Court.

"No, honey," she told a reporter who inquired about her case. "I'm fighting this thing tooth and nail. I admit I got it [the money], but I don't think it's right that we should pay for somebody else's mistake."

Then there was another shock. On the Saturday before Christmas, while this appeal was pending, Mrs. Blakeney looked in her mailbox and found a check from Social Security for $1,813.90. There was no accompanying explanation.

The following Monday she called her local Social Security office. The case worker wanted to know whether it was a gold check or a green check. It was green, the widow said.

The case worker said that meant it was safe to go ahead and cash it because it was from one of Social Security's regular programs. "They don't make mistakes like they do with SSI," she said.

Then, before Mrs. Blakeney had figured out what the green check meant, a computer letter arrived saying that because she had received such a large check she would be deemed ineligible for SSI.

The agency wanted $251 back for the months of October, November and December. This was $100 more than she had received in SSI funds, because the agency had begun taking out $50 a month in November.

In February, the administrative fog that had gathered around the Blakeney case was finally parted. The Appeals Council ruled that she was without fault in cashing the duplicate checks and added that any recoupment attempt would mean a hardship for the widow. And Social Security finally sent her a letter admitting that the $1,813.90 check was issued because she had been entitled to receive her widow's benefits one year before she had been declared eligible. The money had been owed her since 1973. The agency has promised to restore the money that it deducted from her monthly checks. "I'm so happy I could scream," said Mrs. Blakeney. "Now they owe me money."

The Supplemental Security Income program (SSI) is administered, logically enough, by the Bureau of Supplemental Security Income (BSSI) of the Social Security Administration (SSA) of HEW. In essence, what BSSI had to run was a computer program—80 different computer programs, actually. Part of what went wrong is known around SSA (that's right, Social Security Administration) as "The Battle of the Barons." Each "baron," or chief of an SSA bureau, controls a little chunk of what should have been a relatively simple operation.

BSSI, for example, does not control the agency computer system. The Bureau of Data Processing (BDOP) does.

Determining who is entitled to disability payments is up to the Bureau of Disability Insurance (BDI).

Drafting claims policy regulations is the job of the Bureau of Retirement and Survivors Insurance (BRSI).

Case workers in the 1,200 field offices administering the program work under the Bureau of District Office Operations (BDOO).

NATURAL METAPHORS

The man who runs BSSI is not himself a career "baron." His name is Sumner G. Whittier, a former lieutenant governor of Massachusetts, and he was 64 years old when he arrived at Social Security in 1972 to take over the fledgling program. He is a friend of Elliot Richardson (another former Massachusetts lieutenant governor), then head of HEW.

Whittier, who served in the Navy as a lieutenant during World War II, has a penchant for describing things in nautical terms. He also has a penchant for writing memos. "The orders are full speed ahead, and try to ignore the torpedos," he wrote in a memo issued to his staff shortly after he took command of BSSI. "Uncertainty is natural on a shakedown cruise."

In theory, the barons were supposed to work together in what was known as the "coordinative system" under former Social Security Commissioner Robert M. Ball. But Ball retired in March 1973. For six months the Nixon Administration left the commissioner's slot unfilled. Elliot Richardson followed his wandering political star to the Defense Department, and Whittier found himself awash in a sea full of torpedos.

SSI was launched with not one but three field manuals telling the local office staffs how to run the new program. One was drafted by BSSI, another by BDI, and a third by BDOO.

A computer expert retained by Social Security in the winter of 1974, after a year of electronic chaos, found that at least three different bureaus were making changes in the programs without consulting each other and without making records of the changes. One result was that 170,157 cases were found to have been "lost" within the computer's memory banks. Some of them were not located until the summer of 1975, 18 months after the program started.

Whittier's major struggle was with Robert Bynum, the director of field operations (BDOO, you will recall), who insisted that the field force would decide just how SSI should be controlled in the local offices.

"What is BSSI's role?" Whittier asked Bynum in a memo late in 1973. "BSSI has responsibility, but no authority. The actual operation is performed by BDOO in the taking of applications and deciding of eligibility. If BSSI has the responsibility—the responsibility for what? The job description says 'management focus.' I'm in an impossible grind among many strong, tough, experienced forces. My black and blue spots are showing."

MESSIAH OF THE MONTH

Time and time again Whittier was bested by the other barons who knew the ins and outs of the agency's machinery. In his frustration, Whittier himself launched some of the torpedos that damaged SSI.

Unable to shake up the staffs of the other barons, Whittier continually changed around his own staff. One month he would delegate policy making to one person, the next month that person would be frozen out, and another staffer would be placed at the controls. It happened so often that the chosen one was dubbed "Messiah of the Month" by the rest of the staff. Whittier said he did it to encourage greater efficiency, but his fellow barons disagree. "He was playing office over there," sniffs one of the career bureaucrats.

Whittier's incentive system is the oldest one known to bureaucrats. He rewarded people who told him that SSI's development was coming along nicely. Doubters were not likely to be promoted and, of course, could never expect to become Messiah of the Month.

As the hectic year of 1973 wore on, one of the work products of Whittier's shop was a collection of memos mocking the florid, nautical tone of Whittier's memos.

"As we jet along on course, smoke billowing from our sails," begins one, "we realize that we have finally reached our goal. I am very much reminded of the parallels that exist between our splendid BSSI effort and the exemplary deeds of that great American, Christopher Columbus.

"As you remember, when Captain Chris set sail he did not know exactly where he was going; upon arriving at his goal he did not know where he had been. Fortunately, this was accomplished through federal funding."

WE CAN DO IT

While the bureaucrats played their games, the problems multiplied. These are some fairly typical comments taken from routine field reports in August 1975, 19 months after Ed Cramer first noticed that there might be trouble ahead:

"The instructions for this [how to figure out payment formulas] come in daily and from every known resource within the agency," wrote the manager of Salinas, Kansas, office. "We can't tell what supersedes what! We have SSADRS [computer] messages, Bynum memos, SSIH [disability program] transmittals, parallel DO [district office] instructionals, RO [regional office] instructionals, BSSI circulars, Claims Manual transmittals, etc., all on this same subject."

"It is apparent," wrote the manager of the Fort Lauderdale, Florida, office, "that systems-generated overpayments to the extent of thousands of dollars weekly are occurring continuously. . . . we estimate that at least 95 per cent are waivable under current instructions. . . ." He called SSI a "paper-clogged administrative nightmare."

"... the 'we can do it' attitude of the DO staff that confronted any organizational or service problem in the past has been replaced by 'we'll do what we can' or 'whatever you say,' " wrote the manager of the Farmington, New Mexico, office.

"As administrators and taxpayers, we find this not only disturbing, but frightening," wrote the manager of the Springfield, Massachusetts, office, after describing how $70,000 worth of overpayments had been waived in three days.

GRANDFATHER CLAUSE

There was yet another "baron" who felt the need to make "input" on SSI during 1973. This was Russell Long, chairman of the Senate Finance Committee. As originally written, SSI contemplated a uniform maximum payment for all recipients, regardless of where they lived or how much they had been getting under the old state or county programs.

In June 1973, Long learned that the uniform payment scheme meant that, while many would have their welfare payments raised, some would have to take cuts when SSI came into being. Specifically, he was worried about 45,000 voters in his home state of Louisiana who would suffer decreases. The uniform payment system was one of the major bulwarks of SSI. That was what made the program "simple."

Some congressmen spend years trying to pass major changes in social programs. It took Long two weeks.

He worked up a "grandfather clause" that would require Social Security to figure out what a person's welfare check would be under the rules of the 1,149 local welfare programs (many of which have a variety of different payment formulas). If the federal payment was lower than that, the Long amendment forces the state to make a "mandatory supplement" or face a loss in Medicaid funds.

Long tucked it into a bill, "Extending the Renegotiation Act of 1951." It was hardly debated by Congress, but it forced Social Security to replan SSI at a time when the agency had expected to be putting on the finishing touches. Suddenly, the old welfare system had been grafted onto the new system.

Forty of the 80 computer programs governing SSI operations had to be completely rewritten. New information had to be solicited from 48 states, and new contracts had to be negotiated with 31 states which would have to pay the supplement.

The resulting delay meant that some of the computer programs intended for SSI would not be ready when the system began. One of these was the link-up or "interface" between SSI records and records of other government benefits, such as Social Security retirement and survivor's insurance payments and veterans benefits. Knowing that recipients have other government income gives SSI a way to check a client's real needs and reduce his benefits accordingly.

The link-up with regular Social Security benefit records took place 18 months after SSI began. The link-up with records of the Veterans Administration may take place sometime next year. These delays are now believed to be major causes of overpayments.

CAN DO

The "can do" attitude was one that SSA director Cardwell had tried hard to preserve—one that he shared himself. As the January 1 deadline approached, Cardwell refused to exercise the option Congress had given him of delaying the start of the program if there were problems. Cardwell felt the option was really a phantom. Powerful people like Long in the Senate and Caspar Weinberger at HEW had parental feelings about SSI. Cardwell felt he could not disappoint them. As he put it later, explaining his decision to go ahead:

"Our political system, the way it operates—I have difficulty conveying this to people—doesn't permit in a period of, say, 30 to 60 days the development of an abrupt change in this kind of policy. We would have had to prove, I think, beyond the shadow of a doubt, that we couldn't make it happen in order to get a consensus within either the executive branch or the Congress that a delay was necessary."

The scenes in Weinberger's office when Cardwell came to report must have resembled those described in Albert Speer's *Inside the Third Reich:* Goering assuring Hitler more and more confidently, as the situation deteriorated, that the troops at Stalingrad would be supplied by air. "I personally guarantee [it]," he said. "You can rely on that."

So the battle of the barons, the interfering politician, and the misplaced "can-do" spirit all conspired to disable this first attempt at a rational national welfare program.

Dumping $2.6 Million on Bakersfield

Michael Aron

Like the coming of the railroad, the arrival of big federal money in a small, out-of-the-way California town causes a certain amount of uproar, especially when it is dumped in a bundle by an agency that has to get rid of it quick. In this case, the money comes from the Department of Health, Education, and Welfare, for one of its 131 migrant health programs, and the town that has to fight over the grant is Bakersfield.

But it could just as well have been one of the other 130 migrant health programs, or any federal effort where the bureaucrat is mandated both to spend money fast and also to insure that local people control their own destinies. Controlling your own destiny, in these days of decentralization and revenue sharing, really means that the locals can help decide how to divvy up federal money among themselves. Bakersfield is a consequence of the whole idea of community participation in federal projects, but in this instance, the town only began participating after the money was pumped in—for very obvious reasons and with some very disruptive results.

Our story begins in Washington, D.C. in March, 1970, with the passage by Congress of the Migrant Health Act. Senator Walter Mondale's Migratory Labor subcommittee drafted the legislation, authorizing an $11-million appropriation for migrant programs in fiscal 1970, and it was Mondale, personally, who pressed for insertion of an amendment providing that "persons broadly representative of all elements of the population to be served [be] given an opportunity to participate in the implementation of such programs."

Since this was the time the Nixon Administration was striving to decentralize the "vast" federal bureaucracy, it fell to the regional offices of HEW to implement the legislation. Region IX, headquartered in San Francisco, and responsible for seven Western states (it has since lost Oregon and Washington), proposed four areas with heavy migrant "home-base" populations as possible locations for health projects. Three were in rural California counties, the fourth in the state of Washington. One was Bakersfield, Kern County, California.

HEW's plan was to find a chicano community group in each area to become its delegate agency for day-to-day administration of a project, in the same way that local anti-poverty groups became delegate agencies of the Office of Economic Opportunity. But there was a time problem: the legislation had been passed relatively late in the fiscal year, giving HEW only a few months in which to spend the money or else forfeit it back to Treasury. Compounding the problem was the fact that Bakersfield seemed to have no chicano community groups—20,000 chicanos, but no groups.

With the end of the fiscal year only six weeks away, anxious rural health officials turned their attention to a black group, the Kern County Liberation Movement (KCLM). Born six months earlier in the waning hours of a poor people's workshop and designated a consumers' auxiliary of the local anti-poverty agency, KCLM was little more than a collection of low-income citizens. As its first official act, KCLM had applied to HEW for a $70,000 planning grant to assay the health needs of Bakersfield's black ghetto; that application was still in the pipeline when regional HEW asked KCLM if it would accept $2.6 million to immediately establish a health center.

KCLM responded enthusiastically: certainly they would accept a grant—who wouldn't? In late May, 1970, an official from the Rural Health Office of the Community Health Service of the Health Services and Mental Health Administration (HSMHA) of the Public Health Service of the regional office of HEW flew to Bakersfield to help KCLM prepare a formal application. All this was done very quietly, without fanfare. Final contracts were signed in June, three weeks before the end of the fiscal year.

It wasn't until July that Kern County's health establishment got wind of the news—and when they did, all hell broke loose. The entire roster of local health agencies—the county medical society, the dental society, Kern General Hospital, the county health department, the board of supervisors, the state health department, the California Medical Association; and the congressionally mandated regional planning bodies, Comprehensive Health Planning and Regional Medical Programs—vented their spleen because none had been consulted prior to the awarding of the grant. The medical society had a special reason for bitterness: it had been operating its own federally-funded migrant clinic for years in two old trailers outside of town, and HEW was cutting the budget on that program at the same time it was handing $2.6 million to a bunch of poor people with no experience whatsoever in the administration or delivery of health care.

CREATIVE FUMBLING

For five days the flap over the award commanded headlines in the *Bakersfield Californian* (in sky-blue ink, no less); the paper also editorialized against the grant ("More Fumbling and Bumbling") and even ran a two-part feature on the medical society's "wonderful clinic." Bakersfield's two Republican state assemblymen called press conferences to denounce the award. Congressman Robert Mathias sent an angry telegram to HEW Secretary Elliot Richardson questioning how the department could possibly sanction such behavior on the part of its regional office. "Is this what the Administration means by 'creative federalism'?" Mathias asked. For the next three weeks, the Bakersfield health establishment would virtually convulse in an effort to get the grant canceled.

On July 14, Dr. James Cavanaugh, deputy assistant secretary for health, announced a "full review" of the conditions surrounding the awarding of the grant, intimating that the contract would be canceled "if irregularities are detected."

On July 15, Cavanaugh flew from Washington to the regional office in San Francisco. In what is reported to have been a rather stormy session, Cavanaugh and regional officials rewrote the guidelines on community health grants so as to insure consultation with all appropriate state and local agencies. In Washington, meanwhile, Mathias' staff had done some checking and discovered that the Kern County Liberation Movement was not registered with OEO as an official delegate arm of the local anti-poverty agency. Mathias called Cavanaugh to ask if this were sufficiently "irregular" to warrant cancellation of the contract. When Cavanaugh said he didn't think so, Mathias asked if the contract could possibly be renegotiated under the new guidelines just promulgated. Cavanaugh said he doubted it. A Mathias press release the next day called HEW's action "inexcusable" and fixed the blame on "middle-level bureaucrats [who] ignored the letter of the law" (a reference to their failure to consult the congressionally mandated regional planning bodies).

While Mathias was busy reverse pork-barreling in Washington, physicians and politicians in Bakersfield were writing letters to anyone they could think of who might be able to reverse the decision. Let me quote from some of these letters:

Kern General Hospital Administrator Dr. Owen Hatley, to Dr. Vernon Wilson, an HEW official in Rockville, Maryland:

> When an independent, unbiased consulting firm, experienced in developing health delivery systems, presents a program for Kern County, then and only then will I support any sponsoring agency in any of these endeavors. Reputable, experienced consulting firms are available, in contrast to false-front organizations [KCLM] created to obtain desired answers to fuzzy-minded hypotheses conjured up by some social planners.

Congressman Barry Goldwater, Jr. (representing a neighboring district) to Secretary Richardson:

> ... this group [KCLM] has absolutely no experience that would even remotely qualify them for a grant of this magnitude. . . . I request that you immediately investigate this matter and withdraw the grant.

State Assemblyman William Ketchum to HEW Undersecretary John Veneman, his former colleague in the California legislature:

> I object to the "cart before the horse" manner in which this has been handled and request that you immediately stop funding. . . . [HEW's] "better to spend now than undertake planning" philosophy is a classic symptom of the whole OEO syndrome.

On July 27, KCLM held a press conference to refute the "numerous unfounded charges leveled against us in recent days." Considering the group's relative inexperience, it was an artful performance. One moment they were militant: "The low income community of Kern County wants to see a migrant health center that will meet their needs and they want to see it not after a two- or three-year planning study. Frankly we are *tired* of being studied. We want direct medical services now." The next moment, conciliatory: "Naturally we welcome the cooperation and support of any agencies interested in meeting the common goal of comprehensive health care for the entire community."

In San Francisco, meanwhile, regional HEW was kept busy trying to explain its actions to HEW officials in Washington. An assistant regional director recalls: "Washington was not terribly happy with us, and that's the understatement of the year. Of course, we knew what we were doing all along. We were going to get funding into that area no matter who it upset, and not by the traditional route of currying favor with conservative county medical societies. To get things done, you go do them and fight the political battles after—especially in this Administration. We like to think of ourselves as 'bureaucratic guerrillas' fighting for what we believe in."

By July 29, it was compromise time. Cavanaugh and Mathias flew to Bakersfield together to announce that HEW was suspending project funds for 90 days pending a "restructuring" of the KCLM board of directors. The suspension, Cavanaugh told a press conference, would be lifted only when the board, then made up entirely of "consumers," added professional health-care "providers" to its membership. Cavanaugh's, too, was an artful performance (which may help explain why he is now on the White House staff). He seemed genuinely pained by "this unfortunate misunderstanding." He urged the Bakersfield health establishment to play an "activist" role on the consumer-provider board, and assured his good friends that "this sort of thing will not happen again." Privately, he told Mathias that HEW would consider canceling the grant if KCLM should fail in any way to execute its provisions. And when the man from HEW left town that night, KCLM was still the beneficiary of the potential $2.6 million.

Although project funds were technically suspended, regional HEW began sending "emergency" funds to KCLM to keep it on its feet. The grant had called for expenditures of $391,000 in the first year—$248,-000 for staff salaries and the rest for clinic facilities and supplies. (And when they tell you they're putting X million dollars into programs for poor people, remember: professionals, clericals, and private businesses get the money; the poor get services.) Before any of this money could be spent, however, it would be necessary to hire a project director, preferably one who could court the favor of the health establishment and orchestrate a restructuring of the board.

Regional HEW proposed that a young dental school graduate from San Francisco become interim project director until a permanent director could be found. KCLM agreed, and Robert Isman, D.D.S., assumed his duties in August.

Through the fall months Isman worked hard to win the cooperation of local health agencies, but two things were working against him: his longish hair and what they call in Bakersfield "ultraliberal leanings." City officials, whose own budgets only added up to something like $12 million, simply could not understand why HEW would select such a character to supervise a $2.6-million project. He had no experience, either dental or administrative. He showed up for meetings with bankers and lawyers wearing cut-off jeans and thongs. To this day, people talk about Isman as if his eight months in Bakersfield had been profitably spent dealing hashish on the side.

It took much persuasion and several trips to Bakersfield by regional HEW officials, but in November the KCLM board was restructured to include 10 professional health providers representing various agencies in the county, including the medical society, which put its migrant clinic director on the board but instructed him not to vote. (The argument is sometimes advanced that the medical society joined only to sabotage the project, because free health care for the poor takes money out of the pockets of local physicians and the county hospital; but there's too much conspiracy theory there, or at least not enough money involved to make it credible.)

That the consumers still outnumbered the providers 25 to 10 irked some people, however. Mathias' local aide called the restructuring "a token effort to appease the community." Assemblyman Stacey branded it "a sham and a fraud" and joined the ranks of the countless politicians who at one time or another have accused HEW of "strong-arm tactics."

With the board restructured, everyone expected funding to resume, but HEW suddenly attached new conditions to the lifting of the suspension. KCLM either had to demonstrate broad-based community support, or hire a permanent project director.

In the meantime, forces were still at work trying to get the grant canceled. In December, the medical society applied to HEW for $325,-645, ostensibly to expand its existing clinic program, in effect proposing itself as an alternative to KCLM. In Washington, Mathias continued to warn HEW that the project was "doomed to failure" unless local agencies were brought into the fold and given more say in board policy. Quietly, Mathias also asked the Government Accounting Office for a full investigation of the activities of the local anti-poverty umbrella agency, the Kern County Economic Opportunities Corporation.

Three months went by with no progress made toward filling the project director's job and mounting hostility towards Isman from the establishment. Then in April, 1971, HEW decided to step in and temporarily take over the project itself. Vincent Garza, a Mexican-American public health officer stationed at headquarters, was dispatched to replace Isman as interim project director for 90 days. To complement this action, regional HEW abruptly canceled the dental component of the project, thus insuring Isman's complete removal from the scene. Both sides in Bakersfield welcomed the two moves—the health establishment because Garza was a professional like themselves; KCLM because it meant immediate resumption of funding.

From this point on, the struggle ceases to be one pitting organized medicine and its friends against poor people. As you will see, it evolves into a struggle pitting poor people of one race against poor people of another. There are no Machiavellian plots here, no designs by the establishment to divide and conquer. That's just the way it happens.

DUDE RANCH JUNKET

Most of the farm workers of Kern County are Mexican-Americans; maybe 20 per cent are Mexican nationals who came north to follow the soft-fruit season (legally or illegally) and managed to linger longer.

For years, these people have lived in shacks and camps or slept unsheltered on the banks of irrigation canals. Their general health is not good. They get skin diseases from working in fields sprayed with pesticides; they suffer high incidences of venereal disease, eye defects, heart trouble, and nervous disorders; obesity, hypertension, and diabetes are so prevalent that local health authorities believe these conditions to be hereditary in Mexicans; 90 per cent of the children have serious dental problems. "They're learning that an unhealthy body produces nothing," one official said, adding as an afterthought, "They've certainly learned it the hard way." It used to be that when someone got sick, he worked it off or waited it out—unless he got real sick, in which case his family piled him into a car and drove the 20 miles to Kern General Hospital where they would wait for hours in the emergency room hoping that the next intake nurse spoke Spanish. Of course, there was also the medical society's migrant clinic in trailers in Lamont, but it operated only during "the season" (May to September; the actual season is eight to 10 months), and then only three nights a week from 6 P.M. to 10 P.M. At regional HEW the clinic is still referred to as a "band-aid station."

The first thing on Garza's agenda when he arrived in Bakersfield was to find a suitable location for a health center. For several days he, an architect, and Mathias' local aide drove around the Lamont-Arvin-Weedpatch area looking for a site—and immediately a conflict arose. KCLM thought they ought to be looking in the Lakeview district, where blacks live. Garza explained that these were *migrant* funds and that it had been HEW's intention all along to put a health center someplace where the campesinos would have easy access to it. But this had not been KCLM's understanding at all; they had been led to believe, they said, that the center would be located in a black neighborhood and that campesinos from all over the county would be encouraged to use it and think of it as their own.

KCLM felt suddenly betrayed. After fighting off the encroachments of the health establishment for almost a year, they now learned that HEW wanted to put the health center in a part of the country where less than one per cent of the population is black. A bitter pill; several KCLM board members chose to resign rather than swallow it.

To sweeten it, perhaps, Garza organized a weekend outing for KCLM board members at a ranch-retreat 80 miles north of Bakersfield and invited the HEW regional director to come along and to bring some of his staff. A good time was presumably had by all, and the regional director soothed ruffled feathers by promising that no matter what happened in the future, KCLM's efforts would not go unrewarded; but folks in Bakersfield took a different view of the outing. Garza returned to Bakersfield on a Monday morning to find himself being blasted on the front page of the *Californian* for his "$2,500 dude ranch junket" financed by "the tax-payers." (The story was written by the son of the county health superintendent, which says something about small cities.) Three weeks later, Garza left Bakersfield and the Public Health Service and went to Yale on a fellowship.

Garza was replaced in July, 1971, by Charles Pineda, a Mexican-American native of Kern County, the son of a fruit picker and holder of a master's degree in social work. Pineda continued the search for a clinic site and also began to think about recruiting a medical staff.

HMM ... FEDERAL FUNDING

In September, 15 months after the awarding of the grant, a makeshift clinic was finally opened in Lamont. Pineda had found a young doctor from Los Angeles to become clinic physician ($25,000), had lured an aging South American from a hospital in the Bronx to become medical director ($27,500), and the three of them had talked the medical society into renting its trailers to KCLM until a permanent location could be found ($1,600, which has never been paid). As soon as the medical society clinic shut down for the "winter," KCLM occupied the trailers and began treating its first farm-worker patients. Pineda, meanwhile, found an old grocery store in Weedpatch, leased it, and gradually moved the project into it over the next three months.

The clinic in Weedpatch is a shock when you first see it. Somehow the term "migrant health center" leads you to expect a depressing store-front, partitioned in half, and dimly lit, with maybe a purple curtain separating the waiting room from the examining room, and a wizened old doctor inside waiting to grab you in his palsied, age-blotched hands. You walk into the clinic in Weedpatch, however, and your first thought is "hmmm ... federal funding." The clinic is partitioned all right, but partitioned into a large reception room, two intake offices, five examining rooms, a treatment room, a laboratory, a records library, staff offices, and a lounge. The staff numbers about 25. The equipment is brand new, ultramodern, and *clean.* When you open your mouth to say "aaahh ..." in this clinic, you're opening it to an electronic implement coming out of a wall console.

To the campesinos and their families, the clinic is a godsend. It heals them, soothes them, educates them, trains them, employs a few of them —all free of charge, for the time being. HEW wants the clinic to become self-sufficient, so patient billings will begin in the near future; but treatment will still be "free" (sort of) for the 90 per cent who belong to the union's "Robert F. Kennedy Farm Workers' Medical Plan" (for which a small premium is deducted from their paychecks). At last count, the clinic had given treatment to 6,000 patients from 1,200 families, and thanks to the imperatives of bureaucracy, each one now has a detailed record of his medical history, probably for the first time in his life. Ask the campesinos whom they thank for all this, and you get a surprising —no, not surprising—answer. Senator Kennedy, of course. The young one.

CHICANOS IN THE WINGS

But don't get the idea that just because the clinic opened, the infighting ceased. On the contrary, now there was something tangible to fight over.

An interesting bit of correspondence circulated around Bakersfield at this time, copies of an exchange between HEW Secretary Richardson and Senators Walter Mondale and Adlai Stevenson III, past and present chairmen of the Migratory Labor subcommittee. Richardson's letter to the subcommittee requested "clarification of congressional intent" regarding the consumer-participation amendment to the Migrant Health Act. Mondale wrote back: "I was shocked to learn that there is still substantial doubt as to your Department's implementation of an amendment which became effective in March of 1970." Stevenson wrote: "I am extremely concerned that Migratory Health Program relations and guidelines provide the basis for 'meaningful' farm-worker participation, rather than a degree of 'tokenism.' This, of course, requires a policy-making function for the farm-worker participants rather than merely an advisory role."

It was regional HEW that flooded Bakersfield with copies of the exchange. And for a reason. KCLM was still the delegate agency administering the project, but it no longer could be said to represent the true "consumers." Now that the clinic had opened in Weedpatch, the consumers were campesinos. It was *they* who should be doing the community-participating.

This was fine with project director Pineda, a chicano whose father was still out in the fields; it was fine, as well, with the clinic staff, half of whom were Mexican, and others who had to have been sympathetic to the plight of farm workers in the first place in order to have accepted a job in a town as Godforsaken as Weedpatch. KCLM, on the other hand, was naturally upset: first, they had "lost" the clinic itself; now they were faced with possible loss of control over it and forfeiture of their status as a bona fide government delegate agency.

Acting on their own authority, but with behind-the-scenes encouragement from regional HEW, Pineda and several clinic staff members appointed five reasonably intelligent, but non-English-speaking, campesinos to a "campesino board," a kind of shadow cabinet that would wait in the wings ready to take over at the earliest signal from HEW. That they were non-English-speaking meant that they had to rely on people like Pineda to tell them what was going on. This was in October.

On December 14, KCLM voted to fire Pineda. The official reasons are not worth going into—basically they questioned Pineda's competence. The actual reason was that Pineda had been attempting to serve two masters at once, KCLM and the campesinos, and his allegiance to the former seemed to be flagging. Informed of the dismissal, regional HEW immediately ordered him reinstated, saying that KCLM no longer had legal authority to make such a decision (because it no longer represented "consumers").

At its next regular meeting, on December 22, KCLM voted to change its name to the Kern County Health Committee (KCHC). This is not insignificant. It represents a conscious grab at respectability and tacitly acknowledges its new position in the battle configuration. How can you call yourself a liberation movement when you're fighting to preserve a vested interest?

CULTURALLY UNFIT

Two things of consequence happened in January. First, elections for a new campesino board were held in Lamont-Arvin-Weedpatch; four of the five men who had been appointed by Pineda in October won election to the board. (The fifth would have won, too, had he chosen to run.) The board then incorporated itself as Clinica De Los Campesinos, Inc. (CDLC). Second, the clinic's South American medical director failed his state medical board examination, meaning he was without a license to practice in California.

In February, the roof caves in.

On February 14, 24 hours before KCHC was supposed to transfer authority to CDLC, the KCHC board notifies Pineda of his dismissal in a memo listing eight specific grievances, one claiming he hired the South American medical director without consulting the board and another charging him with "loading" the clinic staff with Mexican-Americans.

On February 15: KCHC, citing election "irregularities," rejects the legitimacy of the CDLC board and refuses to transfer control of the project.

On February 16: 200 chicano demonstrators mass in front of the clinic, Pineda and two clinic staff members among them, carrying picket signs and threatening to "shut it down" (in Spanish). The black chairman of KCHC wades into the angry mob and fires the two staff members on the spot. Half of the demonstrators move down the highway to the KCHC administrative office in Lamont. The demonstrations last until midnight without serious incident.

February 17: The clinic has been splattered with paint during the night. There are bullet holes in the plate glass window. KCHC's black chairman appoints himself "acting project director." Regional HEW officials fly down from San Francisco in the hope of restoring order; they put the KCHC chairman on notice that his assumption of the project directorship constitutes a flagrant conflict of interest. Two-thirds of the clinic staff send individual letters to HEW declaring their allegiance to CDLC.

February 18: A provider member of the KCHC board calls the executive secretary of the medical society at midnight and, on behalf of KCHC, pleads for help. The executive secretary calls his 30-year-old assistant, Riley McWilliams, at 2:30 A.M. and orders him to report to KCHC the next day to become interim project director.

February 23: Telegram to KCHC from regional HEW states: actions of KCHC in direct contradiction to agreements; therefore, project funds would be suspended indefinitely and funding to KCHC would terminate on April 15, 1972.

February 24: Local aide sends confidential memo to Mathias in Washington warning of black-brown racial conflict that could engulf the county; says black community promises reprisals if any harm comes to KCHC chairman; surmises that United Farm Workers are involved in demonstrations.

February 26: CDLC writes to Secretary Richardson—letter begins, "Honorable Sire"; informs that Riley McWilliams made project director without HEW approval; ends with veiled threat to close clinic down as "last resort."

February 28: Medical society applies to HEW for $155,891 grant to expand its own clinic; application states, "basic to this proposal is removal of the existing clinic."

February 29: KCHC chairman reports alleged threats to his person.

March 10: CDLC submits application to HEW to take over administration of project; application actually written by four clinic staff members.

March 17: Twelve clinic staff draft joint letter to HEW threatening to resign if CDLC not made delegate agency; claim Riley McWilliams culturally unfit to be project director.

BENT IN THE FIELDS

April 15, the date HEW said it would terminate the project funding to KCHC, came and went, with no word from San Francisco. Three weeks later, the regional director sent letters to KCHC and CDLC proposing a joint luncheon meeting on May 10 at the posh (for Bakersfield) Casa Royale motel. He also sent a letter to the medical society announcing an award of $67,000 to continue their clinic-on-wheels, providing they move it to Buttonwillow, in the southwest part of the county. (Buttonwillow's one physician raised a stink, but that is another story.)

The regional director, the black project officer, and the chicano Public Health Service officer from Los Angeles arrived in Bakersfield the morning of the 10th. At noon they joined the KCHC board for lunch. The CDLC board had been invited to come at 1 P.M., but the hour passed 2 P.M. and the five campesinos had yet to show. Someone suggested that they might have gotten lost, since surely they had never been to the Casa Royale before. Someone else was delegated to go look for them. He found them in their customary positions for that hour, bent over in the fields in 95-degree heat. They said they had not been notified of the meeting. There was reason to think that one of their advisors on the clinic staff had intercepted the letter for reasons she believed to be in their best interests. The meeting proceeded without them. A radical Lutheran minister acted as their unofficial spokesman.

When it was over, an elaborate compromise had been drawn up: 1) the CDLC board would be absorbed into the KCHC board; 2) four providers mutually agreed upon by KCHC and CDLC would join the five campesinos, together to constitute a separate board-within-a-board; 3) the mini-board would serve in a "policy-recommending" capacity and receive the benefit of "whatever training and experience is available"; 4) on or before January 1, 1973, KCHC would transfer administrative control of the project to CDLC, retaining for itself only the role of fiscal intermediary. A fifth provision went unstated, but was well understood nonetheless: in return for its great efforts and considerable sacrifice, KCHC would become HEW's "umbrella agency" for all future projects in the county.

HEW and KCHC signed the compromise that afternoon. In the evening the five campesinos met with their supporters in the basement of the Lutheran Church in Lamont. Heated debate lasted past midnight, but the campesinos finally decided to sign the compromise. "It was not a victory, it was not a defeat," said CDLC chairman, Natividad Arreolo, weary perhaps in the knowledge that he was due out in the fields again at 4 A.M.

IF WEEDPATCH HAD MOVIES

That should be the end of the story. You know it's not. In the months since, there have been controversial hirings and firings, protest resignations, accusations of petty theft, and at least one false rumor of a sexual nature deliberately planted to discredit a potential project director.

The real problem with this project, and, one suspects, with others as well, has been the ease with which political considerations were able to obscure the stated objective, namely, comprehensive health care for farm workers—combined with the fact that HEW would seem to have subordinated the stated objective to an unstated, or at least secondary one, namely, Mexican-American community organization. Thus, it took 15 months of sparring and jockeying before a single patient was seen. And once opened, the clinic had to shorten its hours anytime HEW felt it necessary to suspend funds in order to reprimand this faction or that.

The medical society seems to think that because doctors can save lives on a surgical table, their expertise necessarily embraces all facets of medicine, including how it should be delivered to people whom the doctors barely understand, can't talk to, and don't especially like—and the medical society fights to preserve the integrity of that idea. The poor people, black and brown, want better medical care than they are accustomed to receiving, but they also want power and respectability and anything else that might foster the illusion that they are swimming into the mainstream, and if a government health project is the only game in town, they'll jump at the chance to play it, and they'll play it as fiercely and seriously as they imagine it to be played elsewhere, and so what if the brothers and sisters have to wait a little longer for something they have never had anyway. And the whites on the clinic staff and the others lurking in the background all the time probably wouldn't be so eager to stir up the waters if only Weedpatch had a movie theater.

The government, through all this, has been like a ship captain steering the project towards shores the crew can't see yet. For the crowd in San Francisco, the project has been, and continues to be, "an interesting social experiment" (an assistant regional director's words), originally conceived to meet a singular need, but taking on added dimensions as it unfolds. Can blacks and browns work together? Are illiterate campesinos capable of self-administration? What adjustments can we make to keep the community from blowing apart? "I would say we've basically been more interested in using the clinic as an instrument of long-range social change than in meeting the short-run health needs of the target community," one HEW official admitted, fully aware that this is the kind of statement bureaucrats get roasted for every day.

To date $400,000 has been spent on the project, a mere fraction of the $13 billion HEW spends every year on health programs. One shudders at the thought of KCLMs and medical societies and campesino-equivalents plotting and maneuvering against each other and intramurally in every community where federal grants have been won; and yet, that is probably what happens, and is happening, all over the country at this moment.

"Kern County?" a project officer asked rhetorically. "Oh, it's not so bad there. These things are usually much worse in urban areas."

Why Lindsay Failed as Mayor

Steven R. Weisman

In 1965, John V. Lindsay was elected mayor of New York City with the slogan: "He is fresh and all the others are tired." No one believed those words more than Lindsay himself. In a city nearly 75 per cent Democratic, he was the first non-Democrat elected mayor since Fiorello LaGuardia in 1934. He entered office a dashing patrician and cultivated political figure, but his image was not the only fresh contribution. More important was his notion of the mayor's job and how he wanted to change it.

POLITICAL BUNIONS

Lindsay's predecessor, Robert F. Wagner, Jr., had operated in the traditional manner of big-city Democratic mayors, like Richard Daley in Chicago, in his use of patronage, persuasion, and general finesse to keep things running smoothly. Wagner and his huge bureaucracy functioned on the same wavelength. Like most city workers, Wagner was a Democrat. He had been close to party politics since childhood, when his father, a U.S. Senator, was a leading advocate of labor causes. Mayor Wagner had gone to Yale, like Lindsay, but he grew up in city government and entered City Hall with an almost intuitive sense of the terrain. If a garbage man in Brooklyn had bunions, they used to say, Bob Wagner's feet hurt.

No one, not even Lindsay, denied that Wagner had been a deft administrator. By 1966, however, riots and revolt besieging American cities seemed to undermine all the old ways of doing things. Lindsay, for one, concluded that city government had grown tired and clubby with Wagner's "power brokers," that it had lost its capacity to handle what everyone was now calling "the urban crisis," and that it was not equal, especially, to the bold new tasks he had in mind.

In these perceptions, Lindsay was in the political tradition of the Progressive movement of the turn of the century. Like the Progressives, the Mayor felt that modern government needed to replace the discord of clashing special interests with a new harmony of shared purpose. Lindsay's hero is not Franklin, but Theodore Roosevelt, the activist President with a vision of a new nationalism who saw the presidency as a "bully pulpit."

I am the Mayor!

—John V. Lindsay, 1966

Lindsay's congressional career had taught him little of the need for subtle bureaucratic maneuvering, for understanding an opponent's self-interest, or for the great patience required in a sprawling government. What also became clear in his earliest days was Lindsay's magisterial conception of his own office, a sense that his authority and superior perspective permitted him to monopolize the political process, and that because he was the mayor, everyone else had to defer to his point of view.

Nothing more dramatically illustrates his difficulties in this regard than Lindsay's clumsy dealings with labor.

His first tangle with a city union—in New York's 12-day transit strike —set a pattern that held for years. The huge settlement had national impact.

Though Lindsay emerged from the transit crisis with an enhanced reputation as a combatant for clean government, it is clear in retrospect that the strike hinged more on his imperious attitude than on any issues as he defined them.

For years, Mike Quill, president of the Transport Workers Union, had made something of a tradition of his pre-New Year's Eve strike threats. But his 11th-hour settlements, looking like hard-won union triumphs, were really triumphs of public relations. "Quill always inflated his demands," says one man close to the negotiations. "He needed the strike threat to force a compromise on his union. Actually, his settlements were never that generous."

Lindsay saw Quill's tactics differently. He refused to play the game of negotiations because it clashed with his ideas about his office. "I am the Mayor," he once snapped to a raucous group of reporters who surrounded his limousine, "and you have an obligation to treat me with respect."

With his view that bargaining was a concession to the "power brokers"—"They know who they are," he said—Lindsay could not politically afford a settlement that even looked like a backroom deal. Not until the strike reached catastrophic proportions did he finally negotiate seriously with the unions. Experts agree that the final settlement cost the city twice what Quill would have agreed to at the outset.

In 1967, Lindsay once again refused to recognize the politics of union leadership. The man who had urged a bombing halt in North Vietnam on the basis that the bombing only stiffened Hanoi's will to resist, wanted to call out the National Guard to break a strike by garbage men. Governor Nelson Rockefeller refused Lindsay's request, and an agreement was finally reached. Once again, the Mayor emerged with a political victory masking a costly settlement.

The magic of the Mayor's popular triumphs over unions dissipated the next year in a strike by the city's 60,000 teachers—the worst crisis New York has faced under Lindsay because it fanned racial tension into open violence and created an ugly atmosphere of discord that has not completely receded today.

The teachers' strike was not about wages, but the organization of the school system. The origins are found in the growing demand for "community control" of schools and the liberal response of Lindsay, who, with the help of his friend, McGeorge Bundy, and the Ford Foundation, created three experimental community school districts in disadvantaged areas of the city. The root cause of the crisis was that the relation of these districts to the larger school structure was unresolved. It was also a mistaken upper-class bias, which Lindsay acknowledges today, to select no middle-class neighborhoods for the experiment. From the beginning, no one had bothered to define the powers of the local boards, and Lindsay and Bundy misjudged the stakes that certain other parties had in the situation, particularly the city's powerful, largely Jewish teachers' union.

The strike began in the spring of 1968, when the school board in the black Brooklyn slum of Ocean Hill-Brownsville abruptly dismissed 10 white teachers in their district. A hundred local teachers walked out in sympathy, and they, too, were fired. The following summer, Lindsay misjudged the teachers' willingness to fight for their jobs, and he did nothing to resolve the dispute. In September it was too late, and teachers all across the city refused to work. By this time, the ante had been raised and the Mayor was reluctant to intervene because he feared race riots in Brooklyn if the blacks were defeated. Instead of seeing that the teachers had legitimate grievances in a complex situation, the Mayor forfeited his own role as mediator by denouncing them as lawless, unscrupulous enemies of New York City. His high-handedness was a disruptive factor that prolonged the strike. In the end, the teachers won, returning to work on their own terms.

One of the great myths about city government is that the "old pros," the organization party regulars and the patronage seekers, were skillful, adept managers of city affairs.
—John V. Lindsay, in *The City*, 1970

Because of his mandate, his campaign and his commitment, and perhaps because he fervently believed his campaign rhetoric, Lindsay wanted to be a great mayor, and that meant bringing government into what he saw as the modern era. Lindsay clearly believed in "scientific management"—the notion that, as Walter Lippman wrote in 1914, "as the modern world can be civilized only by the effort of innumerable people, we have a right to call science the discipline of democracy."

Facing his bureaucracy for the first time, Lindsay quickly found reinforcement for his skepticism. That first summer, he learned that City Hall had no permanent lines of communication to New York's tension-filled ghettos, though scores of agencies dealt with the ghettos every day. He was horrified to find that he had no early-warning system to detect potential crises. There was also no formal way for Lindsay to keep tabs on his giant government to see exactly what it was accomplishing. He learned that the work of many departments overlapped, so that one agency might be planning apartments for land already slated for a new road, simply because there was no official information center. There were no statistics on welfare, leaving officials to guess, for instance, how many recipients were actually employable. There was no precise city-wide picture of the garbage problem—no one could clearly demonstrate why some streets were dirtier than others. And if the

Mayor wanted to learn the current status of a school, a library, or a police precinct nearing construction, his aides had to call public works, or the budget bureau, or the purchase department or the legal department, and ask if they had the papers. "There were no manuals!" A Lindsay aide said recently. "There were no manuals on how things worked!"

Confronting these problems, Lindsay made two deductions: his difficulty in establishing what was going on persuaded him that nothing, indeed, was going on; and his inability to see decisions being made led him to think no one was making them. A pragmatic reason for Lindsay's turning to "management science," then, was simply to get information on his desk. He also thought he could use the new management techniques to run the city by circumventing the bureaucracy he distrusted.

PPBS ON BROADWAY

The best way to see management science is through one of the Mayor's most important appointments—his first budget director, Frederick O'R. Hayes, a nervous, intense professional with a clipped mastery of facts who became the Robert McNamara of the Lindsay administration. In fact, Hayes came from Washington and the war on poverty, where he had implemented "systems analysis" techniques first introduced by McNamara in the Pentagon. In New York, he recruited dozens of young generalists to examine and quantify problems in depth, turning the production of each year's budget into a year-round analytic process, known as Program Planning Budget System, or PPBS. He also convinced Lindsay to increase the use of such private outside consultants as the RAND Corporation, the California think-tank that helped McNamara design weapons systems.

In 1968, Lindsay and Hayes established a new city unit, the Project Management Staff, a trouble-shooting group of 40 roving analysts who took on dozens of specific projects to push through the city red tape. For each project, the staff produced a giant organization chart depicting New York's bureaucratic obstacle course: it took 71 steps through 10 different agencies just to order a desk or a garbage truck for the Model Cities program. Then the staff worked at eliminating some of the steps. One assistant recalls: "If you were building a new Police station, you'd go to the engineers in Public Works and say, 'Why do you wait for the architects to finish before you start?' They'd say, 'Well, we have to wait for the plans.' So we'd say, 'Why don't we get a duplicate set of plans?' No one had ever thought of that before."

The Project Management Staff was successful in key areas: it helped cut 100 weeks from construction schedules for police, fire, and library projects and slashed dozens of weeks from the time it had taken to plan sewers and parks. It produced important Lindsay innovations—a massive test of children for lead-paint poisoning, a new bureau to handle parking violations, and a program that puts addicts on methadone. It used computers to analyze data from all agencies—a computer was even fed data from the city's 503 tennis courts to set fees adjusted to each court's use. And it helped the city's uniformed services—police, fire, and sanitation—to reshuffle manpower and equipment to increase productivity.

GRASPING THE OBVIOUS

Yet management science proved to be far from perfect. For one thing, the Mayor's staff saw an illusion of progress just because they were receiving their reports and organization charts. Though many reports were helpful, others told little that wasn't already known. The major conclusion of one 75-page consultants' report on traffic patterns in the Bronx, the city's northern borough, for example, was that traffic tends to flow into Manhattan in the morning and out at night. Another reported that the peak hours of the Staten Island Ferry are the morning and evening rush hours. "A consultant," grumbled one commissioner, "is someone who borrows your watch to tell you what time it is."

A second problem with the new approach was that the experts never told how all their proposals were to be carried out. Lindsay tended to believe that once he and his advisers decided on a new way of doing things he could just give the order and it would be done. That tactic worked no better within his own government than it did with the labor unions. Any bureaucracy is a tangle of loyalties to bosses, unions, subordinates, political parties, and individual careers—not just to the man on top. And since Lindsay all along insisted on circumventing the bureaucracy with his new breed of experts, it is not surprising that the city's regular employees—the ones ultimately responsible for carrying out the orders—would respond with less than complete loyalty to their mayor. Lindsay stumbled worst over this problem with his sanitation department, where Budget Bureau analysts measured garbage on the curbs and pored over figures on production and manpower before they proposed changes of garbage truck routes and the use of much bigger trucks. "We had it all figured out," says a former Budget man. "The figures showed the streets would be 85 percent cleaner in six months. Six months passed and there we were, looking at the same filthy streets. Nothing changed except the statistics."

The problem stemmed in part from flaws in the original analysis, but mostly from a crucial oversight of the fact that the men would still do the same amount of work each day unless motivated to do more.

A GOOD CITY—ON PAPER

The chief inadequacy of management science, however, lies in its assumption that every consequence and detail of each proposal can be measured. That assumption created a political vacuum for decision-making where human nature played no part. Robert McNamara faced the same problem in the Pentagon when his experts designed a swing-wing bomber or strategy for the war that was very logical— on paper.

Lindsay's improvements looked good on paper, too. It was sound logic to coordinate the assortment of 50 departments into a dozen "super-agencies," but once it was done, few things changed and some even got worse. The heads of lower departments retained their titles of "commissioner," and the Mayor didn't help when he frequently overruled a superadministrator in favor of his subordinate. The Housing and Development Administration, the city's first superagency, became so unwieldy that mismanagement festered in a program of city loans for slum rehabilitation and then broke into a scandal, mostly because it escaped the attention of the otherwise preoccupied housing chief.

The same kind of blundering surfaced in other agencies. One report by systems analysts in the police department suggested a reduction of the city's 77 police precincts as an efficiency move to free more patrolmen for street duty. When Lindsay announced the phaseout in one neighborhood, residents there protested and forced him to back down. His retreat was not a sacrifice of a good idea to narrow political considerations. He retreated because his experts' solution had overlooked an important fact: fear of crime has been as harmful to New York as crime itself, and attention must be paid to both.

A final, rather tragic illustration is found in the city's recent move to cut costs at its welfare centers by eliminating the caseworker, who now sees the welfare recipient for special problems only. The caseworker system was loaded with difficulties, but the new one only worsens them because it leaves no one person responsible for a single recipient's problems. Cases that need attention have a greater chance today of getting lost in the bureaucracy. "You see the paper piling higher and higher on people's desks," says one caseworker. "It's worse than it ever was, but the experts will never know why."

If I were writing a book, it would be about the importance of a politician's image.
—former Deputy Mayor Richard A. Aurelio

SHOVELING OUT

But there was a more important event for Lindsay's career in 1969
—a 15-inch snowstorm in February that served as a catalyst for all his
woes, creating the chemistry for one of his most serious political blow-
ups. The storm, the worst in eight years, arrived with unforeseen
strength and shut the city down. Thousands were stranded at airports,
on bridges, and on highways. And in Queens, the city's middle-class
suburban borough, mounds of snow clogged the streets, even the main
ones. Days went by and still the streets were impassable. Then the
Mayor ventured out to tour the area. The vilification he met as residents
gathered by the snowdrifts to boo, jeer, and call him names was something Lindsay never expected and had never before encountered. The
storm had caused something in New York to snap. Years of pent-up
middle-class frustrations over welfare, taxes, crime, and neglect poured
out.

The rest of America may find it amusing that Lindsay was blamed for
a snowstorm, but the blame for the way the city handled it was legitimate. The storm had caused two things to collapse: not just the middle
class's hold on itself, but the whole management-science superstructure
that was supposed to run the city so effectively. Like a Vietnam war
strategist in Washington, Linday had erected an intelligence-gathering
system that neglected people and failed, in the end, to work until it was
too late. Communication with the lower-level bureaucrats had broken
down. "I sat there in Lindsay's office the day after the storm," says
former Budget Director Hayes. "I remember when he got those reports
—they told him the snow was being cleared."

The Shriver Prescription: How the Government Can Find Out What It's Doing

Jack Gonzales and John Rothchild

Sargent Shriver is best known as Kennedy memorabilia and for his ability to win appointive positions, but to some of the old bureaucrats around the Office of Economic Opportunity, he was much more threatening than that. For Shriver is one of two Western leaders in recent times who has actually tried to do something about bureaucracy—the other being Fidel Castro. And in a sense, Shriver's little war may be the more instructive of the two—for while Castro merely shut down his ministries and sent the unemployed into the cane fields, Shriver had to pick and twist from inside the bureaucrats' home territory, hoping not to arouse alarm.

Shriver's role as antibureaucrat has mostly gone unnoticed, or else it has been taken as evidence of his poor abilities as an administrator. The few people who did look into the way he ran the Peace Corps and OEO were more interested in his character than in the nature of the forces he was fighting. That approach missed the point, since he left and they stayed. The bureaucrats always stay, of course, multiplying in the artificial light like coral in heat—that is one of the dilemmas Shriver confronted. And unless somebody else starts scratching down where Shriver began, it will matter less and less about the character of the people at the top. Like the general public, the top people are pleading increasing ignorance about what their agencies are doing.

The most recent example of this comes from General John Lavelle, who was able to dump all over North Vietnam while his superiors had authorized only reaction strikes and the bombing of limited targets.

Lavelle's supposedly unauthorized sorties occurred while the Administration was trying to negotiate, and the North Vietnamese took them as evidence of bad faith. Lavelle got away with the actual bombing for the same reason his superiors later escaped any reprisals for it—Lavelle said he hadn't told the higher-ups, and they said there was no way they could have known. The generals were just like the public—in the dark about it all. Whether or not their story is true, the situation, as we will see, might not have arisen had Shriver's first bureaucratic antidote been applied.

The Office of Evaluation was something that Shriver concocted with William Haddad, an ex-newspaperman, during the early Peace Corps days. The idea was to establish an independent reporting outfit, completely separated from the normal chain of command, to roam the field, find out what was going on, and report directly back to Shriver. The chain of command could be dragged in later to argue and explain itself, but the evaluation reports wouldn't be filtered through it.

This may seem like a trivial measure, and something that had already been practiced by everybody from the Incas (spies for the sun king raced around gathering news of potential uprisings) to the Spanish, the British, and even Stalin's secret police. But Shriver's idea was different from the whisper-in-the-king's ear approach to government information. The reports of his fact-gatherers were public within the agency and everybody had a chance to react to them, correct them, and to confront the accusers. Neither was it a trivial idea to the Peace Corps or the OEO, the only two U.S. agencies that have tried it. The traditional bureaucrats didn't like Evaluation because Shriver's inspectors ruined the whole elaborate sanitizing system that made information gradually more palatable as it passed from the field on up the line. This sanitizing occurs in all government agencies, largely because if your report to your boss doesn't enable him to write an optimistic report to *his* boss, then your boss will be out of a job, and so, presumably, will you. The thought that internal muckrakers would fan out from the agency and pick up the raw scum, right from the silt bottom, and return it to the director's office in unrefined form with everybody stepping back or ducking for cover—was not comfortable to traditional bureaucrats.

So, when Shriver set up the same thing in OEO—where it was called the Office of Inspection, he immediately ran into problems with the Community Action Program (CAP) people. These were mainly cash-flow supporters who saw OEO as a kind of long drainpipe extending from the Treasury. They feared any bad news that might impede the flow, regardless of where the money might end up. The CAP forces, led by a former auto union executive named Jack Conway, soon ran into Haddad and the inspectors, who had discovered, among other things, that white applicants for OEO funds had reneged on promises to hire black staff members. In any other agency this fact would probably not have made it to the director's attention, since it would have had to rise through the hands of the very people who were busy pouring the money downward. It came through OEO courtesy of Haddad and his snoopers. They further enraged Conway by bringing up their reports of false statements on CAP applications at a senior staff meeting, a surprise attack that gave the CAP forces neither advance warning nor a chance to prepare a defense. Haddad's people didn't have to handle it this way. There might have been a lot less intense opposition to their reports if they had provided the CAP a courteous early look—but the struggle that ensued does point up the power that such information has within an agency and the potential threat that it represents.

CAP officials, particularly Conway, never forgave Haddad, and in the eyes of many bureaucrats he became just another Jack Anderson—with fink overtones since Haddad was inside the agency. Shriver supported the Haddad forces by refusing to sign Community Action grants unless Inspection approved them first. CAP, meanwhile, went to its client communities and contacts with complaints about Shriver's disregard for channels. (Without such strong support from the boss, the report-writing system would never have worked. The whole process of putting out evaluations gutsy enough to make CAP people mad was encouraged by the idea that Shriver would not only read them, or possibly reward somebody for producing them, but even might take action on them.)

PUMPING THE IRON LUNG

Shriver's slap at bureaucratic etiquette was also a challenge to CAP's view of the agency as Santa Claus. CAP partisans didn't see the point in digging up dirt about a program, since they believed that grants should be given even if the recipient used them in contradiction of the purposes of the agency. CAP mounted enough resistance to Shriver that the 1965 conference of U.S. mayors came close to adopting a resolution accusing OEO of "trying to wreck local government by setting the poor against city hall." This meant trying to cut off money.

CAP also started leaking stories to the press about Shriver's "poor administrative ability," and curiously, it was the liberal press that picked up on the charges. *The New Republic* slashed at Haddad's attack on "administrative order," a criticism that was probably true; the magazine also indicted Shriver for "administrative weakness." These charges were echoed in various ways through newspaper accounts of the OEO chaos, and you got the sense from reading them that the place was falling apart for lack of respect for the machinery. The machinery and the meddling of Inspection was the level on which the whole Conway-Shriver tussle was debated, but underlying that debate was the role of government itself. Was government to be a place to live, a secure provider of jobs, a national iron lung that must be protected from jolts and shocks so it could continue to pump out its sustenance to all those who depended on it? Or was government a catalyst, an experimenter, a change agent, a gambler that would cut in or out of projects at will, depending on whether those projects were working or whether the goals were still valid? The Conway iron lung view was essentially the same as that of the people who support Lockheed—give them the money even though the planes aren't working, don't make trouble because jobs are at stake. The Shriver Inspection office was based on the second view—in projects like OEO, government was not a warm tit. You couldn't support Inspection, and the shake-ups it might cause, without believing that programs could conceivably be reformed or even canceled—and you had to accept the second role of government for that.

FAKING OUT JACK ANDERSON

It is ironic that Shriver's Inspection office ultimately gave him a bad press, because newspaper clippings were largely the reason the office was established in the first place. Shriver saw Inspection not as a way to change OEO's mode of thinking, but as an "early warning system," to get the bad news from his own Jack Andersons before the real one caught him in *The Washington Post* without a defense. As a by-product of this public relations move, grass-roots problems of the agency would be brought to his attention, and many of them would be solved. But Inspection also helped Shriver learn where his Pakistans were, so his people could enthusiastically lead reporters away from them. This technique was perfected in the Peace Corps, where many inquiring journalists were pushed off to the success story in Ethiopia while there was a volunteer revolt going on in Peru.

We often think of the struggle between the press and the bureaucracy in terms of information hidden from the public—that they are all sitting over there, in smug knowledge, joyously slamming our fingers in their file cabinets. But even if he didn't establish it for precisely the right reasons, Shriver's Inspection office underscored the deadening effect that fear of the press can have inside the bureaucracy itself. From an agency perspective, the bureaucrat's main job is not only to hide facts from the public, but also to keep them from fellow bureaucrats up the line. When bad news gets into the papers, the superiors will read it too. If the heat is on and there might be leaks in the pipes, the best thing to do is not to send any adverse information through. Both the public and the agency's directors end up suffering from the same ignorance.

It also turns out that the greater the potential for being burned in the press, the less government officials want to know about what is happening at the lower levels. Which brings us back to Lavelle. His bombings brought a strange chorus line to Senator John Stennis' Armed Services Committee, all in a scramble to prove their ignorance. The boss' lack of awareness that his hireling was bombing the hell out of a country might be grounds for charges of incompetence, but Stennis found it reassuring, even laudable, that Abrams didn't know. The fact that the commander of the U.S. forces in Vietnam hadn't the foggiest idea what Lavelle, the commander of the Seventh Air Force, was up to, was enough to convince Stennis and most other senators that Abrams was qualified for the top post in the Army.

It is doubtful that the military brass ever heard of Shriver's inspectors, but the Lavelle case caused some of them to think of the idea on their own. Robert Seamans, Secretary of the Air Force, was concerned that the public might lose confidence in the military when it learned that some guy was wiping out a country without Pentagon knowledge. He talked of investing Air Force inspectors with more credibility by separating them from the line of command. He pointed out that there might be a problem in the fact that the Air Force inspector general closest to the Lavelle case was also the vice commander of Lavelle's air base. "That's the kind of thing we've got to take a look at," Seamans said.

The question is, who's going to look? Certainly not the inspectors, whose past performance will be brought into doubt. Certainly not top staff people like Abrams, whose protective decapitation from the rest of the military is often their only defense. Inspection won't be adopted in most agencies because it makes it harder for officials to deny that they knew what was happening all along. The way things are going in government, the only accepted defense these days is ignorance. For a government that bases its claim to wisdom on superiority of information, the recent record is startling—generals didn't know about Mylai, the Nixon finance committee didn't know about the Mexican bank accounts or how hundreds of thousands of dollars got into its hands, the antitrust people didn't know about ITT's talks with the White House, the secretary of agriculture didn't know about people benefitting from grain deals—the roll of ignorance is endless. On another level, Washington, D.C. police officials didn't know that the crime statistics were being lowered by a deliberate undervaluation of larcenies by cops on the beat. Put in inspectors who would get all this muck back to the top, and administrators everywhere would flee from the reports as if they were so many subpoenas.

CLOGS IN THE SYSTEM

Shriver-style inspection has a very short future in bureaucracy because it runs against all the grains. Information from the field flows up, but almost everything else—paychecks, status, power, influence, GS ratings, rewards—flows down. The whole GS system is powered on the energy generated by everybody caressing the bottom of the chair of the person above. Far from finding ways to get more unpleasant information to the top, the bureaucratic market in finding ways to avoid just that is growing very fast. Several have tested out well over the last decade:

Banishment. The usual fate of whistle-blowers and others who persistently demand that an agency do what it is supposed to. Too well-understood to elaborate.

The Sandwich. As discovered by reporter Frye Gailliard after investigating the Bureau of Indian Affairs. Dissident Indians were recently brought into the Bureau, but their questioning was effectively buffered by putting a traditional Bureau supporter on either side of a critical Indian. You ended up with a multilayered sandwich (dissident-loyalist-dissident-loyalist . . .) so that information from any Indian could not get any further than the next office.

Tell Me On My Own Terms. One of the beauties of Shriver's technique was not that it brought information from the field—which thousands of bureaucrats were doing every day—but the kind of information it brought. Most agencies have cleverly devised the questions so that the answers deliberately hide the real story without actually lying. It was a hard lesson for officials to learn, as David Halberstam shows in his book on the makers of Vietnam *The Best and the Brightest.* Halberstam says that on one of his first trips to Vietnam, McNamara was confronted with a barrage of glowing reports, until finally he arrived at a province in the Delta where:

Rufus Phillips' people had reported enormous Vietcong progress. A copy of the Phillips report had been made available to McNamara in the morning when the military briefing began. Taylor was standing there impressive, asking helpful leading questions: Major, we know what a good job you're doing and that this situation is under control, and we wonder if you could tell us about it? . . . McNamara had tried to penetrate these briefings in the past without much success but this time he was prepared, he had read a pessimistic paper on this same province. Had the major, McNamara asked, read the report of his civilian colleague in the Hamlet program? Yes, sir. Did the major agree with the civilian appraisal? Pause. Finally the officer said yes, he did. Why, then, asked McNamara, hadn't he reported it himself? Because his civilian colleague reported it and because he himself had reported only the military situation as set by guidelines from MACV.

This was fine as far as it went: here was McNamara, finally cutting through to the truth, and presumably he would no longer be duped by the self-serving military reports. But that optimistic conclusion misses a central point: even when accurate reports filter to the top, there is that final and most important barrier to the officials' understanding of the news—his own mind. While McNamara could be enraged at the system that kept lower-level people from getting their points across, he reacted in the following manner (a year after the Phillips incident) to this CIA briefing:

> Fitzgerald, an old Asia hand, was made uneasy by McNamara's insistence on quantifying everything, of seeing it in terms of statistics, infinite statistics. One day after McNamara had asked him at great length for more and more numbers, Fitzgerald told him bluntly that he thought most of the statistics were meaningless, that it just didn't smell right, that they were all in for a much more difficult time than they thought. McNamara just nodded curtly, and it was the last time he asked Fitzgerald to brief him.

The McNaughton Effect. There are also reasons that people along the line might not want their views to get to the top, especially middle-level officials who derive power from knowing the important players. Halberstam describes the hypnotic effect that Robert McNamara had on one of his most articulate advisors, Harvard Professor John McNaughton. In the Pentagon Papers, McNaughton comes off as the most strident hawk of all, but Halberstam shows him as one of the most intelligent and troubled doves during the early years of escalation. McNaughton pours his doubts out to one trusted friend in the Pentagon, Michael Forrestal, and then a few moments later, confronting a few colleagues who are using precisely the same arguments that he expressed to Forrestal, he tears his arguments to shreds. Halberstam outlines the forces that move the McNaughtons to keep even their most passionate opinions to themselves:

In 1964 McNaughton was very unsure of his relationship with McNamara, he was newer in his position than McNamara was in his. He was almost mesmerized by McNamara: he had never seen anything like him and admired the Secretary without reservation, being almost slavish in his subservience. That and being extremely ambitious, and wanting, now that he was operating in the big and fast world of Washington, to remain there. So he became at once the man in the government where two powerful currents crossed: great and forceful doubts about the wisdom of American policy in Vietnam, and an equally powerful desire to stay in government, to be a player, to influence policies for the good of the country, for the right ideas, and for the good of John McNaughton. Though he was a Harvard law professor, there was no more skillful player of the bureaucratic game than John McNaughton, for he understood the bureaucracy very quickly and how to play at it, and he learned this, that his power existed only as long as he had Robert McNamara's complete confidence, and as long as everyone in government believed that when he spoke, he spoke not for John McNaughton but for Bob McNamara. That, with its blind loyalty and totality of self-abnegation, meant bureaucratic power, and John McNaughton wanted power. Any doubts he had were reserved for McNamara, virtually alone, and perhaps one or two other people that he knew and trusted, who would not betray him with gossip, so that the word would not go around Washington that McNaughton was a secret dove.

. . . Later, after the war had been escalated and he had become more confident of his relationship with McNamara and more sure that the war was wrong, some of his close aides began to wonder what would happen if the President ever asked him what he, John McNaughton, thought about an escalatory move, not what the Defense Department thought, not what McNamara thought. In 1966, when the question of bombing the oil depots at Haiphong came up, and the President was going around the room trying to get a consensus, one after another they all signed on, McNamara said yes, it was time to take them out. The Chiefs and then Rostow signed on. Ball dissented. And finally Johnson turned to McNaughton, who had been arguing violently in private against this, and McNaughton said simply, "I have nothing to add, sir."

The Field Syndrome. Shriver's inspectors in OEO and the Peace Corps found that people working out on the end of government's fingers often were not all that anxious to get the facts back to Washington. Some of them were worried about how those facts might be mangled and twisted on what seemed to be the increasingly distant trip from the field to the home office. Often it was less a matter of facts than a matter of culture; the field people were concerned that their views would be understood about as much as a German pun translated literally into English.

There is also a sense—at local levels of agencies—that keeping Washington out of things is a good idea, both because you ought to be able to solve your own problems, and also because once Washington gets into it, complications generally arise. Almost every bureaucrat in the capital is hired to facilitate work somewhere out in the hinterlands. The gratitude that the field generally has toward all this aid was summed up in a report that HUD commissioned last year on the effectiveness of its field support activities: "The Assistant Secretaries seem to get much more out of Field Support than does the Field."

For their part, Washington officials are uncomfortable with the people they are actually supporting. They would much rather follow a strict find-em, field-em, fund-em, and forget-em policy, where there is no danger that an irate local official or a government caseworker who doesn't understand the system, will make trouble for the higher levels. Higher-level bureaucrats also make the mistake of thinking that a lower-level bureaucracy is actually the field. This happened in the Peace Corps, where early programmers would go to a foreign country, talk to the minister of agriculture, agree to send 30 cattle experts into an area, and come home confirmed that they had accomplished some grassroots-level planning. The 30 volunteers would arrive in their area to find that there was no cattle farming in that region.

This happens a lot, because the solution to the field problem—from the bureaucratic point of view—is always to bureaucratize the field as much as possible. You set up enough chains of command and memo flow charts so you know you are talking to a real office down there in Topeka, and not to somebody who only works out on the streets. Decentralization is accomplishing this, and there will be more and more reports from field offices, but they will sound more and more like the ones already concocted in Washington. There will probably be very little of the kind of reporting that Shriver had in mind.

I. F. STONE ON YOUR HEELS

These five bureaucratic tendencies to squash information are formidable obstacles to making inspection work in other agencies around the government, where the rubber cement is thicker and the GS trenches are deeper, and where the bosses are less willing than Shriver to admit their own mistakes, or to look closely at those made down the line. But the method did work in the Peace Corps and OEO, and while the entire bureaucracy won't unravel when one string is pulled, Shriver also yanked at a couple of others in the process.

Through the five-year plan at the Peace Corps, he challenged the tenure system. One thing he did recognize was that career instincts are the main cause of all the backing and filling and covering of tracks. If bureaucracies weren't seen as careers, there would be no need for all

the self-protection through inertial force. Shriver found a special way
to deal with the career problem in the Evaluation offices, where many
of the reports were written by journalists and other outsiders under
part-time contract. This was supposed to make the reporting tougher
and more independent, but in the Peace Corps, at least, the outsiders'
evaluations tended to be less critical than those done by permanent staff
people. But the presence of outsiders did have an effect on the regular
staff investigators, who wanted to make sure they turned in an uncom-
promising account this year because I. F. Stone might be sent to the
same place next year.

Beyond the Evaluation staff itself, Shriver proposed, and won for the
Peace Corps, the stipulation that no employee could stay around longer
than two two-and-a-half year stints. As a result, the agency was able
to attract noble transients with no niche to protect. The five-year plan,
however, had no future at OEO, which was set up by normal, level-
headed bureaucrats, and it has about as much chance of being adopted
in any other part of government as the Gay Liberation Front has of
getting invited to a White House dinner.

Inspection, and the five-year rule, were hardly enough to turn
Shriver into a bureaucratic abolitionist, but the amazing thing is that
they were the only attempts at getting around what is a growing problem for everybody. Shriver's antidotes stand out because nobody else
in government leadership over the last decade has done anything except start new agencies or talk about cutting down the size of old ones
—which never happens, for predictable reasons. Shriver's experience
tells us how far we have to go, especially since it was rewarded with the
lasting impression that he was, in the end, a bad administrator.

part 3
BUREAUCRACY
AND ITS
CONSTITUENCIES

"Constituency" is a word that ordinarily is associated with elected officials. A congressman's constituency, for example, is made up of the people who live in his district. His relationship with those constituents is a delicate one: though they give him the power he exercises in Washington, they also place limits on the ways he can use it.

Bureaucratic agencies also have constituencies which both enhance their power and limit their discretion. As Francis Rourke observes, "strength in a constituency is no less an asset for an American administrator than it is for a politician, and some agencies have succeeded in building outside support as formidable as that of any political organization. The lack of such support severely circumscribes the ability of an agency to achieve its goals, and may even threaten its survival as an organization."

Where do agencies get their support? Ironically, the most abundant source of nurture is also the least critical and, constitutionally, the least likely: Congress. As Morris Fiorina argues in "Big Government: A Congressman's Best Friend," the electoral success of legislators actually requires a bureaucracy that is both large and inefficient. Under such a system, congressmen win votes by creating new agencies and programs, then win more votes by helping voters who are victims of the new agencies' mistakes. "Congressmen take credit coming and going," concludes Fiorina. "They are the alpha and the omega."

The political parties also prop up bureaucracy rather uncritically, according to Walter Shapiro in "The Two Party Pork Barrel." Nowadays Republicans and Democrats rarely quarrel about whether government should be big or small. Instead, they argue only over which parts of it should be bigger, and which smaller. Republicans tend to support the "military pork barrel;" Democrats the "social pork barrel." "When either party talks of cutting the federal budget," writes Shapiro, "it is invariably referring to the opposition's pork barrel programs, not its own." The usual result, though, is that both barrels overflow.

If Presidents (see James Fallows' "Why Presidents Like To Play with Planes Instead of Houses" in the preceding section), congressmen, and the political parties are bureaucratic constituencies that provide powerful but generally uncritical support for bureaucracy, which constituencies impose direction on it? The answer lies in a suggestion that George F. Will once made: if you want a short lesson in American politics, pick up the District of Columbia telephone book, turn to page 357, and read four pages of listings beginning with the word "National" (for example, National Education Association, National Association of Realtors, National Association of Food and Dairy Equipment Manufacturers).

Private interest groups keep a very close watch (unlike the rest of us) on the daily activities of the particular bureaucratic agencies whose activities affect them directly. They also monitor congressmen on the committees and subcommittees who are responsible for overseeing those agencies' actions. By marshalling political pressure from their members in the form of campaign contributions for the "deserving," for example, private interest groups generally are able to persuade the agencies to see things their way. One such relationship is described in James Risser's "The U.S. Forest Service: Smokey's Strip Miners," another in Stephen Chapman's "The ICC and the Truckers." In both cases, agencies that were established to protect the public interest—in protected forests and fair shipping rates, respectively—eventually were "captured" by the very groups (the lumber companies and truck companies) whom they were supposed to be regulating.

Recently, a number of public interest groups, such as Common Cause and the various Nader organizations, have formed. Many people hoped that they would counter the influence of the private interests—after all, the distinguishing feature of the public groups was that the actions they sought from government would benefit not their members in particular, but society in general. But these groups pose problems of their own, problems of a kind anticipated by Henry Thoreau when he said that, "If I knew for a certainty that a man was coming to my house with the conscious design of doing me good, I should run for my life." Marjorie Boyd describes one such problem in "The Protection Consumers Don't Want."

In serving its various Washington constituencies—Congress, the President, the political parties, and the interest groups public and private —it becomes easy for bureaucratic agencies to overlook the rest of the country. Thus, Nicholas Lemann shows in "The View from a Small Town," by the time the government's many programs actually get to grass-roots level of implementation, they sometimes are more resented than appreciated. The bureaucracy, it seems, exacts taxes and other burdens from people with far greater efficiency than it displays in returning benefits to them. As for the individual, says Robert Taylor in "Chronic Epistlitis," he can easily get lost in the shuffle.

Big Government: A Congressman's Best Friend

Morris P. Fiorina

In this article I will set out a theory of the Washington establish-ment(s). The theory is quite plausible from a common sense standpoint, and it is consistent with the specialized literature of academic political science. Nevertheless, it is still a theory, not proven fact. Before plung-ing in let me bring out in the open the basic axiom on which the theory rests: the self-interest axiom.

I assume that most people most of the time act in their own self-interest. This is not to say that human beings seek only to amass tangible wealth, but rather to say that human beings seek to achieve their own ends—tangible and intangible—rather than the ends of their fellow men. I do not condemn such behavior nor do I condone it. I only claim that political and economic theories that presume self-interest behavior will prove to be more widely applicable than those that build on more altruistic assumptions.

What does the axiom imply when used in the specific context of this article, a context peopled by congressmen, bureaucrats, and voters? I assume that the primary goal of the typical congressman is reelection. Over and above the $57,000 salary plus "perks" and outside money, the office of congressman carries with it prestige, excitement, and power. It is a seat in the cockpit of government. But in order to retain the status, excitement, and power (not to mention more tangible things) of

Morris P. Fiorina teaches political science at California Institute of Technology. This article is excerpted from his book, *Congress Keystone of the Washington Establishment,* published by Yale Univ. Press.

office, the congressman must win reelection every two years. Even those congressmen genuinely concerned with good public policy must achieve reelection in order to continue their work. Whether narrowly self-serving or more publicly oriented, the individual congressman finds reelection to be at least a necessary condition for the achievement of his goals.

Moreover, there is a kind of natural selection process at work in the electoral arena. On average, those congressmen who are not primarily interested in reelection will not achieve reelection as often as those who are interested. We, the people, help to weed out congressmen whose primary motivation is not reelection. We admire politicians who courageously adopt the aloof role of the disinterested statesman, but we vote for those politicians who follow our wishes and do us favors.

What about the bureaucrats? A specification of their goals is somewhat more controversial. The literature provides ample justification for asserting that most bureaucrats wish to protect and nurture their agencies. The typical bureaucrat can be expected to seek to expand his agency in terms of personnel, budget, and mission. One's status in Washington is roughly proportional to the importance of the operation one oversees. And the sheer size of the operation is taken to be a measure of importance. As with congressmen, the specified goals apply even to those bureaucrats who genuinely believe in their agencies' missions. If they believe in the efficacy of their programs, they naturally wish to expand them and add new ones. All of this requires more money and more people.

And what of the third element in the equation, us? What do we, the voters who support the Washington system, strive for? Each of us wishes to receive a maximum of benefits from government for the minimum cost. This goal suggests maximum government efficiency, on the one hand, but it also suggests mutual exploitation on the other. Each of us favors an arrangement in which our fellow citizens pay for our benefits.

With these brief descriptions of the cast of characters in hand, let us proceed.

THE FIRST PRIORITY

What should we expect from a legislative body composed of people whose first priority is their continued tenure in office? We should expect, first, that the normal activities of its members are those calculated to enhance their chances of reelection. And we should expect, second, that the members would devise and maintain institutional arrangements that facilitate their electoral activities.

For most of the twentieth century, congressmen have engaged in a mix of three kinds of activities: lawmaking, pork-barreling, and casework. Congress is first and foremost a lawmaking body, at least according to constitutional theory. In every postwar session Congress "considers" thousands of bills and resolutions, many hundreds of which are brought to a record vote (over 500 in each chamber in the 93rd Congress). Naturally the critical consideration in taking a position for the record is the maximization of approval in the home district. If the district is unaffected by and unconcerned with the matter at hand, the congressman may then take into account the general welfare of the country. (This sounds cynical, but remember that "profiles in courage" are sufficiently rare that their occurrence inspires books and articles.) Politicians have propounded an ideology that maintains that the good of the country on any given issue is simply what is best for a majority of congressional districts. This ideology provides a philosophical justification for what congressmen do while acting in their own self-interest.

A second activity favored by congressmen consists of efforts to bring home the bacon to their districts. Many popular articles have been written about the pork barrel, a term originally applied to rivers and harbors legislation but now generalized to cover all manner of federal buildings, sewage treatment plants, urban renewal projects, etc. as sweet plums to be plucked. The average constituent may have trouble translating his congressman's vote on some civil rights issue into a change in his own personal welfare. But the workers hired and supplies purchased in connection with a big federal project provide benefits that are widely appreciated.

The importance congressmen attach to the pork barrel is reflected in the rules of the House. That body accords certain classes of legislation "privileged" status: they may come directly to the floor without passing through the Rules Committee, a traditional graveyard for legislation. What kinds of legislation are privileged? Taxing and spending bills, for one: the government's power to raise and spend money must be kept relatively unfettered. But in addition, the omnibus rivers and harbors bills of the Public Works Committee and public lands bills from the Interior Committee share privileged status. The House will allow a civil rights or defense procurement or environmental bill to languish in the Rules Committee, but it takes special precautions to insure that nothing slows down the approval of dams and irrigation projects.

SPEEDING UP THE PROCESS

A third major activity takes up perhaps as much time as the other two combined. Traditionally, constituents appeal to their congressmen for myriad favors and services. Sometimes only information is needed, but often constituents request that their congressmen intervene in the internal workings of federal agencies to affect a decision in a favorable way, to reverse an adverse decision, or simply to speed up the glacial bureaucratic process. On the basis of extensive personal interviews with congressmen, Charles Clapp writes:

"Denied a favorable ruling by the bureaucracy on a matter of direct concern to him, puzzled or irked by delays in obtaining a decision, confused by the administrative maze through which he is directed to proceed, or ignorant of whom to write, a constituent may turn to his congressman for help. These letters offer great potential for political benefit to the congressman since they affect the constituent personally. If the legislator can be of assistance, he may gain a firm ally; if he is indifferent, he may even lose votes."

Actually congressmen are in an almost unique position in our system, a position shared only with high-level members of the executive branch. Congressmen possess the power to expedite and influence bureaucratic decision. This capability flows directly from congressional control over what bureaucrats value most: higher budgets and new program authorizations. In a very real sense each congressman is a monopoly supplier of bureaucratic unsticking services for his district.

BLEEDING ALL OVER THE CAPITAL

Every year the federal budget passes through the appropriations committees and subcommittees of Congress. Generally these committees make perfunctory cuts. But on occasion they vent displeasure on an agency and leave it bleeding all over the capital. The most extreme case of which I am aware came when the House committee took away the entire budget of the Division of Labor Standards in 1947 (some of the budget was restored elsewhere in the appropriations process). Professors Richard Fenno and Aaron Wildavsky have provided extensive documentary and interview evidence of the great respect (and even terror) federal bureaucrats show for the House Appropriations Committee. Moreover, the bureaucracy must keep coming back to Congress to have its old programs reauthorized and new ones added. Again, most such decisions are perfunctory, but exceptions are sufficiently frequent that bureaucrats do not forget the hand that feeds them. The bureaucracy needs congressional approval in order to survive, let alone expand. Thus, when a congressman calls about some minor bureaucratic decision or regulation, the bureaucracy considers his accommodation a small price to pay for the goodwill its cooperation will produce, particularly if he has any connection to the substantive committee or the appropriations subcommittee to which it reports.

From the standpoint of capturing voters, the congressman's lawmaking activities differ in two important respects from his pork barrel and casework activities. First, legislative programs are inherently controversial. Unless his district is homogeneous, a congressman will find his district divided on many major issues. Thus when he casts a vote, introduces a piece of non-trivial legislation, or makes a speech with policy content, he will displease some elements of his district. Some constituents may applaud the congressman's civil rights record, but others believe integration is going too fast. Some support foreign aid, while others believe it's money poured down a rat hole. Some advocate economic equality, others stew over welfare cheaters. On such policy matters the congressman can expect to make friends as well as enemies.

In contrast, the pork barrel and casework are relatively less controversial. New federal projects bring jobs, shiny new facilities, and general economic prosperity, or so people believe. Snipping ribbons at the dedication of a new post office or dam is a much more pleasant pursuit than disposing of a constitutional amendment on abortion. Republicans and Democrats, conservatives and liberals, all generally prefer a richer district to a poorer one. Of course, in recent years the river-damming and streambed-straightening activities of the Army Corps of Engineers have aroused some opposition among environmentalists. Congressmen happily reacted by absorbing the opposition and adding environmentalism to the pork barrel: water treatment plants are currently a hot congressional item.

Casework is even less controversial. Some poor, aggrieved constituent becomes enmeshed in the tentacles of an evil bureaucracy and calls upon Congressman St. George to do battle with the dragon. Again, Clapp writes:

"A person who has a reasonable complaint or query is regarded as providing an opportunity rather than as adding an extra burden to an already busy office. The party affiliation of the individual, even when known to be different from that of the congressman, does not normally act as a deterrent to action. Some legislators have built their reputations and their majorities on a program of service to all constituents irrespective of party. Regularly, voters affiliated with the opposition in other contests lend strong support to the lawmaker whose intervention has helped them in their struggle with the bureaucracy."

Even following the revelation of his sexual improprieties, Wayne Hays won his Ohio Democratic primary by a two-to-one margin. According to a *Los Angeles Times* feature story, Hays' constituency base was built on a foundation of personal service to constituents:

"They receive help in speeding up bureaucratic action on various kinds of federal assistance—black lung benefits to disabled miners and their families, Social Security payments, veterans' benefits, and passports.

"Some constituents still tell with pleasure of how Hays stormed clear to the seventh floor of the State Department and into Secretary of State Dean Rusk's office to demand, successfully, the quick issuance of a passport to an Ohioan." Practicing politicians will tell you that word of mouth is still the most effective mode of communication. News of favors to constituents gets around and is no doubt embellished in the process.

In sum, when considering the benefits of his programmatic activities, the congressman must tote up gains and losses to arrive at a net profit. Pork-barreling and casework, however, are basically pure profit.

A second way in which lawmaking differs from casework and the pork barrel is the difficulty of claiming credit for the former as compared with the latter. No congressman can seriously claim that he was responsible for the 1964 Civil Rights Act, the ABM, or the 1972 Revenue Sharing Act. Most constituents do have some vague notion that their congressman is only one of hundreds and their senator one of an even hundred. Even committee chairmen, let alone a rank-and-file congressman, may have a difficult time claiming credit for a piece of major legislation.

THE SNAP TO ATTENTION

Ah, but casework, and the pork barrel. In dealing with the bureaucracy, the congressman is not merely one vote of 435. Rather, he is a nonpartisan power, someone whose phone calls snap an office to attention. The constituent who receives aid believes that his congressman and his congressman alone got results. Similarly, congressmen find it easy to claim credit for federal projects awarded their districts. The congressman may have instigated the proposal for the project in the first place, issued regular progress reports, and ultimately announced the award through his office. Maybe he can't claim credit for the 1965 Voting Rights Act, but he can take credit for Littletown's spanking new sewage treatment plant.

Overall then, programmatic activities are dangerous, and programmatic accomplishments are difficult to claim credit for. While less exciting, casework and pork-barreling are both safe and profitable. For a reelection-oriented congressman the choice is obvious.

The key to the rise of a semipermanent Washington establishment (and the fall of the non-safe congressional seat) is the following observation: *the growth of an activist federal government has stimulated a change in the mix of congressional activities.* Specifically, a lesser proportion of congressional effort is now going into programmatic activities and a greater proportion into pork-barrel and casework activities. As a result, today's congressmen make relatively fewer enemies and relatively more friends among the people of their districts. Hence, more safe seats.

To elaborate, a basic fact of life in twentieth-century America is the growth of the federal role and its attendant bureaucracy. Bureaucracy is the characteristic mode of delivering public goods and services. *Ceteris paribus,* the more the government attempts to do for people, the more extensive a bureaucracy it creates. As the scope of government expands, more and more citizens find themselves in direct contact with the federal government. Consider the rise in such contacts upon passage of the Social Security Act, work relief projects, and other New Deal programs. Consider the millions of additional citizens touched by the veterans' programs of the postwar period. Consider the untold numbers whom the Great Society and its aftermath brought face to face with the federal government. In 1930 the federal bureaucracy was small and rather distant from the everyday concerns of Americans. Nowadays it is neither small nor distant.

As the years have passed, more and more citizens and groups have found themselves dealing with the federal bureaucracy. They may be seeking positive actions—eligibility for various benefits and awards of government grants. Or they may be seeking relief from the costs imposed by bureaucratic regulations—on working conditions, racial and sexual quotas, market restrictions, and numerous other subjects. While not malevolent, bureaucracies make mistakes in their dealings with the citizenry, both of commission and omission, and normal attempts at redress often meet with unresponsiveness and inflexibility and sometimes seeming incorrigibility. Whatever the problems, the citizen's congressman is a source of succor. The greater the scope of government activity, the greater the demand for his services.

CREATIVE PORK-BARRELING

In addition to greatly increasing casework, let us not forget that the growth of the federal role has also greatly expanded the federal pork barrel. The creative pork-barreler need not limit himself to dams and post offices—rather old-fashioned interests. Today, creative congressmen can cadge LEAA money for the local police, urban renewal and housing money for local politicians, and educational program grants for the local education bureaucracy. There are also sewage treatment plants, worker training and retraining programs, health services, and programs for the elderly. The pork barrel is full to overflowing. The conscientious congressman can stimulate applications for federal assistance (the sheer number of programs makes it difficult for local officials to stay current with the possibilities), put in a good word during consideration, and announce favorable decisions amid great fanfare.

In sum, everyday decisions by a large and growing federal bureaucracy bestow significant tangible benefits and impose significant tangible costs. Congressmen can affect these decisions. Ergo, the more decisions the bureaucracy has the opportunity to make, the more opportunities there are for the congressman to build up credits.

The nature of the Washington system is thus quite clear. Congressmen (typically the majority Democrats) earn electoral credits by establishing various federal programs (the minority Republicans typically earn credits by fighting the good fight). The legislation is drafted in very general terms, so some agency, existing or newly established, must translate a vague policy mandate into a functioning program, a process that necessitates the promulgation of numerous rules and regulations and, incidentally, the trampling of numerous toes. At the next stage, aggrieved and/or hopeful constituents petition their congressmen to intervene in the complex (or at least obscure) decision processes of the bureaucracy. The cycle closes when the congressman lends a sympathetic ear, piously denounces the evils of bureaucracy, intervenes in the latter's decisions, and rides a grateful electorate to ever more impressive electoral showings. Congressmen take credit coming and going. They are the alpha and the omega.

The popular frustration with the permanent government in Washington is partly justified, but to a considerable degree it is misplaced resentment. *Congress is the linchpin of the Washington establishment.* The bureaucracy serves as a convenient lightning rod for public frustration and a convenient whipping boy for congressmen. But as long as the bureaucracy accommodates congressmen, they will oblige with ever larger budgets and grants of authority. Congress does not just react to big government—it creates it. All of Washington prospers. More and more bureaucrats promulgate more and more regulations and dispense more and more money. Fewer and fewer congressmen suffer electoral defeat. Elements of the electorate benefit from government programs, and all of the electorate is eligible for congressional ombudsman services. But the general, long-term welfare of the United States is no more than an incidental by-product of the system.

The Two Party Pork Barrel

Walter Shapiro

Since Dwight Eisenhower was elected President in 1952, the United States has been ruled, more often than not, by Republican Presidents and Democratic Congresses. Up to now, political analysts have tended to dismiss this pattern of divided government as little more than a short-term aberration. Typical is Kevin Phillips, the author of *The Emerging Republican Majority* and perhaps the most interesting current political theorist. In his recent book, *Mediacracy,* Phillips acknowledges that "debunkers of the idea of a 'new majority' [Phillips' theoretical obsession] raise a telling point: Based on historical precedents, no new presidential majority could be taking shape without bringing a Congressional majority in its wake." Phillips responds much like a Ptolemaic astronomer faced with the Copernican Revolution. Rather than abandon his theory, Phillips tries to save it with a few minor adjustments. He largely blames the failure of the Republicans to win control of Congress in 1968 and 1972 on the increase in ticket-splitting —yet develops no convincing rationale to explain why Nixon voters across the country felt compelled to vote for Democratic congressional candidates.

In their elaborate efforts to divine the national will, Phillips and other less inventive electoral theorists have neglected a much simpler explanation for the continuation of divided government: it's what the voters want. The combination of a Republican President and a Democratic Congress provides a majority of the electorate with tangible benefits they couldn't get if one party controlled both the White House and Capitol Hill. To understand what these benefits may be, we must first take a slight detour to discuss the real differences between the two parties.

A generation ago, the differences seemed apparent—the Democrats were advocates of big government and the Republicans weren't. It was as simple as that. A look at the federal budgets of the last Republican administration reveals how outmoded these distinctions have become. Under Nixon and Ford, federal spending swelled to more than $400 billion—over double the size of Lyndon Johnson's biggest budget.

By the late 1960s, social issues provided a new shorthand for distinguishing between the two parties. The Democrats took the high road, the Republicans the low. The orthodox interpretation of the McGovern debacle is that his campaign seemed so obsessively concerned with abortion, amnesty, gay rights, and the lettuce boycott that it drove Democrats who were conservative on social issues (many of whom had voted for George Wallace in 1968 and the 1972 primaries) to support the reelection of the President. It's an interesting theory, but it doesn't seem to have much relevance for 1976, since the social issues that promoted cleavages during the 1960s generally disappeared. Remember campus disorders? The only activism on college campuses these days comes from students protesting that they aren't getting enough job training. Amnesty was defused by none other than Jerry Ford. Drugs are no longer the center of national attention: marijuana use is increasingly accepted and the use of "hard" drugs has become less visible. Crime is still a serious problem, but voters have grown increasingly sophisticated about simplistic political solutions. Just because Frank Rizzo is mayor of Philadelphia doesn't mean that the city is filled with brotherly love.

This emphasis on social issues has tended to blur much more significant differences between the two parties. To my mind, the important distinction is that Republicans support the "military pork barrel" and Democrats are wedded to the "social pork barrel." When either party talks of cutting the federal budget, it is invariably referring to the opposition's pork barrel programs, not its own. Kevin Phillips, whose prose sometimes seems a parody of modern social science, puts it this way: "The important distinction appears to lie between that segment of the knowledge sector *essentially engaged in social and human resources endeavors*—academicians, urban planners, journalists, social-welfare experts—and *those whose expertise is spent in the direction of military and aerospace research, product marketing, and industrial technology.*"

THE SOCIAL PORK BARREL

We all have a fairly good sense of who benefits from the military pork barrel, but the concept of "social pork barrel" requires a bit more elaboration. In the early 1970s Edith Green—a Democratic congress-woman from Oregon who grew increasingly disenchanted with liberal social welfare nostrums—began using the phrase "Education-Poverty Industrial Complex." The actual term "social pork barrel" comes from David Stockman, a former aide to Republican Congressman John Anderson, who used it as the title of a compelling article in the spring 1975 issue of *The Public Interest.*

Stockman argues that wasteful subsidy programs for social services have replaced rivers and harbors legislation as the way in which legislators can deliver pet projects to their constituents: "The billions that pass through the social welfare budget each year are anchored in place by political sinews as sturdy as those which line the Internal Revenue Code. . . . The care and maintenance of the social welfare spending pipeline that extends to each of the 435 Congressional districts in the nation have now become a central preoccupation of Members and their staffs." Stockman's thesis is that in an era of limited government resources, we won't be able to finance expensive liberal social programs like national health insurance and a guaranteed annual income unless we eliminate many of the other subsidies that make up the social pork barrel.

While interesting in its own right, Stockman's concept of "social pork barrel" can also be used to characterize the philosophy of the Democratic Party.

There is now an awareness that a large portion of the electorate would be adversely affected by any significant cuts in the military budget. In addition to the three million soldiers and civilians on the Pentagon's payroll, there are another 1.5 million Americans directly employed by defense contractors. When you add those indirectly dependent on military spending, the number is many times larger. Shifts in federal funding patterns can plunge entire cities into mini-depressions like that of Seattle in the early 1970s.

What is not so clearly recognized is that there are millions of Americans who are equally dependent on the social pork barrel. Most of these people are convinced that they are working to solve the nation's pressing social problems, much as the executives at Grumman Aircraft are probably genuinely concerned about the growth of Soviet military strength. While those with strong ties to the military tend to be disproportionately Republican, those whose jobs are provided by the social pork barrel are understandably likely to be active Democrats. One telling illustration is provided by Daniel Moynihan's account of *The Politics of a Guaranteed Income.* Moynihan makes clear that the most damaging opposition to Richard Nixon's Family Assistance Plan came from the left, rather than from Republican conservatives concerned about "welfare chiselers" getting something for nothing. In hindsight, it is easy to understand why a group like the National Association of Social Workers would be deeply threatened by a plan to provide cash grants to the poor, rather than services. Lyndon Johnson's Great Society is now ridiculed for having provided more jobs for middle-class "poverty professionals" than direct aid to the poor. Kevin Phillips is close to the mark in *Mediacracy* when he notes that "various studies of Great Society programs have shown how little money—often 10-25 percent —actually made its way through the maze of bureaucratic, consultant, and business-contractor overhead into the hands of the poor."

Stockman's article provides some telling examples that this pattern did not end with the Great Society. In fact, it can be argued that these middle-class subsidy programs were accentuated by eight years of a Republican President and a Democratic Congress. Take the amendments to the Social Security Act that were designed to provide a broad range of social-psychological services to public assistance recipients. The goal was to help the poor become independent of welfare, but the result has been to annually provide $2.5 billion of federal funds to help support a host of day-care centers, recreation programs for the elderly, summer camp programs for the young, family counseling services and job-training centers. Rather than reducing dependency on welfare, this program has made thousands of social service workers dependent on the federal budget for their jobs. What makes matters worse is that often these services are no longer even targeted at the poor. The program has been reorganized since Stockman's article appeared. The new legislation (known as Title XX) is so complicated that consulting firms have had a field day interpreting it for states and local governments. A report commissioned by the Child Welfare League explains that "low income people" are "the basic target group for the Title XX support." But it then goes on to define "low income people" as anyone "at or below 115 percent of the state's median income level. . . ." This means —believe it or not—that probably 70 percent of the population is now eligible for federal assistance under a program designed for welfare recipients.

'FORCES OF CHANGE'?

Public employees are yet another beneficiary of the Democratic Party's social pork barrel. The federal civil service has had a definite liberal bias since the New Deal, but only recently has the identification of government workers with the Democratic Party become pronounced. In Congress, it is the conservative Republicans who mount the generally futile efforts to delay cost-of-living bonuses and raises to already overpaid federal workers. Another significant trend is the growing importance of the American Federation of Teachers (AFT) and the American Federation of State, County and Municipal Employees (AFSCME) within the Democratic Party. No major Democrat seems uncomfortable in the embrace of these unions—although they are largely responsible for New York's harrowing financial crisis.

Stephen Schlesinger's recent book, *The New Reformers,* provides an ideal illustration of the widespread failure to make a connection between unions like AFSCME and the increasing size of government budgets. Schlesinger's book is largely an uncritical paeon of praise for the "forces of change" within the Democratic Party. Along with obligatory chapters on the blacks, the women, the gays, the Chicanos, and the Puerto Ricans, Schlesinger delineates the schism in labor between those unions loyal to George Meany and those identified with the reform wing of the party. It makes for unintentionally revealing reading. Jerry Wurf, the president of AFSCME, is described in glowing terms as a "vibrant, sparkling iconoclast." Schlesinger then goes on to quote one Victor Gotbaum, "a dark, shaggy, articulate man, one of Wurf's principal lieutenants who heads the influential New York local of AFSCME." Gotbaum's predictable tirade against George Meany is not worth repeating. But while portraying Gotbaum as a liberal hero, Schlesinger neglects to mention that the exorbitant contracts won by Gotbaum's union are a major cause of New York's budget deficit. Nowhere in *The New Reformers* is there even a hint that the interests of the average taxpayer and those of Victor Gotbaum's AFSCME may not entirely coincide.

RATIONAL SELF-INTEREST

None of this, however, explains why the American voter may be displaying rational self-interest when he elects a Republican President and a Democratic Congress. Divided government means that the military pork barrel is dominant in the White House and the social pork barrel in Congress. The advantages of this arrangement over one-party control should be evident. It must be remembered that Democrats also tend to be critical of military spending and Republicans are likely to be skeptical about new social programs. If the Democrats controlled both the White House and Congress, the military pork barrel might be threatened. Conversely, if the Republicans somehow managed to obtain a congressional majority to go along with their hold on the presidency, the continuation of the social pork barrel might be jeopardized.

But the underlying ideology of both parties is "Don't Rock the Boat." For example, Hubert Humphrey's surprisingly strong showing in the 1972 California primary can be attributed to widespread fears that George McGovern would cost defense workers their jobs.

Conservative opposition to the social pork barrel is also often more theoretical than real. David Stockman notes that in Congress "the political maintenance capabilities of the system are so strong that all except the most extreme and idiosyncratic conservatives are eventually brought into the consensus. . . ." They may protest when a program is initially proposed, but before long they are voting for annual appropriations just like their Democratic colleagues.

The best indication that the American voter wants both subsidy programs going full blast is the political fate of Barry Goldwater and George McGovern—the only two presidential candidates who really threatened the status quo. In 1964 it was feared that Goldwater would dismantle the entire social welfare bureaucracy. In 1972 McGovern was portrayed as a man who would decimate the military budget. Both times the election results were overwhelmingly pro-subsidy.

THE SUBSIDY PARTY ALWAYS WINS

With this hold over both political parties, the millions of beneficiaries of the federal pork barrel should be sanguine about the future. But when your livelihood depends on the vagaries of the political process, it's dangerous to be over-confident. The anti-military rhetoric of most Democrats is enough to arouse some fears. And the budget-cutting efforts of governors like California's Jerry Brown raise the spectre of a possible new alliance between disenchanted liberals and old-fashioned conservatives.

That's why a divided federal government is needed to minimize the chances of any significant alterations in either subsidy program. Divided government alone is not sufficient—the Republicans must control the White House and the Democrats the Congress. The survival of the military pork barrel requires a sympathetic President and Secretary of Defense. An administration committed to trimming the military budget could probably prevail against a pro-Pentagon Congress. In contrast, Congress is the key to the social pork barrel. As the legislative problems of Harry Truman and Jack Kennedy indicated, social welfare programs can be easily throttled by a conservative coalition in Congress.

The U.S. Forest Service: Smokey's Strip Miners

James Risser

The director of a prominent conservation organization angrily picked up the telephone in his Washington headquarters and dialed the office of White House adviser Charles Colson. The conservation leader was worried because the U.S. Forest Service, guardian of the 187-million-acre national forest system, had endorsed a timber industry plan to vastly increase logging in the already depleted federal woodlands. The proposed "timber supply act" of 1969 appeared headed for certain passage in the House of Representatives. If the supposedly conservation-minded Forest Service could not be counted on to head off the legislation, the only hope was to persuade the White House to come out against it.

Mr. Colson was in conference, his secretary said politely. But could she help? The caller explained that he and other environmental leaders were anxious to talk to Colson, and perhaps to President Nixon himself, about the pending timber legislation.

"Oh," said the secretary, "you'll have to talk to Ralph Hodges about that. He's handling all the timber matters for us. I'll give you his phone number."

Ralph D. Hodges, Jr., is vice president and general manager of the National Forest Products Association, the timber industry's powerful Washington lobbying organization.

"That's when I knew how things really stood," the conservationist recalls.

Things stand poorly in the national forests, where the timber industry is shaving away huge quantities of public trees, while making grossly inadequate efforts to restore the barren lands. Of the 97 million acres in the national forests on which tree-cutting is allowed, there is already a backlog of 20 million acres that need reforestation or timber-stand improvement. Yet the Forest Service and the White House, to the joy of the timber industry, have recently called for a 60 per-cent increase in timber-cutting on the public forests in this decade.

The remarkable fact about the conservationist's call to Charles Colson is that he had written off the Forest Service, the once-proud agency where conservation was really born in the federal government more than 50 years ago. But his judgment was correct. For, as a half-dozen reports have documented, the sad truth is that the Forest Service has developed a saw-log philosophy toward managing the national forests since World War II. Although it is supposed to permit judicious use of the forest resources while preserving them for future generations of Americans, the Forest Service has become instead "a federal agency which measures success primarily by the quantity of timber produced weekly, monthly, and annually," according to an investigation by a University of Montana Forestry School task force.

The story of how all this happened is a sad and complex tale of an agency that has been taken over by the industry it is supposed to regulate, an agency that dances to the tune of timber-state congressmen, an agency that has forgotten that its first duty is to the long-time public interest and not to a short-term private gain. Smokey the Bear is still guarding the national forests from fire, but he would do better to protect the trees from the chain saws.

The technique that has made the chain saws more devastating as they buzz through the forests is clear-cutting—in which all trees are stripped from an area by machine whether the trees are mature or not, destroying the productivity of huge stretches of the national forests. The practice also claws esthetic horrors into the land: a clear-cut forest looks like a bomb has been dropped, with effects closely akin to those of strip mining.

As a district ranger on the Monongahela National Forest in West Virginia, Ralph O. Smoot felt the insistent pressures to provide more public trees for clear-cutting. The companies that log that area's prized hardwoods were not satisfied with the time-tested "selective cutting" methods that allowed them to harvest the older mature trees but left smaller trees to grow larger. They wanted more wood, and in 1964 they persuaded the Forest Service to adopt clear-cutting as the dominant harvesting method on the Monongahela. Clear-cutting is quick, and when the cut-over land grows back, it produces trees of the same age and size, which can be logged more easily next time and handled with speed in modern sawmills. "In other words, it's efficient, but that doesn't mean that is the way a national forest should be operated," says Smoot. He says that during his years in the Forest Service the philosophy changed, under pressure from the timber industry, to the point where a ranger "is graded on whether he meets a quota for cutting timber." Allowable cuts became goals to be achieved, rather than a maximum timber-cut figure. Smoot recalls with disgust a sale he handled in the Hunters Run section of the Monongahela—a selection cutting with only the mature hardwoods removed. "Eight years later, because the pressure was on, they went back in and clear-cut," he said.

The local citizenry around Richwood, West Virginia, rose up, complaining of the esthetic damage to the forest, the killing of wildlife, and the abrupt change in the forest ecosystem from a mixed hardwoods forest to a monocultural tree farm. They also charged that Forest Service officials had described clear-cutting as experimental and had lied to them about the extent to which it was to be used. One devastating cut covered 549 acres and laid bare what had been an important habitat for bear and wild turkey. The West Virginia Legislature responded by creating a special forest management practices commission. The commission determined that the Forest Service had become "timber-oriented" and had deliberately planned "that every single acre of the 820,000-acre Monongahela National Forest could be clear-cut sooner or later, regardless of whether an area was used predominantly for recreational activities of camping, fishing, hunting, hiking, or boating, as scenic vistas, peaceful brook, or meandering stream, or was an area in which the flora and fauna depended on the trees for cover and food." The timber industry is all-important to Richwood, whose small business district is dominated by a large Georgia Pacific mill, and it took considerable courage on the part of a small contingent of local conservationists to force the issue. "We are not preservationists," insists Izaak Walton League member Howard Deitz, who runs a Richwood shoe store. "We support use by the timber industry of the Monongahela. But we are tremendously concerned by the rapid liquidation of the remaining mature timber on the forest." Clear-cutting, he said, "is just dead wrong in a mixed eastern hardwoods forest" and, in the case of the Monongahela, was proceeding at a pace that could eventually have depleted the forest and brought economic ruin to the area.

While the Forest Service hacks away, Interior's Bureau of Land Management has taken some important strides toward reducing or eliminating massive clear-cutting of Douglas fir on its own lands in Oregon and California, and this year the Bureau reversed a trend toward more and more logging by reducing the allowable cut on its Oregon forests despite intense pressure from the timber industry and Governor Tom McCall. Disturbed by the failure of clear-cut lands in southwest Oregon to regenerate, Bureau scientists found that the fir seedlings were being burned to a crisp by the intense sunlight that was supposed to aid their growth. They then began to experiment with a new technique they call "continuous canopy" management, which leaves enough mature trees after logging to provide a partial forest appearance, to give some shade, and to permit natural seed-cone regeneration. The young Douglas fir are "growing to beat the band," in the words of one Land Management official, and an inspection of the experimental sites near Tillamook, Oregon, bore out his claim. The contrast with nearby clear-cut areas was striking. The Bureau is hesitant to say flatly that the experiments disprove the claim that clear-cutting is the only way to regrow Douglas fir, but the studies are being expanded and the Bureau already has reduced its maximum allowable clear-cut to 40-acre patches.

Robbed of some of its major justifications for clear-cutting, the industry has revealed its true economic motives. George R. Staebler of Tacoma, Washington, a forester for the Weyerhauser Company, told the Church subcommittee that "clear-cutting relatively large blocks of trees (100 acres, rather than 40-acre or 10-acre plots) requires less investment in equipment and access roads and reductions in other logging costs, as well as greater per-acre yield and more certainty and greater quality of reforestation." Charles Kirkwood, deputy commissioner of public lands for the state of Washington, warned the Senate subcommittee that "an instant moratorium against clear-cutting could cripple our forest industry and wreck the state's economy." He even came up with an esthetic argument. "Proper clear-cuts," he said, "provide opportunities to enjoy vistas otherwise hidden by the forest itself."

EROSION OF THE LAND ETHIC

The Forest Service has not always parroted the timber industry's positions on conservation, or dedicated itself to providing the loggers with trees. For the first 50 years of its existence, the Forest Service took to heart the words of its first chief, Gifford Pinchot. "Conservation is the foresighted utilization, preservation, and renewal of forests, waters, lands, and minerals, for the greatest good of the greatest number for the longest time," he wrote. Today, the Forest Service remembers well the word "utilization" but has forgotten the rest of Pinchot's maxim.

The change came gradually, but basically it dates from the post-World War II years, the era of a burgeoning national economy and a housing boom. The demand for lumber was fierce, and genuine, and the Forest Service responded. The agency has raised the annual "allowable" cut of timber on its 154 national forests from 5.6 billion board-feet in 1950 to a current level of about 14 billion board-feet. There has not been a corresponding increase in reforestation. The beleaguered chief Cliff has confessed to a congressional committee that it would take $900 million just to wipe out the backlog of national forest lands that need replanting, seeding, thinning and other stand-improvement tasks—assuming the efforts could work. Regarding the five million acres of land which currently need reforestation from scratch, Cliff told the Congress that it would take 38 years to replant them at present rates.

The Forest Service's change in direction has led to flagrant violations of the Multiple Use-Sustained Yield Act of 1960, the law that governs the national forests. The act requires the renewable resources of the forests to be managed on a sustained yield basis, which, put simply, means that timber and other resources are to be used only at a level that will never result in their being used up. The multiple use section of the law is designed primarily to insure that the national forests will not become solely a commercial logging operation but will be dedicated to other public uses as well. Both parts of the law are being freely violated by the Forest Service.

The change in direction was also a radical departure in philosophy, and Forest Service personnel who adapted to it found themselves on the way up. This has had a serious and lasting impact on the agency. Chief Cliff and his top assistants represent the new philosophy, and they are running things today. The trouble is primarily at the top, not down in the forests where many of the district rangers and forest supervisors are appalled at what has happened. Trying to run the forests on a scientific and ecological basis, and with a love for the land, they are faced with orders like that which came down from President Nixon in 1969 to put up for sale an additional 1.1 billion board-feet of national forest timber. The order was obtained through pressure from the timber industry, and the Forest Service obediently complied.

One of the many foresters who are deeply troubled at what has happened is G. M. Brandborg, who served for 20 years as supervisor of the Bitterroot National Forest in Montana until his retirement in 1955. Raised in the traditions of Pinchot and Theodore Roosevelt, "Brandy," now 78, recalls: "In my day, the forester was imbued with a 'land ethic' that no generation could be allowed to damage or reduce the future wealth by the way it uses natural resources. There was never any fear then in speaking out against the special interests and in making decisions that were for the good of the public. But the leadership in the Forest Service and other public land agencies has capitulated to the timber barons and other economic forces. The Forest Service now is operating under a system that precludes scientific forestry, but it will not admit it." The white-haired forester and a small outspoken band of what he proudly calls the Bitterroot Valley "hard core" raised a hue and cry about the massive clear-cutting that was threatening the existence of the Bitterroot Forest and the fact that the Forest Service had permitted loggers to exceed the forest's allowable cut by six million board-feet in 1968 and nearly 13 million board-feet the next year. Aided by the aggressive reporting of environmental columnist Dale A. Burk of *The Missoulian,* their outcries resulted in a request by Montana Senator Lee Metcalf that the University of Montana Forestry School investigate. The school agreed and produced the Bolle report, named after forestry school dean Arnold W. Bolle. It was a scorcher. On the Bitterroot Forest, the report concluded, "multiple use management, in fact, does not exist as the governing principle.... Quality timber management and harvest practices are missing. Consideration of recreation, watershed, wildlife, and grazing appear as afterthoughts." The Forest Service, the report charged, had permitted loggers to clear-cut on steep slopes with fragile soils, land which then had to be terraced to prevent serious soil erosion and where reforestation efforts were often in vain.

There is encouraging evidence that not all Forest Service personnel like what has happened to their beloved agency. Because of local controversies, the Forest Service set up agency task forces to study timber management in the Bitterroot Forest in Montana and in four national forests in Wyoming. The task force members were Forest Service employees, but they were given free rein to call the shots as they saw them without submitting their reports to top agency officials for review. The result was two remarkably candid reports. The one on the Bitterroot, although not going as far as the Bolle report in its criticisms, provided insights into an agency gone sour.

"The emphasis on resource production goals [timber cutting] is not unique to the Bitterroot National Forest and does not originate at the national forest level," the task force wrote. "It is the result of rather subtle pressures and attitudes from above.... The insistence of this pressure is indicated by the fact that the Forest Service is required, once a week, to report accomplishments in meeting planned timber sale objectives to its Washington office, in order to keep the Secretary of Agriculture, Congress, and outside groups informed of progress in meeting timber-cut commitments." The report reveals the triumph of a kind of "body count" mentality within the Forest Service—more trees for the trucks, more numbers for the charts, more emphasis on the "outputs" that can be quantified and targeted and maximized. In any public agency like the Forest Service, the numbers syndrome is a sure sign that other values are being crowded out. "It seems clear," said the report, "that until sound land management receives top priority in fact, as well as in principle, from the leaders of the nation on down, the handling of the public lands will always leave something to be desired."

THE PULPWOOD PUSHERS

In recent years the timber industry, often allied with the homebuilders and the trade unions, has exerted a strong influence on the management of the national forests, working both by direct contact with the Forest Service and through friendly congressmen. Compared with some other industry lobbies, the gifts by the Forest Products Political Education Committee are relatively modest. ($28,000 divided among 42 senators and congressmen in the 1970 election). The fact is, however, that the committees of Congress which handle timber legislation and decide on the Forest Service budget are so tightly controlled by timber-state congressmen that the industry doesn't have to put up a lot of cash to win support in key places. Julia Butler Hansen of Washington chairs the House appropriations subcommittee which holds the Forest Service pursestrings. She is extremely friendly to the needs of the timber industry, and fellow subcommittee member Wendall Wyatt of Oregon is an even more ardent spokesman for the timber lobby's views. On the Senate side, the Forest Service must come to Nevada Senator Alan Bible for its appropriations and has been forced on several occasions to obey his orders not to make timber sale reforms that were strongly opposed by the timber companies. There were some signs for a time that the Senate Interior Committee might look favorably on Senator McGee's bill for a clear-cutting moratorium, until Senator Henry Jackson of Washington passed the word along that he did not like the bill at all.

The principal organization of the timber lobby is the National Forest Products Association, whose executive vice president, James R. Turnbull, complains that Forest Service critics are "preservationists" who want to lock up the national forests and ban all logging. The lobby's educational arm, called the American Forest Institute, puts out brochures pushing the industry's views, takes willing members of the news media on expense-paid tours of industry logging operations, and buys newspaper advertising to answer its critics. And there are a number of allied organizations representing the pulpwood, paper, pine, plywood, and other specialized segments of the industry. H. P. Newson, public affairs man for the timber lobby, says the whole purpose of the industry is "to meet the social needs of the country for decent housing." To accomplish that goal, "we have to build some public backfire against the hysteria of setting all this land aside," he says.

The stress on housing needs touches a sensitive chord in many listeners because the United States undeniably has a tremendous amount of substandard housing, and Congress has set a goal of 26 million new or rehabilitated housing units in a decade. The trouble with the argument is that it is used to justify increased logging in the national forests far beyond what constitutes wise and legal use. Furthermore, Montana forestry dean Bolle says the projection of 26 million homes is "an unrealistic estimate" that has been seized upon by the timber industry in concert with the Forest Service. "The Forest Service and/or the timber industry has been crying 'timber famine' for 75 years," he told the Senate public lands subcommittee. "Scare tactics have been effective in the past, but they are becoming less so as the years pass and the impending crisis never seems to materialize. . . . But shortages of other forest values (wilderness, quality of water yield, wildlife habitat, etc.) seem to be very real possibilities to many Americans, and the Forest Service did not warn us or did not act very aggressively in these cases. The result: some Americans have lost faith in the Forest Service and perhaps the forestry profession."

TREE BANDITS

The timber executives constantly complain about high prices and about lumber shortages. But as Dean Bolle has pointed out, the shortages that do exist are partly of their own making. Rising timber exports are, according to some critics, a major factor behind the demands on the national forest and they provoke a debate that has at times split the industry. Some segments of the timber industry are making lucrative profits from selling raw logs to Japan, where softwood lumber is acutely needed for housing. This has driven up the price of national forest timber, for which commercial timber firms bid competitively. The loggers who have little land of their own, or who have overcut their own lands in past years, desperately need the public timber. (An industry witness, representing the Western Wood Products Association, told the Church subcommittee that only five member companies of the association are now capable of supplying their timber needs without cutting on public forests.)

The timber lobby also works hard to oppose creation of new wilderness areas in national forests because it would prevent logging, and has persuaded the Forest Service to oppose a proposed executive order designed to protect "de facto" wilderness areas from the saws while they are studied for possible inclusion in the wilderness system. The lumbermen seem to have trouble even understanding the concept of wilderness areas. "Forests consigned to the whimsical attention of nature alone fall into neglect and ultimate disaster," says Lowrey Wyatt, president of the National Forest Products Association. Boise Cascade Corporation president Robert Hansberger says that a forest tree which grows to maturity, falls, and dies, "has been wasted and has not fulfilled its ultimate purpose for the people."

The timber lobby does not concentrate on the Forest Service alone, but attempts to obtain domination over state agencies that regulate forestry. A recent Nader report on land use in California points out that six of the eight members of California's forestry board represent timber or other commercial interests. California forests, both public and private, are being "leveled," says the report, "with an utter disregard for the integrity of the land and its relationship to man." In California and elsewhere, privately owned forests are being bought up by large timber companies, logged, and then turned into quickly built, sprawling, housing developments. More private timber land thus disappears, creating even more demand for public-land timber.

Evidence has begun to emerge that the timber industry is involved in collusive bidding practices in its purchases of national forest timber. At the Portland Senate hearing, Richard Schloemer of Victor, Montana, a former industry timber buyer, testified that in his five years of bidding on national forest timber "31 of the 34 sales with which I was connected were predetermined as to who would buy what, and at what price." Representatives of competing sawmills would meet to discuss their timber needs and upcoming sales of national forest trees, he explained. Then they would decide how to divide up the sales, agreeing in advance how much each would bid, he said. Asked why Forest Service personnel do not move to stop collusion, Schloemer explained, "One thing is, it is hard to prove, and second, they, in fact, in a lot of cases are directly involved." Collusive bidding is a federal criminal offense, but the Forest Service shows little inclination to pursue the matter.

Out west, in Montana's Bitterroot Valley, old Fred Waylett found that the Forest Service was actively inclined *not* to pursue matters of timber fraud against the public. The loggers, under the complacent eye of the Forest Service, have been "stealing logs" from the national forests, he said. Wearing a lumberjack shirt and sitting crosslegged on the floor of his modest Hamilton, Montana, home, 68-year-old Waylett told a visitor how he had been drummed out of the Forest Service when he tried on his own to straighten things out. Waylett had risen through the ranks to take charge of a Bitterroot National Forest scaling crew, the men who measure the trees removed from the forest by timber firms under contract with the Forest Service. What offended Waylett's uncomplicated sense of justice was that the loggers were getting a lot of wood free. The scaling sticks, which the Forest Service crews use to determine the amount of board-feet in each log and the amount the logger must pay, were hopelessly out of date. With modern sawmill methods, the industry, which once used only the large logs and then wasted perhaps one third of each log, was utilizing everything, including chips, sawdust, and bark. What didn't make lumber was turned into pulp or fiberboard or a host of other products. Yet the loggers were still paying on the basis of the huge allowable waste and the minimum usable log sizes that prevailed years earlier.

Furthermore, the Forest Service had ordered a change in the log-scaling procedures, and now only about one in every 20 truckloads leaving the forest was sample-scaled. Resourceful timber firms had taken advantage of the change by finding out in advance which load was the one to be measured and purposely loading that truck light. Everything was becoming weighted in favor of the timber industry and "it was like they were stealing logs," Waylett decided. His objections ignored, he devised his own system of adjusting the log measurements to accurately reflect the amount of usable wood the logger would obtain. The loggers howled in protest, and the Forest Service regional office in Missoula jumped. Waylett's check-scaler certificate was revoked, he was demoted, and his pay cut. He resigned rather than accept the decision. "I was forced out because I was too honest," says Waylett, who lives now on a small pension and spends his days fishing and doing odd jobs.

When Rep. John Culver of Iowa learned of this legalized thievery of the public forests, he demanded an explanation from Agriculture Secretary Clifford Hardin, whose department includes the Forest Service. Back came a reply from Hardin's righthand man, executive assistant E. F. "Fritz" Behrens, that the whole thing was blown out of proportion and that Waylett was simply "disgruntled." Behrens' objectivity was subject to some question, though. Before joining the Agriculture Department he was manager of general operations for the National Forest Products Association. At any rate, Fred Waylett was fully vindicated early this year when the Department's Inspector General, Nathaniel E. Kossack, issued a toughly worded report charging the Forest Service with sloppy and antiquated scaling and sales procedures and concluding that timber companies were getting substantial amounts of national forest timber free or at less than full value.

CUT AND RUN

Amidst the clear-cutting, the denuded hills, the silt-choked streams, the dead fish, and the eroded soil, organizations like the Sierra Club, the

Wilderness Society, and Friends of the Earth are constantly fighting rear-guard actions to stem new incursions into unlogged virgin areas of the national forests.

As long as the timber industry maintains its hold over the Forest Service and over the key congressional committees, and as long as the protests come mainly from the remote areas of our smaller states, the chances for real reform seem slim. But the word is spreading and citizens are beginning to make more noise.

The ICC
and the Truckers

Stephen Chapman

In all the agencies of government in Washington, there is probably no worse example of federal regulation than the Interstate Commerce Commission. Over the course of its 90-year existence, the commission has compiled an almost spotless record of guarding and promoting the interests of the dominant companies and unions in its jurisdiction. Created in 1887 to regulate the nation's rail traffic, it later was given authority over waterways, pipelines, and highways as well, making it one of the most powerful agencies in the federal government. It has held rates above their normal levels, inflated the costs of doing business, contrived to shut out newcomers, encouraged inefficiency, and made a thorough mess of surface transportation in the U.S.

The commission's beginning, despite its fervent support from antibusiness progressive circles, was really a victory for the railroads. The establishment of a regulatory agency had strong support among railroad executives, who were frazzled by frenetic competition and disillusioned by the failure of price-fixing and cartelization agreements. The commission was given broad authority to enforce "reasonable and just" rates, and stocked by President Cleveland with an undistinguished group of men who had strong ties to the railroad industry.

For all intents and purposes, the industry became a government-

protected cartel. Subsequent court rulings, however, badly under-
mined the ICC's authority, forcing Congress to shore it up again by
passing new laws against rebates, discriminatory pricing, and rate-cut-
ting. Chief among them was the Transportation Act of 1920, which
supplemented the agency's power by giving it absolute control over all
rates and entry measures intended to ensure a sufficient profit to rail
companies.

A SHORT-SIGHTED SOLUTION

But government protection of the railroads soon proved a short-
sighted solution. The 1920s brought the rise of a new, unregulated
competitor, the trucking industry. The way to control this unwanted
competition was clear: bring trucks under the ICC's protective umbrella too. Beset by intense lobbying by the ICC and the railroads,
dismayed by record financial losses in the rail industry, Congress in
1935 widened the commission's scope to include commercial motor
carriers, hitherto left to the states. With only a few changes and addi-
tions—most notably the Reed-Bulwinkle Act of 1948, which exempted
carriers under ICC regulation from federal antitrust laws—the 1935 act
is still the basis of the federal government's regulation of surface transportation.

Since then, of course, the railroads have become the victims of their
own short-sightedness and indirect government assistance of the trucking industry, and the ICC is now the instrument of truckers, not rail
barons. In the early years of trucking regulation, the rail companies
underestimated the competitive threat of trucks, says Jim Ritch, a lobbyist for deregulation. "In the 1930s, the railroads wanted a floor on
rates, to prevent trucks from undercutting them. They didn't appreci-
ate what was happening to them until long after the war." State construction of highways, to handle the millions of cars Americans bought
during the post-war boom, made trucking easier, quicker, and more
efficient. The crippling blow to the railroads was the construction of the
interstate highway system, which permitted truckers to compete seriously with the railroads in long-distance freight carriage. Delivery times
fell, and the door-to-door service trucks offered persuaded many shippers to switch from rail to trucks. "With this you also began to see a
resettlement of industry away from rail sites and out into the suburbs
and rural areas, which were serviceable by trucks," Ritch says. "The
railroads were also hurt by the industrialization of the South, which had
few railroads to begin with and had to rely on trucks for most shipping."
By the time the rail companies realized they were being destroyed by

the very regulations they had promoted for their own protection, it was too late to do anything, for with the loss of rails' dominant position came the loss of their influence in Congress and with the ICC.

ABSOLUTE CONTROL

Perhaps the ICC's most important power today is its absolute control over entry into the trucking business (no one wants to enter the rail industry anymore). In order to be admitted as a "common carrier"— essentially a commercial trucker—an applicant must obtain a certificate of "public convenience and necessity," generally granted only when the newcomer can demonstrate that existing firms can not provide the service specified. If established carriers can show they have the capacity to handle the traffic, the application is normally rejected, regardless of whether or not the applicant might provide a cheaper or more efficient service. The burden of proof is on the applicant, and it is often an impossible one.

MORE IMPORTANT THAN TRUCKS

The difficulty of obtaining new certificates is suggested by their value on the market (the certificates, once obtained, can be sold to other firms without further ICC approval). When one company, Associated Transport Inc., went bankrupt, it sold its operating rights for more than $20 million. The American Trucking Association says operating rights quadrupled in price between 1962 and 1972 and admits that they are a trucker's "single most important asset"—more important, one gathers, than trucks. Allan Mendelsohn, a lawyer for the Colorado Meat Dealers Association, says many meat-hauling trucklines "have gotten rid of their employees and have likewise gotten rid of their tractors and refrigerated trailers," preferring simply to rent their operating rights to independent truckers. The independent trucker does the work, but the firm with the operating rights gets a sizable cut of the take—generally 25 per cent, but sometimes as much as 50. Mike Parkhurst, editor of *Overdrive*, a magazine aimed at independent truckers, calls this practice "sharecropping," and the analogy is far from unreasonable.

Trucking licenses work similarly to another government outrage, the federal Communications Commission's operating licenses to radio and television stations. These licenses are enormously valuable—having one is commonly compared to having a license to print money. *The Wash-*

ington Post recently sold its radio station in Washington for the staggering sum of $6 million. FCC licenses don't get much attention in the press, although most large publishing operations own and profit from them. If the granting of FCC and ICC operating certificates is deemed a public matter, why should their exchange be an extremely lucrative private one?

Defenders of the status quo, such as the American Trucking Association, scoff at the notion that certificates are hard to get, noting that upwards of 80 per cent of applications are approved by the ICC But Stan Sender, a lobbyist for Sears Roebuck, says that figure means little: "Only about 30 carriers a year are given general commodity, unrestricted rights. Most are only short extensions of authority for existing carriers. And that 80 per cent figure doesn't tell you that it takes the ICC 14 months to handle an average case." Jack Pearce, a lawyer whose clients include several black truckers, mentions one client in Dallas who is applying for a certificate to provide household moving service in 40 states: "He's spent a year trying to get the money together just to apply, and it will probably take another three to six months before he has enough. Then it will probably take him another year or two to get the authority, and he'll probably get it, because he's black and there are only a few black movers with ICC authority. If he were my brother or cousin he'd have to pay $20,000 to $50,000 for the legal work involved in getting through the ICC and it would take two to four years, and he probably still wouldn't get it. He might be allowed to operate from Texas to Oklahoma. And all that money—well, that's not even talking about putting the trucks on the road."

IN SELF-INTERESTED HANDS

Equally important is the ICC's authority over rates. This it usually places in the self-interested hands of regional rate bureaus made up of representatives of companies in each mode of surface transportation. These bureaus set rates on all services, and while each firm is supposedly free to deviate from the established rate, few have much choice but to go along, since undercutting the fixed rate is expensive, time-consuming, and usually futile. If any company cuts its price below the standard, the local rate bureau or another company can—and usually does—challenge its right to do so. The classic case is the time a frustrated company filed a rate to carry yak fat, an imaginary product, from Omaha to Chicago. Though no one had ever heard of yak fat, much less carried it, no fewer than 13 carriers protested the rate.

THE PICTURE IS ILLUSORY

The ICC places numerous nonprice restrictions on each operating certificate too, specifying what commodities can be carried, which points served, and so on. The American Trucking Association points to the 15,000 different firms engaged in trucking as evidence of competition, but that picture is illusory. The operating restrictions work to prevent direct competition among different companies. A shipper may have little choice in which firm to hire to ship a particular commodity, since companies do not receive rights to carry all goods, but only a few specific ones. Moreover, the specific authority is often even more specific than it seems to be. A firm with the right to transport "fruit and vegetable juices," for instance, cannot carry frozen juices. A company granted the authority to carry "machinery" will find that designation doesn't include carburetors, generators, distributors, and electrical motors. Some trucks are allowed to carry exposed film but not unexposed, and companies authorized to carry lead pipe are prohibited from handling plastic pipe.

To guard further against firms competing for the same traffic, the ICC imposes restrictions on which highways each company may use. These rules often force trucks to take long, roundabout routes that waste time and money. One Dallas firm has to send its trucks to California by way of Kansas, which adds an extra 12 hours to the trip. Another company in Duluth, Minnesota is required to run its carriers to Chicago through Clinton, Iowa, a route 120 miles out of the way. The only possible justification for this kind of route regulation is the one the Civil Aeronautics Board uses—that it's the only way to assure the continuation of what would otherwise be unproductive service for small cities. The American Trucking Association argues that in a free market the Springfields and the Fresnos would lose their trucking service, but in fact these towns are already perfectly well served by unregulated carriers, who wouldn't be affected by deregulation.

These rules promote further waste by guaranteeing that trucks will run empty or only partly loaded much of the time, since a truck carrying one category of goods to a given city may not be able to find anything to carry on the way back. One study suggested that half of all trucking capacity is unused. The ICC also has rules prohibiting some carriers from carrying anything at all on return trips.

A WHOREHOUSE IN BOSTON

This sort of cost inflation doesn't reduce profits by much, though. Certified truckers traditionally have had a high return on investment, because of the protected environment in which they operate. In 1977 the average return on equity for carriers under ICC control was better than 16 per cent, with many firms reporting returns of 30 to 40 per cent. One lobbyist tells the story of the late Paul Cherington, then an Assistant Secretary at the Transportation Department, meeting with a group of certified carriers, who complained that deregulation would diminish the value of their operating rights. Unsympathetic, Cherington retorted, "You people are making a 40 per cent return on equity! A whorehouse in Boston doesn't make that!"

How does the trucking industry get away with it? There are two crucial reasons for its domination of the ICC, one related to necessity, the other to the commission's self-interest. The rate-setting bureaus, though perhaps the most flagrantly objectionable feature of the truck and rail regulation, are indispensable as long as the federal government chooses to fix prices. There is simply no way the ICC could ever come up with a fair, reasonable rate on each of the thousands upon thousands of commodities shipped between hundreds of different points on hundreds of different routes. Plainly the commission, with its relatively small budget and staff, could not even begin to try, so it has no choice but to turn the decisions over to the firms who ship the goods. The best the commission can do is to use its authority in a few instances to prevent especially blatant abuses by the rate bureaus.

In any case, the ICC would profit little by vigorously promoting competition. What would happen in a competitive environment? Rates would fall, surely, but some companies would find themselves outmatched by more efficient rivals, forcing them to go out of business, dismiss workers, close offices—all those things that usually provoke editorial outcries and congressional investigations. Competition is often bloody, leaving the corpses of inefficient firms strewn in its path, so the ICC runs the other way at first mention of it. As long as it restricts competition to ensure the prosperity of the bulk of the firms in its jurisdiction, the ICC can count on being ignored most of the time. A neat and tidy cartel, from the point of view of the regulators, is clearly preferable to the messy, unpredictable "chaos of the marketplace."

Skippers and consumers are not the ICC's only victims; ironically, railroads also suffer. After pressing for ICC regulation of trucking to protect themselves from competition, the railroads have found that the sword cuts the other way too, giving trucking companies a tool for suppressing their rivals in the rail industry. The railroads have declined steadily since the 1930s, both in health and competitive ability. Between 1939 and 1967, their share of regulated intercity freight dropped by a third. During the same period, the total volume of freight carried by trucks rose six times as fast as that carried by rail.

There is no inherent reason why railroads cannot compete successfully with trucks, since they have appreciably lower costs on medium and long hauls—those over 200 miles. The longer the trip, the greater the cost advantage of rail. In a free market, most medium- and long-distance traffic would go by train.

Right now it doesn't. The reason is that the rate bureaus base their rates on the time-worn principle of "value-of-service" pricing, which means that expensive goods travel at higher rates than cheap goods, regardless of the actual cost of transporting them. Besides preventing monopolistic pricing and rate wars, value-of-service pricing was designed to promote development of the West by holding down rates on the low-value bulk goods that farms and mines produce. Hay, for instance, which takes up a lot of space, was made cheap to ship, while gold, which is compact, was made expensive. Both the railroads and the public saw this as a way of stabilizing the industry. The problem today is that rail and truck prices are based on the same rules, which keep their rates roughly equal—that is, the rates are based on the kind of product carried, rather than the cost of carrying it. Shippers have a choice between sending their cargo by truck, which can provide door-to-door service, or by train, which can deliver goods only to a particular city or town. Trucks can offer better service than railroads, but only at a higher real cost on most hauls. Present pricing thus both hobbles the railroads and deprives the shipper of the choice between superior service and lower rates. (Railroads have not, by the way, pressed for deregulation, apparently preferring the known—however unprofitable —to the unknown.)

UNREGULATED TRUCKS

A look at the differences between regulated and unregulated trucks dramatizes the wasteful consequences of regulation. Under current law, there are three kinds of commercial trucks exempt from federal regulation. The first kind is trucks carrying agricultural products. When during the 1950s the courts ruled that frozen fruits and vegetables, frozen poultry, and fresh dressed poultry were exempt goods, their rates fell sharply—for frozen fruits and vegetables, 19 per cent in two years; for frozen and dressed poultry, 33 per cent. When Congress removed the exemption, rates went right back up.

The second kind of unregulated trucks are those owned or leased by companies that want to ship their own goods. If Safeway, for instance, wants to buy its own trucks it can ship its products anywhere it wants. The only restriction is that it can't carry anyone else's goods. This can be a tremendous money-saver. Ann Friedlaender of the Brookings Institution notes that one paper manufacturer "was able to cut freight costs by 45 per cent by using leased equipment. Another company saved between 25 and 45 per cent on freight."

The final variety of unregulated truckers is what's called "contract carriers." These are companies who have only a few long-term clients and usually charge more than common carriers. In return for the higher price, shippers who use contract carriers can send their goods anywhere they want, rather than having to figure out which common carrier has the rights to which route. It's like the difference between taking a bus and taking a cab. Like a bus, a common carrier is cheaper, but it follows only one specific route, and you may have to transfer several times to reach a faraway destination. While common carriers can carry the goods of one and all on their prescribed routes, contract carriers have to apply to the ICC for special permission each time they take on a new client, and this process can take two years. So while contract carriers have freedom of movement, common carriers have freedom of clientele.

A comparison of the United States with countries in Western Europe suggests that relatively unregulated truckers provide better service at lower prices than regulated ones. In Great Britain, following complete deregulation in 1971, rates fell by five per cent—even though the government had controlled only entry, not rates, points served, or routes. The lowest rates are in Belgium and Sweden, both of which permit an essentially free market in trucking. West Germany, which has the most pervasive regulation, also has the highest rates: in 1973, they were 50-percent higher than anywhere else in Europe. German rates, in fact, run a full 25-percent higher than those in Britain, even though Britain has one of the continent's worst highway systems and West Germany one of the best.

The Carter Administration has endorsed deregulation of the nation's rail and trucking industry. ICC deregulation was also a pet cause of President Ford, who found allies of assorted philosophical persuasions, from the Consumer Federation of America to Common Cause to Ralph Nader to laissez-faire Republicans. Nader has suggested that the ICC be simply abolished, as has Senator William Proxmire.

Any change in that direction would be to the benefit of American consumers and shippers, and most likely would help revive the railroads as well. Eliminating value-of-service pricing to allow them to undercut truck rates on a lot of freight traffic would do more for the rail industry than a dozen Penn Central bailouts. After years of trying to compete with their hands tied, the railroads deserve a fair fight.

Trucking interests say deregulation would lead to chaos, but the evidence of unregulated trucking argues the opposite. Most critics of the ICC believe a freer transportation market would force prices down. Stan Sender adds that the reductions would not necessarily be across the board: "Sometimes a shipper wants fast service; other times he'll sacrifice that for a lower price. In a competitive marketplace you can shop at an expensive store, a discount store, or one somewhere in between. In a freer trucking marketplace, you would have a much greater range of price and service options." In other words, the customer would get what he wants, and what he can afford.

From its beginning, the ICC has failed to promote healthy competition, falling instead into a pattern of protecting the strong, hindering the weak, keeping out those who aren't already in, and letting the public be damned. The real culprit, however, is not the commission itself, which, given the American experience with regulatory agencies, could hardly be expected to do otherwise. The source of the problems that regulation causes is the original Interstate Commerce Act, which is designed to create and maintain a cartelized industry. As long as the ICC is authorized to limit entry, fix rates, prescribe routes and commodities, and generally restrict competition among supposed rivals, it will do so. In order to introduce some simple elements of free market capitalism into truck and rail transporation, those powers should be abolished.

The Protection Consumers Don't Want

Marjorie Boyd

Congress' reluctance to pass legislation creating a Consumer Protection Agency has been widely denounced. President Carter led the bill's supporters in blaming the defeat on the lobbying of powerful special interests, and some editorialists followed suit. But that is a distorted view; this is not just another case of members of Congress dancing to any tune played by the U.S. Chamber of Commerce. Many congressmen who previously supported the idea of a Consumer Protection Agency were surprised to find opposition to the bill growing among their constituents—congressmen were increasingly hearing from the advisers and friends who serve as political barometers in their districts that people are not so keen on consumer legislation as they once were. The bill suffered a severe blow when a convention of the Federated American Women's Clubs passed a resolution opposing the consumer agency. What has happened to make consumers leery of the government's protection? Is it a general unease growing out of an anti-Washington mood? Or is it something more specific?

It was in the mid-1960s that Congress discovered the consumer. Polls showed that Ralph Nader was held in the highest public esteem, and his various organizations, staffed with bright young men and women, were producing a multitude of proposals to help consumers. Congress, in its excitement at finding a sizable constituency that posed no political risks, quickly passed Nader-inspired laws with names like the Fair Labeling and Packaging Act, the Truth in Lending Act, the Flammable Fabrics Act, the Poison Prevention Packaging Act, the Refrigerator Safety Act, the National Traffic and Motor Vehicle Safety Act, the Federal Caustic Poison Act, and the Hazardous Substances Act. The Consumer Product Safety Commission was set up and given broad powers to ban unsafe products from the market. Also, other laws designed by the Nader groups to protect workers were passed—for instance, the Occupational Safety and Health Act and the Employee Retirement Income Security Act, which reformed private pension plans. Each of these laws, while meeting real needs, pushed government a step closer to the day-to-day lives of businessmen and consumers.

As a result of the congressional interest in the consumer, there are now 33 federal agencies and approximately 400 bureaus and sub-agencies operating more than 1,000 consumer-oriented programs. If there is indeed a declining public confidence in the government's ability to protect the consumer, it stands to reason that it is in some way connected with the operation of these programs. An examination of how the consumer laws really work shows why the government's bear-hug of protection, which was at first so warmly received by all consumers, now seems stifling.

SOMETHING HAS GONE AWRY

One of the first consumer laws passed was the Truth in Lending Act of 1968. It was heralded as a great breakthrough. Creditors would be required to disclose the true cost of credit, and, congressional sponsors and consumer advocates pointed out, once the true cost of credit was known, consumers would choose to buy from businesses offering the lowest interest rates, thus helping to fight inflation.

Now, it is clear that something has gone awry—so far awry that the Senate Banking Committee has called the law in for an overhaul. The original idea for a Truth in Lending Act was simply to require a creditor to disclose the true annual rate of interest he was charging. But as the bill went through Congress other disclosure requirements were added, and when the Act got to the Federal Reserve Board, the bureaucrats there, charged with writing regulations for the new law, quickly added many more requirements, some so complicated as to be unintelligible.

Now banks and businesses seeking to meet the law's requirements send out lengthy and confusing statements to consumers, who are more puzzled than ever about exactly how much interest they are paying.

Some of the Nader-inspired laws have created problems because they were designed with big corporations in mind and had unanticipated effects on medium-sized and small businesses. For instance, the Employee Retirement Income Security Act (ERISA), which reformed private pension plans, is perhaps the most complicated piece of regulatory legislation ever devised—the annual reports required by the law arrive at the Labor Department in packing crates.

The major impetus behind the reform of private pensions were Studebaker's bankruptcy, which left 8,500 workers without pensions. There were no representatives of small or medium-sized businesses present at hearings on the legislation, and when the law went into effect a huge outcry arose from these businessmen, who complained they could neither understand nor comply with ERISA. Senator Gaylord Nelson's Small Business Committee held hearings for which planeloads of angry businessmen descended on Washington, all testifying that complying with the law would cost them enormous legal and clerical fees, in a few cases higher than their companies' annual contributions to their pension plans. Several senators threatened to try to repeal the law, or at least to exempt small businesses from it. As this was going on, it was learned that since the bill's passage, four times as many companies as usual had terminated their pension plans because they could not afford the legal fees and clerical personnel necessary to assure compliance. The Labor Department finally responded with shorter, simplified forms for small businesses, and private consulting firms sprang up to help the smaller companies bring their pension plans into conformance at prices lower than lawyers would charge.

Confrontation was avoided. But by this time, two years after the Act's passage, more than 10,000 companies had dropped their pension plans and 320,000 workers had lost their pensions.

So while the costs of complying with the consumer laws are a nuisance to General Motors and Nabisco, they are a real burden for small businesses—and their employees. Of course, businesses eventually pass legal and clerical costs on to consumers through higher prices. But this takes time, during which legal bills must be paid and payrolls met. For the businessman with a narrow margin of profit, the cumulative expenses of complying with several different government regulatory programs can change ink from black to red.

And we forget that America is still a land of small and medium-sized businesses. According to the Small Business Administration, 55 percent of all jobs in the private sector are in small businesses. These businesses produce 48 percent of our output of goods and services and account for almost 43 percent of the GNP. There are actually more businessmen working for small businesses than for large corporations.

ARTHRITIC FINGERS

Other consumer laws have had unfortunate side effects that have annoyed or angered various groups of the consumers they were supposed to help.

The Poison Prevention Packaging Act, passed in 1970, required, among other things, that aspirin bottles have caps that could not be opened by a child under five years old. The law provided that aspirin could be sold for use by the old and handicapped in bottles without safety caps, as long as it was labeled "This package for households without young children." But retailers cannot always keep on hand a supply of the aspirin without safety caps, so many senior citizens have been forced to try to manipulate the "child-guard" caps with arthritic fingers as they struggle to get their dosage of aspirin every four hours.

The banning of hazardous substances is provoking increasing skepticism among consumers. Of course, no one has questioned the advisability of banning extremely toxic chemicals, but there are a large number of substances that fall somewhere between safe and unsafe because acceptable levels of exposure cannot be precisely determined. Public reaction to the saccharin ban has been fully explored in the press, and there are other less well-known cases that illustrate the various facets of this problem.

In October 1973, the Consumer Product Safety Commission banned certain brands of spray adhesives because of a researcher's work that concluded that the sprays, when used by pregnant women, would cause birth defects in their unborn children. Seven months later, the Commission lifted the ban. Doctors across the country were horrified, because on the basis of the ban they had advised pregnant women who had used the spray adhesives to undergo abortions.

Consumer advocates themselves are sometimes sharply divided over a particular product's safety. Some groups have been working to have smoke detectors made mandatory, and several local ordinances requiring them have been passed. At the same time, other consumer advocates, including Ralph Nader, are working to have smoke detectors banned because they believe they emit cancer-causing radiation.

One consumer-protection law that totally backfired involved childrens' sleepwear. In 1972 the Consumer Product Safety Commission in the course of carrying out the Flammable Fabrics Act, required that all children's sleepwear under size 6-X be treated with a flame-retardant chemical (sizes 7 through 14 were added in 1975). Millions of parents, already hard-pressed to keep their growing children in pajamas and nightgowns, watched prices jump by 20 percent overnight. Some manufacturers attached labels explaining that the flame-retardant chemicals and the processes necessary to apply them were responsible for the price hike, and stores posted signs to the same effect. Then, in spring, 1977 when the Consumer Product Safety Commission banned the chemical Tris, which had been used to treat over 40 percent of children's sleepwear, parents were understandably shocked to learn that they had been paying a higher price in order to expose their children to a cancer-causing agent.

The Flammable Fabrics Act has left an incredible imbroglio in its wake. Incensed fabric makers and sleepwear manufacturers have gone to court to try to get the government to make up their losses. Spring Mills, one of the country's largest fabric companies, announced it was ceasing production of fabrics for children's sleepwear because of "unpredictable governmental policies," a development expected to drive up further the prices of children's pajamas and nightgowns, at least temporarily. To bring the fiasco full circle, a federal judge enjoined the Consumer Product Safety Commission from enforcing its ban on Tris because it didn't follow its own regulations in issuing the ban. And a group of scientists is warning that the other chemicals used to make fabrics flame retardant are almost as dangerous as Tris.

Sometimes the Consumer Products Safety Commission seems to be *trying* to make consumerism look bad. For instance, it announced plans to require all manufacturers of power lawnmowers to equip each of their machines with a safety device that will automatically shut off the motor every time the mower stops. This means that when you pause to move a tool or toys out of the way or even to answer a question from a passing neighbor, you have to tug at the inevitably balky cord starter. And manufacturers say the device will add an average of $60 to the

price of a new lawnmower. Granted, Americans suffered 160,000 cut
fingers and toes and other injuries while mowing lawns last year, but the
Commission admits that the device "might have prevented only about
half of those." No figures are available to show how many of these
accidents were caused by carelessness. Some sense of perspective
should be brought to bear on this problem, since there are 40 million
power mowers in this country, most of which are used about once a
week in the summer months.

THE ISSUE OF INTERFERING

It's clear that a large part of the problem is that consumers define
their problems differently from the consumer advocates. For instance,
consumers tend instinctively to resent intrusions even if they're for
their own good—seatbelts that had to be buckled in order for cars to
start were extremely unpopular. Consumer advocates are blithely unconcerned with the issue of interfering in people's lives, and don't mind
the government acting *in loco parentis*. Also, Ralph Nader and other
consumer advocates who played major roles in designing consumer
legislation have always focused primarily on safety. But many people
simply do not see safety as the most important consumer problem. To
them, consumer problems are the new electric frying pan that fails to
work after only two uses; or the unbelievably high price of coffee; or the
television set that always seems to be in the repair shop; or the house
paint that peels after three months. Laws that restrict their personal
freedom for what the government has determined to be their own good
are not what they had in mind.

Besides the annoyances they cause, it is possible that the consumer
laws are producing detrimental effects that are not so readily apparent.
The Wall Street Journal, Business Week, and other business organs have
long warned editorially that the laws are actually hurting consumers
instead of helping them because the expense of meeting their myriad
regulations is added on to the prices consumers pay. But the cost of the
government regulatory process is a subject that most consumer advocates, government officials, and liberals would prefer to avoid. When I
asked an expert on inflation at the Brookings Institution if he had done
any studies on the cost of the consumer laws or their effect on inflation,
I was told curtly, "We don't do that sort of thing."

One of the largest costs of government regulation in the consumer
field, legal expenses, is rarely mentioned. One does not have to be a
statistician or an economist to see how this works. The consumer laws
are heavily weighted toward the use of the legal system. Government

investigators search out violators of the various regulations and when they find one, the accused business can either pay the assigned penalty or challenge it in court. Businesses must also hire lawyers to represent them at government hearings on ever-changing rules and regulations and to interpret the flood of new rules that pour out of Washington. Wronged consumers are also encouraged to go into court—some of the laws provide for the payment of legal fees by either business or the government. The proposed Consumer Protection Agency would add a new dimension to this legal round robin because it would be permitted to sue all other government agencies.

From the standpoint of the legal enthusiast who is convinced there is no human problem the adversary system can't solve, these laws offer the wondrous opportunity for government, business, and consumer to have the full extent of each and every right and responsibility defined in court.

While a system that assures everyone's day in court makes uplifting reading in a legal textbook, litigation is an expensive and time-consuming process, usually viewed as a last resort. Who is paying for all these lawyers? When you ask consumer advocates this question, you hear such soothing phrases as "negligible expense" and "absorbed by business." But this fails to mollify anyone who has had recent experience with lawyers. "Negligible expense" is not a term associated with that profession's work, and since business is not a charitable activity, it does not "absorb" substantial new costs but passes them along to consumers.

Now it's true that most consumer legislation has a point and that some of it is eminently worthwhile. American businessmen too often confirm the most vulgar Marxist's view of free enterprise, so the public does need protection against fraud, against products that endanger health, or, as Nader put it, are "unsafe at any speed." The magazine *Mother Jones* has, for example, revealed that Ford was knowingly producing Pintos with gas tanks that, if the car were hit from the rear, had an excellent chance of incinerating the cars' occupants. Action was needed. But every action taken by government, whether it succeeds or fails in achieving its stated purpose, will inevitably produce unintended effects. The more lengthy and complicated the legislation—and consumer legislation is very lengthy and complicated—the more unintended effects there are.

And it is these unintended effects, which range from the laughable to the horrendous, that eat away at the confidence of citizens in their government. The cumulative effect of 320,000 workers telling how a program designed to protect pensions wiped theirs out; of thousands of businessmen complaining about what consumer laws cost them; of women recounting how a faulty government decision led them to have abortions; of the elderly talking about aspirin bottles and parents about Tris; and all the other word-of-mouth about the failings of consumer laws—it all adds up to a disillusionment that's quite widespread. The way to combat the disillusionment is to attack it at its source, by either accepting limited goals or devising laws that are not maddeningly complicated and whose effects have been well thought out in advance. This would be in sharp contrast to our present system of writing laws whose goals are understood fully only by their authors. And the system heaps confusion upon confusion as each law is loaded down with pages of regulations written by bureaucrats who speak a different language from the rest of us.

The View From A Small Town

Nicholas Lemann

Early on in the new Washington novel by Ben Wattenberg, who became famous as a man attuned to the hearts and minds of average Midwestern Americans, a White House speechwriter has lunch at Sans Souci with a savvy *New York Times* reporter, the kind of character who's obviously there to say what's on the author's mind. The reporter is just back from several weeks of traveling around the nation to sample the simple folks' attitudes, and the speechwriter straightaway asks her, "How are things in the country?" Which elicits the following response:

" 'Strange.' Her brow furrowed. 'I'm always amazed at how different the rest of the country is from Washington. In this town, you'd think politics was at the heart of the universe. Out there'—she waved her hand—'people manage to hold jobs, have babies, and wash their cars without thinking about Congress or the President or Washington for days—hell, years—on end.' "

It is doubtless true that the daily concerns of the people out there are not those of Joseph Kraft and James Reston, but it's hard for anyone to live in complete blissful ignorance of the federal government. The long arm of Washington touches almost everybody in one way or another.

At President Carter's town meetings, people were too busy asking about federal programs that touched their own lives to worry about the burning issues of the big-think set. In Louisiana, towns live and die according to two-cent fluctuations in federal sugar supports and import taxes. In Indiana, a town closed down because of federal water-treatment requirements it couldn't meet. In California, the cancellation of the B-1 bomber threw thousands out of work.

And in La Plata, Maryland, population 1,800, the town manager says the federal government "is involved in every facet of life that we have." La Plata is the county seat of Charles County, Maryland, population 50,000, which sits astride the Potomac south of Washington and west of the Chesapeake Bay. Charles County is an old farming area, and La Plata is the kind of town that serves most agricultural regions. Everybody knows everybody. A couple of old families (the Diggeses and the Bowlings) run most major enterprises. There is a main street, a high school, and a few stores and offices, all of which make up a commercial district about five blocks long. For half a mile on either side of the main street there are single-family houses and a few apartment buildings, which give way to miles of farms—tobacco (the county's original economic base) and corn and soybeans.

La Plata is the kind of place that's usually written about these days in sepia-tinted prose that is meant to indicate a quaint, remote, placid, and dying way of life; it's well known, after all, that America is now 75-percent urban. But that's a misleading statistic; a full 40 percent of the population still lives outside cities of more than 50,000 and their suburbs. To people in Washington there's a certain mystery enveloping these areas. They are known to vote against Washington—they formed the solid backbone of the Nixon-Ford constituency—but that's usually chalked up to a general pastoral conservatism. The possibility that it might be the government's fault is left unexamined.

$2,000 A PERSON

The first striking aspect of the federal presence in a small, mind-its-own-business county like Charles is how large it is. These may be proud and independent people, but in the 1976 fiscal year the government spent $97.2 million in Charles County, which works out to about $2,000 a person. In addition, it lent out $26.3 million. All this is considerably more than the county pays the government: nationwide, federal taxes in 1976 were $1,328 per capita, and in Charles County, which is fairly low-income, they were probably less.

The government's largesse to Charles County has come gradually over the last 50 years; there have been three major waves of federal domestic spending in this century, and a county like Charles is in a position to have profited from all three.

The first wave was the New Deal, under which Social Security ($10 million a year in Charles County) and various relief programs began. The New Deal's social programs were aimed first and foremost at building a firm economic floor under agricultural America, which they did quite effectively. The Department of Agriculture is today the most visible federal presence in Charles County, with a brand-new office building in La Plata, and it guarantees decent housing and a farm to every citizen who makes less than $15,600 a year. The chief agency of this generosity is the Farmers Home Administration (called, for some reason, the FmHA, which, its genial county director, Thomas Potter, says, can "do just about anything in a rural area as far as financing.")

As long as they've first been turned down by a bank, anyone under the income ceiling, even single people, can get from the FmHA a loan to buy or rent a house or farm, at low interest and long terms, that can cost as much as $45,000 (which still does buy something in Charles County). Loans are also available to cover farm operating costs, start businesses in town, and build community facilities like sewage and water treatment plants, roads, and drainage systems. Through its price-support system, the Agriculture Department also guarantees the county's corn and soybean farmers that they'll never have a bad year. Should drought or heavy rain destroy the crops altogether, the government will step in with disaster relief—in fact, there are two programs, the FmHA's and the Small Business Administration's, that provide identical disaster loans to the same people, the only restriction being that nobody can be on both agencies' caseloads simultaneously. In 1976, the SBA lent farmers in Charles County $28,000 in disaster loans after heavy spring rains, the FmHA (which seems to be winning the bureaucratic battle on this front) $187,000. The FmHA also lent out $300,000 to cover farm operating costs; $64,000 to buy farms; and, to farmers and townspeople, $2.5 million to buy houses.

The second and third waves of government spending—military, starting with World War II and continuing apace in the years thereafter, and social-services, taking off during Lyndon Johnson's presidency—have bestowed their gifts on Charles County too. The Defense Department spends $50 million a year there, most of it in pay for the 2,500 employees of a Naval Ordnance Station in the town of Indian Head, and the Department of Health, Education, and Welfare chips in nearly $25 million, the biggest single chunk of which goes to Medicare ($2 million) and Medicaid ($6 million). Another $2 million in social-services programs—mainly food stamps and school lunches—comes through the

Agriculture Department. Rural areas get more than their share from the federal government because it's hard to build military installations in cities; and social-services grants, usually thought of as aimed at big cities, do a lot for the low-income country as well.

Otherwise, federal spending in Charles County is a miscellany—$6 million in insurance for low-income homeowners from the Department of Housing and Urban Development, $329,000 in unemployment compensation, $824,000 in highway construction grants. Two-and-a-half million dollars comes in from the Veterans Administration for pensions and training; $1.2 million from the Treasury in revenue sharing; $6.1 million from the Civil Service Commission in pensions on federal salaries. All eleven Cabinet-level departments and ten independent agencies put some money into Charles County.

Overall, the federal government's spending in Charles County breaks out like this: this: $35 million in salaries, mostly to Defense employees (who average about $16,000 a year); $20 million in pensions; and $25 million in loans, most of which help low- and moderate-income people buy houses. In other words, the government primarily helps its own (which in turn helps the local economy, but also leads to resentment and inflation), the retired, and the housing industry. By comparison, only $6 million a year is for the kind of payments to poor people that could conceivably be called the dole—Medicaid, food stamps, welfare, and the like.

THE SHORT END OF THE STICK

For all this government generosity, Charles County does not send its gratitude back toward Washington. In fact, both by their votes (conservative Republican) and in conversation, the county's residents make it clear that they think they're coming out on the short end of the federal stick. Most don't realize that the government spends more on the county than the county gives it, but even if they did, it's a fair bet that they'd insist the relationship isn't worth it. The people of La Plata are glad to enumerate their theories about the federal government: that it pays people to sit around and do nothing, and that the money it puts into the county is less than what the county has contributed because bureaucrats skim a large percentage off the top for themselves before giving it back. They resent the high salaries paid the county's federal employees. The government "is to Charles County what Con Ed is to New York," says Daniel Kennedy, editor of the *La Plata Times-Crescent*. "Everybody blames them even when they're right."

All these are general complaints, often arising out of no more specific

a burden than paying taxes; but they certainly show that the government has a public-relations problem even if they don't explain why.
More particularly, people in La Plata, especially businessmen, complain
that they are overburdened with federal regulations that were designed for giant corporations, crush the small ones, and make it impossible to earn a profit. That kind of griping goes on all over the country
(the giant corporations that the rules were designed for complain the
loudest) and probably always has. Recently the small-town businessman
has even obtained a spokesman, in the person of Billy Carter, whose
complaints about OSHA inspectors, hiring regulations, the minimum
wage, unemployment compensation, and, generally, federal "paperwork" are echoed by businessmen in La Plata.

There's no doubt that the state of bureaucratic affairs small businessmen allude to can come about; in France, reports Alain Peyrefitte in his
book *Le Mal Francais*, the federal government closed down a small
town's only store, a cafe-grocery-general store, because it is illegal to
serve liquor less than 200 meters from a school and the store was ten
meters too close. But while that kind of horror story is worth keeping
in mind for its cautionary value, in America the government's oppres-
sion of the small businessman seems to be exaggerated. Its truth is
mostly symbolic; to an entrepreneur who is accustomed to answering
to nobody at all, even the slightest intrusion takes on an importance that
those of us who are accustomed to drawing a paycheck would find hard
to understand. And small-town life is a mixture of two strains, the
independence glorified in *Our Town* and the xenophobia condemned
in *Babbitt* and *Main Street;* sometimes the two work in opposition, but
whenever government regulation is involved, they gang up and damn
it.

A case in point is James Hancock, a weather-beaten, articulate man
who runs La Plata's shoe repair shop out of a tiny, cinder-block building
on the main street. Hancock started his shop in 1949 and, he says, has
made less money every year since then—mainly because the government has swamped him in regulations and paperwork. He says he'd
expand his business except that, with all the regulations involved, it just
isn't worth it.

But asked to produce some of the paperwork that plagues him, Hancock can only shrug his shoulders—all he does at the government's
behest is keep books, "just like I was Ford Motor," for income-tax
purposes, something he wouldn't otherwise do. The rest of the paperwork is more in the realm of threat than reality. It is worth noting,
though, that for a really small businessman—not Billy Carter, but Hancock—the minimum wage is a genuine hindrance. He and his assistant
are both below the poverty level, and the assistant has to be hired as

a subcontractor rather than an employee because he can't be paid the minimum wage.

A LITTLE MORE COMPLICATED

Hancock's perceptions are shared by most people around La Plata. A defender of the government would say life has to be a little more complicated in order to bring about a better society—for instance, aren't OSHA inspectors worth it if they'll stop industrial accidents? But in Charles County there's no perception of a reason behind the complication, and it's seen as better just to avoid it, to keep life simple. A local lawyer told me he gave up his real-estate practice rather than comply with the "paperwork and nuisance" of the truth-in-lending act, and reported with great umbrage that the government "sent a man around with a tape measure to measure my damn farm." The manager of the La Plata Chamber of Commerce says solemnly that there are "government agencies created just for the purpose of making more rules." Being brought into a complex society of guarantees and strictures and subsidies designed to bring the greatest good to the greatest number is not what the people of Charles County have in mind.

The question this raises is, are perceptions of overwhelming paperwork and government interference a valid cause for concern if in fact they're only perceptions? Surely government officials shouldn't spend their time trying to keep imaginary dragons away from small businessmen. More broadly, is Charles County, despite its sentiments to the contrary, really getting a good deal from the federal government when everything is taken into account?

Despite all the money that flows in, the answer is not a sanguine one for the government. What it takes out, it takes with impressive efficiency from one and all, but what it puts back, other than salaries and pensions, it does in a way that leaves much to be desired. The money that is spent to help the people in the county who need help, while generous in theory, is often bungled in practice. The fact is that when the government is bestowing its direct gifts on the citizenry, there really *are* a lot of rules to follow and forms to fill out—enough of them to make people shy away from the gifts, acting against their economic interest. In cases like that, the sincerity of sentiments against the government can't be doubted, and something must be wrong.

The two major giveaway organizations in the county—the FmHA and the county department of social services (which is largely federally funded) both have caseloads that are far smaller than they should be. At the social services agency, a supervisor named Sarah Mitchell says, the forms that must be filled out to get on welfare and other public assistance programs, designed in Washington, are "quite detailed—people have difficulty filling them out, and they're bothered by the requirement of a personal interview with a caseworker." Welfare recipients have to submit proof of income, and forms having to do with their housing and children. "Any time you have outside forces dealing with your life in that way," she says, "you'll resent it."

At the FmHA the caseload is only 650, just one of which is a loan to a local business. In 1976, Thomas Potter handed out 700 loan applications, but only 112 came back for processing, and at least part of the reason is that the applications must have held the promise of some future pain. For a housing loan to go through, for instance, the house must conform with a detailed code that specifies the kind of beams that must be used and requires a smoke detector in every room. The Agriculture Department's farm storage loan program, which provides funding for the storage of crops, has had no applications so far—"a lot of people don't understand it and don't want to be bothered with the government," the program's director says. HUD's block grants program is far under-utilized because, the people who run it in the county say, there is so much paperwork involved—every application has to have at least 12 forms, six statistical reports, and three copies of lease agreements, just for a grant for one house.

THE GOOD THE GOVERNMENT CAN DO

The largest-scale case of a government program not helping people as it should in Charles County is the new sewage treatment plant in La Plata. A sewage plant project in a rural area—improving the environment, providing jobs, a big capital investment—is the kind of project liberals are accustomed to pointing to proudly as an exemplar of the good the federal government can do, and indeed there is a whole range of programs through which a town like La Plata can fund such a plant. But the plant, now under construction, is being financed locally—not out of ignorance of the government programs or blind mistrust of outsiders, but because local financing is faster and almost as cheap for the town as federal funding.

The story of the sewage treatment plant begins in 1970, when the town of La Plata hired an intense young man from Utah, John Newman, for the one full-time administrative job in its government, town manager. At that time La Plata was short of drinking water, so Newman set out to get a new water treatment plant built—with federal money. The plant was originally estimated to cost $380,000, of which the Department of Housing and Urban Development would fund 90 per cent, leaving the town with a cost of only $38,000. Five years later, the plant was built, at a cost of $1,150,000, of which the town paid $347,500.

The huge increase in cost was due in large part to inflation, although government building requirements also played a large part. Of course, the requirements and the inflation are intimately connected; every requirement means paperwork, every piece of paperwork means delays, and every delay, in inflationary times, means the cost of a project goes up. Newman has the paperwork for the plant in a cardboard box in his office; the box is four feet long and is filled with the most detailed sort of requirements, preapplications, applications, impact assessments, engineering reports, promises of nondiscrimination. Newman says for four years he "practically lived" in the HUD regional office in Baltimore.

So in 1973, when La Plata started having sewer problems, Newman was already not kindly disposed toward the federal government. But since the town was low on money, and the plant would cost more than half a million dollars, he decided to give it another try.

First Newman took his project to the Environmental Protection Agency, which had a program that would pay directly for 75 per cent of the cost of the plant and arrange for the state to contribute another 12½ per cent. EPA decided that perhaps a sewage plant for all of southern Charles County, rather than just La Plata, might be a good idea, so it had the County Sanitary Commission look into it. The commission contracted for a $106,000 study, which turned out to take three years to complete and to conclude that a county-wide plant *wasn't* needed. In the middle of this, with annual inflation well over ten per cent, Newman decided he couldn't wait any longer and pulled out.

He next looked into getting an HUD community facility grant, although with extreme trepidation, because from his experience with the HUD-funded water plant he knew all his plans, bids, and pay vouchers would have to be federally approved at great additional time and cost. But in the midst of the application process HUD replaced its community facility grants with block grants, which were billed as a streamlining of the bureaucracy. To get a block grant, a small community had to have a certain level of unemployment, which La Plata, though above the national average, then did not meet (it now does). Newman had to go elsewhere.

Having given up on the idea of a grant, he went to the FmHA for a loan—the terms were good (40 years at five-percent interest) and he imagined that a loan would be simpler in the processing than a grant. In April 1976 he approached Tom Potter about applying.

Here came a rude awakening for Newman, for he found that the instructions for filling out the loan application ran to 50 single-spaced pages. Among other forms, he had to fill out a pre-application, a full application, a balance sheet, an engineering contract, an operating budget, contracts for professional services, evidence of compliance with various rules, preliminary reports, and a project summary—quite a load on a one-man government. All plans had to be reviewed by FmHA architects and engineers. Every step of the process took time. For example: Newman had to send all his plans for approval to a state clearinghouse, which in turn sent them to five separate state agencies for *their* approval. Everybody approved in the end, but the process took months.

Finally, in April 1977, the FmHA sent the town a request for form FmHA 442-46, Letter of Intent to Meet Conditions; this was a final step to make sure the town understood it had to submit to the FmHA details like all construction contracts, an accountant agreement, monthly progress reports for each contractor, and non-discrimination reports. (Bear in mind, this is a program only for towns of less than 5,500 people, a group in which La Plata is a rarity for having any full-time administrative staff. In most places, all these forms would have to be filled out after hours by someone with a full-time job.) A month later, the grant was approved.

'FOR *OUR* APPROVAL'

In the meantime, however, as Newman grew impatient, he had been talking to a local financial firm about floating a bond issue. He found the terms wouldn't be quite as good—20 years at 5.85 per cent—but that the bonds could be out on the market by July 1. He submitted a short report on the financial condition of the town, which the firm used to write a bond issue report. That was the only information La Plata had to submit. When the bond issue papers were ready, Newman says, *"They* brought it down for *our* approval"—and he decided to forget about the FmHA. On June 3, he wrote Tom Potter that he was going on the open market. "I'm appalled," Newman wrote, "at the amount of paperwork that is required by the United States Government through the FmHA for a loan . . . levels and levels of bureaucrats seem to feed on themselves as make-work projects to justify their own existence."

Potter says now that the processing of the La Plata loan application was among the fastest he's seen. As for the plant, construction is now well along and should be finished by the first of the year.

The forms and regulations in which the government enshrouds its gifts are not without some logic, of course: the theory is that if Washington is going to pay for something, it is its duty to make sure the project conforms to various noble social goals. Would it be right, the planners think, to fund a building on which there's discrimination by the contractor, or faulty construction, or an incompetent architect, or unsafe working conditions? But what this attitude does is effectively take federal programs out of the reach of small-scale America—there are few small towns whose governments can keep up with all the paperwork for every federal program they're eligible for. By not being able just to grit its teeth and give away money, Washington is short-changing small-town America on a major category of its benefits.

A good example of the problem is the impoverished shoemaker, James Hancock, who complains that the government is biased against a small businessman like him. To be sure, Hancock suffers a little under the burden of taxes and the minimum wage law—but that ought to be countervailed by a helping hand from the government when he can't make ends meet. Poor as he is, he's eligible for a number of federal loans and perhaps even subsidies to finance the expansion and operation of his business—and personally, he could get food stamps and housing subsidies. The government should buoy him up far more than it grinds him down.

But Hancock participates in none of these programs designed to help people like him. "I haven't looked into it," he says. "I think it's wrong. If the government robs you so you have to go beg 'em for something to eat, that's wrong. You don't take anything free without controls." Maybe that's an emotional view, but the evidence in Charles County shows that there's a lot of truth to it.

Chronic Epistlitis

Robert L. Taylor

Before me on my desk, in a red vinyl folder marked "confidential," is a congressional inquiry. It is addressed to the director of the National Institute of Mental Health. I am not the director, but my task is to act as if I were and compose a reply. Directors never write their own replies. Instead, inquiries are routed throughout the Institute along somewhat lawless traffic patterns, and the loser is the one with nobody to pass them to.

This time, I lost. That's why I'm sitting at my desk, staring at the wall, wondering what the director would say to the Senator from Texas, concerning his constituent, John Dingee of Waxahatchie, who suspects that the Institute doesn't evaluate its programs and challenges us to prove him wrong.

Dingee sought a congressional escort for his question only after a long series of frustrating exchanges with me. I kept hoping the director's office would refer his letters to somebody else, but each time, like homing pigeons, they found me in the recesses of the Institute. Answering the letters of concerned taxpayers could perhaps provide valuable communication, but the Institute's output can always outmuscle and outequivocate even the most dedicated letter-writer's input. I held Dingee off for months with letters about how we were studying the problem, and, when he asked about the specific studies, I countered with the privileged communications ploy—the studies were being finalized and the information was not available.

That's when Dingee escalated to his senator. Dingee's words were robed in red vinyl with the attached senatorial note: "Please inform me concerning the question raised by my constituent." It is through such

"Congressionals"—thousands a year at the Institute, 206,241 in 1970 at the Department of Defense, 85,000 at HEW—that the act of letter-writing ceases to be a matter of grammar and becomes a matter of Zen Buddhism.

The once simple dialogue between Dingee and me, or between Dingee and the director, now becomes a game of multi-dimensional chess. On the base level, I am still writing to Dingee—it is his question, after all—but answering Dingee becomes the least of my problems. It doesn't matter if my answer satisfies him. It is layers of bureaucrats I am writing to, people who must okay the letter before it can be forever removed from my desk.

The Congressionals move horizontally, but our task is to write them vertically. Not only do I have to worry about what the director would say, if he ever personally wrote his own replies, but also what the director would think the Senator would say if he ever read his own mail. And since neither the Senator nor the director will ever hear of Dingee, the game enters a fourth dimension—my letter must impress not the director but the highest subordinate to the director who will approve or reject it. I must therefore write what the highest subordinate would think the director would say to the Senator, or better, what he would think the director would think the Senator's aide would think the Senator would say. Dingee, as you have gathered, disappears in all of this.

The frustration leads me to consider a direct, even creative answer:

Dear Senator:
Tell Dingee we are going to throw his ass in the asylum if he keeps raving about psychiatric incompetence.

But such responses go unwritten. The political consequences are inevitably brought into the equation. There is hardly any chance that Dingee, his suspicions aroused back in Waxahatchie, could put enough pressure on the Senator to threaten the mental health appropriations, but there is no point in taking useless risks. But then perhaps I should use the grandiose global ploy, where the specific question is disregarded and instead the answer refers repeatedly to the "Institute's undying battle for mental health and well-being." Or perhaps I should just say it straight. I recall previous letters I had written stating unambiguous positions, all returned from the director's office with notes listing ways "this information can be used against us" and the curt directive, "Needs to be more vague. Please redo."

Aside from the paralyzing policy problems of Dingee's inquiry, there are the technical questions. Does the director know the Senator personally, addressing him by first name and closing with "Yours truly" rather than "Respectfully"? Should the closing line really retain the standard form insisted upon by the director for all 12,000 letters that go out over his name each year: "If I may be of any further assistance, please let me know"?

This Congressional, I conclude, is too complicated to be answered. So I give in to the reverse Peter Principle (as incompetence rises, so problems fall) and hand the project over to my secretary. Hardened by past experience, I find the secretarial solution easier and easier. I present it to her nonchalantly, as if the matter is too trivial for my own efforts: "Wonder if you might draft a reply to this. Pretty much the same as before. If you have any difficulty, pull the file on old Congressionals." Old Congressionals, no doubt, were written by her, anyway.

Three hours later, she has a draft ready. It seems all right to me, sufficiently noncommittal, but I must not let it pass untouched. I ask her to make a few changes, even though they are unnecessary, to restore my sense of dignity and my faith in government job levels.

It would seem that the Institute has done its duty to John Dingee. We have probably spent more man-hours' worth of highly paid public service on answering Dingee's letters than he contributes in federal taxes, proof enough of the government's interest in serving the individual citizen. But Dingee has also given in return—he has given several federal employees something to do. For if lower divisions are for writing letters, then upper divisions are for editing them, and still higher echelons exist to undangle participles and rephrase sentences. And what is a director for if not to sign final copies? On each level, the simple question from John Dingee plays its small part in justifying the layers of personnel, the paychecks, the appropriations, and the typewriters.

Three days later the letter reappears in my in-box, having been returned from the next level of bureaucracy, with words scratched out, sentences transposed, and numerous suggestions for inconsequential changes scribbled in the margins. So "the" becomes "this" and "as you know" is changed to "as you *well* know." "If I may be of any further assistance, please let me know *immediately*" is substituted for "If I may be of any further assistance, please let me know" in order to convey real concern.

At this point I could not care less. What the letter says is strictly secondary; the original question is long forgotten. Once again, I hand the letter to my secretary, with instructions to make the changes indicated. The ping-pong process continues: the draft to me and back to her with an "O.K." for the second "final" copy. But at last, in victory the secretary appears with the copy. I check it for "perfection," and it passes. The final product.

And now for the last hurdle. The letter is sent in full regalia to the

Office of the Director. An official "letter secretary" records receipt of the letter. It is ushered into the Office of the Special Assistant to the Director who has final responsibility for making sure that all is correct with these labors of creative vaguery. Suddenly, he sees a dangling participle. Back the "final" copy goes into its red folder with the terse note of righteous indignation: "Please correct!" The letter passes from special assistant to secretary, to interdepartmental mail, to secretary, to me. At least the mistake was a good, solid one. The last Congressional came back because of an unnecessary comma.

This time I deliver the "final" myself to the director's office. Upon leaving there can be no complete peace of mind; there is the haunting possibility of another dangling participle or split infinitive lurking somewhere in that reply.

Days pass before I receive a phone call: "Remember some Dingee letter you were writing for the director?" It's his special assistant talking to me. "Before I had a chance to look it over again for corrections, the director informed me that the Senator's office had called, asking why he hadn't received a reply to his inquiry of four weeks ago. The director assured him of an immediate, personal reply. So I drafted a new letter, expressing his considerable concern."

Thus relieved, I can return to my work—preparing papers on new ways of looking at things at the Institute. Like the next Congressional, they must go through channels.

part 4
GOVERNMENT SERVICE, CIVIL AND OTHERWISE

Nicholas Lemann has compared the civil service to "an overcrowded banquet where you have to fight to get a seat but can feast in peace once seated." Three bits of data demonstrate the truth of Lemann's analogy: in fiscal year 1977, only 9,034 of the more than 250,000 people who applied for white-collar civil service jobs got them—an acceptance rate to the "banquet" of 3.7 percent. But of those already in the civil service, 99.94 percent received "merit" pay raises. And only one-seventh of one percent of those who had held their jobs for at least a year were fired. Getting a federal job is hard; losing one, it seems, is even harder.

Working for the government was not always that way. Throughout the first century of our history, bureaucrats were appointed and dismissed by elected political officials. This meant that most of them were members of the incumbent President's political party, beneficiaries of what came to be called the "spoils system." But politics did not necessarily conflict with the selection of able people, as is sometimes thought. Presidents had every incentive to appoint good federal officials and get rid of bad ones. As George Washington wrote shortly after becoming President, "if injudicious or unpopular measures should be taken by the Executive under the New Government with regards to appointments, the Government itself would be in the utmost danger of being utterly subverted by the measures."

Nevertheless, some political appointees were grossly incompetent or corrupt, and during the national crises of Civil War and Reconstruction, their scandalous shortcomings were highly publicized by reformers. When President James Garfield was assassinated in 1881 by a "disappointed office-seeker" who had worked in his election campaign, opponents of the spoils system seized the moment and secured passage of the Pendleton Act, which created the civil service. Only 14,000 low-grade employees were originally covered by the new merit system of appointment, but Presidents were given the power to extend the Civil Service Commission's domain even further. Ironically, it was politics that usually led them to do so. As the end of a President's term neared, he would bring more federal employees into the civil service in order to prevent a new President of the opposite party from stocking the government with his own supporters. Today, nearly all government workers are immune from what some might call "politics," others "democratic accountability."

Ann Pincus describes "How to Get a Government Job" in terms that are equally depressing for jobseeker and taxpayer alike. Not only are civil service jobs extremely hard to get, she explains, but the influence of "friendship networks" within the government sometimes undermines the merit system of hiring as effectively as politics once did.

The demand for government jobs surprises some people. Until a few years ago, civil servants were commonly regarded as people who had traded the possibility of high earnings for long-term job security. But half that equation has changed, according to Marjorie Boyd. As she shows in "What's Wrong with the Civil Service," federal employees are now paid an average 20 percent more than workers in the private sector. Equally important, says Leonard Reed in "Firing a Federal Employee: The Impossible Dream," the other side of the equation has *not* changed. In fact, if a small business employing ten people discharged workers for cause at the same rate as the federal government, it would fire only one person every 70 years!

One serious consequence of providing civil servants with such comfortable employment is that it makes it that much harder for them to "blow the whistle" when they see wrongdoing in their agencies. Albert O. Hirschman argues in "Exit, Voice, and Loyalty" that in theory a member of an organization has three ways of expressing dissent. He can "exit," or quit; he can raise his "voice" in complaint; or he can do both —resign and protest.

Each of these options has its advantages, depending on the situation. Undoubtedly, the country as a whole benefits when a government bureaucrat exposes improper activities from within. (The news media rarely covers the bureaucracy with anything near the thoroughness that it devotes to the President and Congress; thus, our reliance on the insider for information is even greater.) But the risk of losing a lucrative, secure job via "exit" often outweighs the benefits of abandoning the unsavory activities such a job requires. And, as Taylor Branch shows in "Courage without Esteem: Profiles in Whistle-Blowing," the personal costs inflicted on the person who uses his "voice" to "go public" are enough to discourage all but the most courageous.

The supreme irony, of course, is that the whistle-blower is punished while the civil servant, competent or not, enjoys all but absolute job security. Compounding the irony even more is the fact that the greatest reward of all goes to those who leave the government and use the expertise and inside knowledge they gained there to manipulate the government on behalf of their new employers in the private sector. John A. Jenkins describes how Washington lawyers make this formula for success work for them in "The Revolving Door between Government and the Law Firms."

How To Get a Government Job

Ann Pincus

You are a decent, public-spirited American, without obvious defects of character or intelligence, and you want to work in Washington for the government.

Your ambitions are limited. You don't want to be a National Highway Traffic Safety Administrator, or executive director of the Marine Mammal Commission, or a member of the Railroad Retirement Board.

What you have in mind is something on the order of Executive Assistant to the Federal Disaster Assistance Administrator of the Department of Housing and Urban Development—a medium-level civil service job, in other words. Or maybe you're even willing to settle for the lowest administrative job on the ladder.

So you turn to the Civil Service Commission, which was established in 1883 to help and protect people like yourself, and you attempt to apply for a job that suits your interests and qualifications.

Entering the Civil Service building, you are directed to the Federal Job Applications Center, a reassuringly bureaucratic anteroom, where a series of display cases are filled with descriptions of job openings in the various agencies. You notice that the best sounding ones all seem to have "closed" stamped over the cover, which means that the job has been filled.

Surveying the Federal Job Applications Center, you come upon a group of people standing in front of a television set. Someone pushes a button, and the face of Jim Vance (black anchorman on NBC's local evening news show) comes on the screen with a 90-second explanation of how to get a federal job. He outlines the competitive process and advises: "The government does not have jobs for the people, it has people for the jobs." The truth of that statement will become clearer to you in time.

But for the moment, you are just another job-seeker, and you stand behind 20 other applicants (the average number of walk-ins is 718 per day) in the information lines where a member of the Civil Service personnel staff advises you what forms you need. There is an express line for those who already know what forms they want.

You go home, fill out the forms, send them to the Civil Service Commission, and wait up to six weeks to hear whether you are qualified for the GS level for which you have applied. (Anything below GS-9, you must also take a written test.) If you are qualified, you receive a letter from the Civil Service, informing you that you are now on the register and that they will let you know if anything turns up.

You should frame the letter, because the odds are very high that it is the last you'll hear about that federal job you hoped to get.

Consider the statistics. Around 300,000 people apply for civil service jobs through the Washington office each year. Only ten per cent get jobs. And barely more than one per cent get administrative jobs.

Let's start with the PACE (Professional Administrative Career Examination) level of jobs, which are GS-5 and GS-7 with base salaries of $8,925 and $11,046. To qualify for a PACE-level job you must take a written examination. Each year there are between 1,600 and 2,000 PACE jobs in Washington listed on the Civil Service register. That is not all the PACE jobs that are available, because many others are filled from within the agency, in-house promotions, transfers from other agencies or persons coming back into government. Of the 1,600 to 2,000 filled from outside the government, many are "name requested," that is, when an agency sends over a personnel request to the Civil Service Commission, they also send over a name to fill the job. (More on how this works later.) To make the PACE system even more complicated it should be pointed out that high marks on the exam alone do not get you into the civil service. There is something called the quota system, which means that every state has a certain number of jobs—based on population—it can fill in the Washington office.

Soooo ... You can have a 100 achievement rating and be from Virginia and not get the job; on the other hand you can have a 75-percent score on the test and possibly be hired because you are from Iowa. Not only that. There are 50,000 people on the Civil Service register who have passed the PACE exam, which means that approximately 50 people are competing for each available PACE job.

The next step up the competitive career job scale is to mid-level, which is grades 9 through 12. The mid-level base pay is $13,482 to $19,386, compared to PACE base of $8,925 to $11,046 (1976 figures).

You do not take an examination for mid-level jobs in Washington, but you still must compete with about 15,000 others on the register. There are certain qualifications necessary to get on the register, such as education or years of experience. There are an average of 1,600 mid-level jobs available each year to persons not already working in government. Many of those jobs are "name requested," however, which leaves 320 to be filled—presumably—by matching a person's qualifications against his or her job description and subsequent interviews.

Senior-level jobs, GS-13 through 15 (base pay $22,906 to $31,309) are also on the Civil Service register, but, again, nearly all the jobs are filled from within the government itself—95 per cent of them, in fact. This leaves 480 senior-level jobs, but don't get your hopes too high. Civil Service personnel insist that name requests don't automatically get hired, but they admit that "most" of them do.

The final category to be considered is super grade: GS-16, 17, and 18 (base pay: $36,338). These jobs come in two categories: career and schedule C, the latter meaning by political appointment. In 1974 nearly all the career super-grade jobs—92 per cent of them—were filled from within the government. That left only 60 career jobs to be filled by persons outside the government. What is more startling is that, of the *political* appointments to this grade, only 12 per cent were filled from the outside. That is, 88 per cent of the political patronage at the super-grade level was "dispensed" by the bureaucracy itself.

Anyway, the combined annual job openings for GS-9 through GS-18, when all the "in-house" and "name request" slots are filled, amounts to a mere 476 vacancies. Unfortunately, it so happens that there are 30, 000 persons on the Civil Service register who qualify as GS-9 or above. In other words, the odds against you are about 65 to one.

Clearly, then, your only rational hope of getting a government job is to find out what a "name request" is, and try to become one yourself. Meanwhile, you could pause to reflect that the Civil Service Commission employs 3,414 people in Washington, D.C., which is not far short of the 4,000 or so that it hires each year at the GS-5 through GS-18 levels for the entire government.

If you had understood Washington better, you might have started your quest for a "name request" government job on Capitol Hill and saved yourself a lot of trouble.

Your senator or congressman would probably have been willing to act as your job placement counselor—especially if you worked in his campaign or contributed money to it. The system works this way: you visit your elected representative and remind him of his obligations to you.

He in turn puts pressure on someone in the agency or department where you want to work. Your application is then circulated with "must hire" written on it, and someone somewhere finds room for a GS-13. He writes up a job description and a name request and sends it over to the Civil Service Commission.

If all goes well, the job description is written so cleverly that *only you* qualify for the job. Presto! You are hired. Usually. Occasionally there is a mixup, as when officials at the Department of Defense wanted to hire a certain man and 19 others with identical qualifications came up on the register before him, so they had to hire all 20 persons.

A House subcommittee studying the workings of the merit system has filled eight file cabinets with "must hire" letters to the General Services Administration from various members of Congress seeking jobs for constituents or friends. Senator Hugh Scott, the former Republican Minority Leader, was especially adept at using the GSA, thanks to his close friendship with former GSA chief Arthur Sampson. Bob Woodward and Carl Bernstein, in their book, *The Final Days*, quote former White House Special Counsel Fred Buzhardt as saying that Scott and Sampson ran the GSA "as a private employment agency." But for all their meddling, the congressmen—especially the Republicans—are still outsiders, and this has been especially true of late. The politicians now are more cautious than before—they have become fed up with being exposed in the press and accused of participating in crooked deals.

A much more common and effective way of getting your name requested is to know someone inside the agency where you want to work. Agency insiders will be the first to know about a job opening and, knowing both you and the job, they can tailor the description to your experience. The people you need to know to use the "buddy system" are mostly Democrats—people who got their government jobs under the Roosevelt and Truman Administrations, when the civil service grew from 600,000 to 2.2 million—the friends they subsequently hired, and the friends of those friends. (This helps explain why you seem to be meeting the same person over and over again in Washington—someone with the ideology of Eleanor Roosevelt and the working habits of Step 'n Fetchit.) Eisenhower and Kennedy had little impact on the civil service. It grew by 600,000 under Lyndon Johnson, but the hiring was done mostly by the old Roosevelt-Truman bureaucrats, with LBJ's Marvin Watson just trying to make sure the top appointees weren't pro-Robert Kennedy or at least weren't anti-LBJ.

Richard Nixon became the first president to challenge the control of the civil service by Roosevelt-Truman appointees and their friends. Nixon wanted to do more than just pay off political debts, he wanted to "clean out the Democratic-infested civil service," as one of his biographers put it. First, he established political personnel contacts in most of the federal agencies, whose jobs were to refer Republicans into job vacancies, and to make the agencies' personnel policies more "responsive" to the Administration's wishes.

After the '72 elections Nixon wanted an even firmer hold on the bureaucracy. His Cabinet officials had less and less control over who was hired in their agencies, and most hirings went from the White House to the special referral offices in the agencies. For example, former Secretary of HUD James T. Lynn has stated that he knew nothing about the special referral office with 13 workers in it which operated only two doors down from his own office.

White House staff members Alan May and Jerry Jones sought to "improve" the referral system. They coauthored the now famous "Malek Manual," a 600-page booklet designed to instruct top-level political appointees how to fill career jobs with Nixon types, outlining ways to rid the civil service of career personnel, in general how to activate the "responsiveness program." (The manual was called the Malek Manual because it was found in Fred Malek's files.)

The disclosure of the "Malek Manual" caused a minor panic among the federal political appointees and nearly everyone began to point a finger at someone else. General Accounting Office revelations forced the Civil Service Commission to inquire into violations of the merit system in the General Services Administration, HUD, the Small Business Administration, and CSA (Community Services Administration, formerly Office of Economic Opportunity and now part of ACTION). GSA officials immediately turned an accusatory finger back on the Civil Service Commission. They charged the Commission chairman, Robert E. Hampton (a Nixon appointee), with participating in a political patronage ring. Charles L. Ryan, a special assistant in the Commission's Bureau of Recruiting and Examining, said in a deposition that he had personally processed job references from congressmen, White House officials, and even the Civil Service commissioners themselves between the years 1969 and 1973.

Gordon Freedman, who has worked in the House Manpower and Civil Service subcommittee for a year, believes that the real subverters of the civil service concept are the civil servants themselves. "Sure, some politicians get jobs for their friends," he says. "But you could have put all the Nixon referral people on the Sequoia and it would still float. But if you put all the people involved in the buddy system on the carrier *Enterprise,* it would sink."

Freedman says the public has no real protection from the growing force of the bureaucracy itself: "Agencies in general, to protect their turf, develop their own language. They snow politicians. Many more personnel come in through" the buddy system than through political pull.

"Face it," he says, "bureaucrats can work this system any way they want to. And there's no coherent group you're talking about. They don't socialize together. It's just common practice.

"Sure, it's bad when Nixon deals in political purity, but some of the Civil Service Commission attacks on the White House were so dishonest and self-righteous that they were almost as bad as the White House itself."

What's Wrong with the Civil Service

Marjorie Boyd

Anti-bureaucratic sentiment may be abroad in the land, but so is the desire for the government's services; so big government is usually blamed on the constant creation of new programs designed to help the general populace. Politicians often present government growth as an insoluble, illusory dilemma: the federal government has actually grown very little in the past ten years, they say, and what growth has taken place has only been in response to the public demand for new programs and services.

But the federal budget has grown in the last decade from $170 billion to $500 billion, twice as fast as the cost of living, at the same time that many huge programs have been cut back or ended. And if the public desire for services can't be lessened, there are obviously other things that can. One major culprit in the growth of the federal budget that has nothing to do with the desires of the American people is the civil service system. Everybody knows that the civil service was originally set up to get the hacks out of government, which it has done. But because it has become so enormous, complex, and shrouded in confusing language it hasn't gotten much attention.

Behind its aura of virtue, however, lurks the most wasteful organization in America. The civil service is at the very heart of government growth.

Between 1955 and 1965 the civil service white-collar work force grew from about 1 million to about 1.8 million. Since then it has stayed relatively stable in size; the growth has been in its cost. The line of a graph charting the rise in payroll costs for all federal workers looks like the trajectory of a rocket launch. The increases have raised the average government salary to $12,521, while the average salary in private industry is only $10,522. Of course, there are still government workers who are not paid as well as their counterparts in private industry—Cabinet officers, top management, and research scientists—but these are few in number, and they are all on the highest rungs of government. Paying these people handsomely is at least a reasonable position, assuming that they do have very special skills and abilities. What isn't reasonable is paying the hundreds of thousands immediately below the top well over what they would get outside of the federal government.

The rise in government salaries is the product of a system that is ongoing, so it can be expected that the gap will widen in the future. To understand that system, it is necessary to understand how the civil service works.

White-collar government workers are classified in 18 civil service grades, and grade is the sole determinant of salary. Grades 1 through 4 are generally clerical and low-level technical workers. Grades 5 through 12 are called "administrative" and cover a wide range of workers described as "the college graduate type," though a college degree is not required. Grade 5 is where young administrative workers usually enter the government, but some start out higher. Grades 13 through 15 are called "supervisory," and grades 16 through 18 "management." The bulk of the civil service is in the lower and middle grades; of the 1,349,104 graded federal civil service employees, only 4,605 are in the top three grades and only 363 are grade 18s (1977 figures).

Within each grade there are ten "longevity levels," each at a progressively higher salary. For instance, a grade 10 at the lowest longevity level is paid $15,524, while a grade 10 at the highest level makes $20,-177. These longevity salary increases are granted at one- to three-year intervals according to a set formula. While poor job performance could theoretically cause a worker to be denied his longevity increase, I could find no one in the government who had heard of such a case. "All you have to do is breathe," said one official.

It stands to reason that an administrative employee entering the government at grade 5 would move up the grades one by one, but that isn't the way it works. Grades 6, 8, and 10 are reserved for "special employees," such as administrative secretaries, bookkeepers, and technical designers; so all administrative employees go from grade 5 to grade 7 to grade 9 to grade 11 before their grade-by-grade ascent begins. The average time it takes to rise from grade 5 to grade 11 is nine years, but ten per cent do it in as little as three years. The lowest level for a grade 5 is $9,303, and the lowest salary for a grade 11 is $17,056. Holders of master's degrees enter government at grade 7 ($11,523) and lawyers enter at grade 9 ($14,097), so their ascent is even more rapid.

Until 1962 most civil servants were underpaid because they had to depend on the caprice of Congress for pay increases. But that year the entire system of government salaries was overhauled, and ever since, according to the Brookings Institution, federal pay has been rising faster than pay in private industry.

The post-1962 system is called "comparability," and it is based on an idea that, on paper, seems scrupulously fair to both taxpayers and government workers. The system starts in the Bureau of Labor Statistics, which each year makes an extensive survey of salaries in private industry. Taking descriptions of government jobs provided by the Civil Service Commission, the Bureau of Labor Statistics identifies "comparable" jobs in a range of industries spread over a wide geographic area and arrives at an average figure for each job. The Civil Service Commission then fits the jobs into the grade system and sets up a new pay scale by grades. The process is repeated each year and a new salary scale is constructed and presented to the President. If he does nothing, the raises go into effect every October. If the President feels the increases are too high, he can make another proposal that goes into effect unless it is vetoed by a majority of one of the houses of Congress.

Something happens in the translation of this system from paper into practice that results in an average government salary about 20 per cent above private industry's average. It's a problem of definitions. While the Civil Service Commission prints stacks of books purported to contain exact descriptions of the jobs in each grade level, those descriptions are sufficiently vague and elastic as to cover, if the need arises, almost any human activity. Take accounting, a profession whose work should be easy to classify and quantify. It ought to be possible to state clearly the activities of a grade 12 auditor, but here's how the Civil Service Commission does it: "Characteristic of this level are assignments that require the ability to develop audit plans and analyze policies, functions, procedures, internal controls, and accounting systems of complex activities primarily in terms of evaluating the future impact of current practices and proposed actions." That kind of gobbledygook is used to describe each grade level, and is complemented by a sprinkling of sentences here and there pointing out that "the work of a grade 12 is more complex than the work of a grade 11." All judgments are relative.

Mike Causey, *The Washington Post*'s civil service columnist, says, "There's no such thing as a typing pool in the federal government any more. It's been replaced by a 'word processing unit.' If you're a supervisor, you don't mind giving a GS-3 or GS-4 to a typist, but you feel rotten giving it to a word processing specialist."

In the personnel office of each government agency is a job classifier who is responsible for the grade classification of jobs. A classifier is an administrative employee, typically a grade 11. Some classifiers are responsible for as many as 4,000 low-level jobs; a few classifiers oversee unusually technical or varied jobs and may cover as few as 500; but the average is around 1,000. The Civil Service Commission provides the classifiers with voluminous written "standards" and offers counsel as well as conducting periodic reviews of the classifiers' work.

Because the only way to get a substantially higher salary is to get a different job with a higher grade classification, government offices are in a constant state of reorganization and realignment. New sections and new jobs are perpetually springing up. While bureaucrats contend, even to each other (perhaps especially to each other), that these ever-changing arrangements enable them to perform their tasks more efficiently, the reorganizations also have the effect of rapidly raising salaries. If a supervisor works up an idea for a new, improved section, it usually entails creating several up-graded positions. The new job descriptions are sent to the agency classifier for approval. Some agencies have permissive classifiers who approve supervisors' plans without checking further; others conduct "desk audits," visiting the reorganizing offices and questioning both supervisors and employees. In agencies that have strict classifiers, a newly up-graded employee is coached extensively in preparation for the classifier's visit.

EVEN MORE ENTICING

Since the comparability system went into effect, the salaries of the higher grades (except the management grades) have risen much faster than the salaries of the lower grades because salaries for "comparable" jobs in private industry have been rising faster. This has made the prospect of moving up the grade ladder even more enticing.

Thus over the years the distribution of federal workers in the grades has changed drastically. While the number of workers in the top three "management" grades has remained about the same and the number in the lower grades has either grown slightly or declined slightly, grades 12, 13, 14, and 15 have all undergone enormous booms. There are now 300,000 workers in these four civil service grades—that's more than the total population of Birmingham, Alabama or Tucson, Arizona—all of whom make between $20,442 and $43,923 a year. Grade 13, which had only 65,000 workers in 1965, now has 105,000—a 62-percent increase.

The increase in grade 13s has affected not just government's cost, but its size as well. Because grade 13 is the first "supervisory" grade, the civil service regulations make it clear that, except in rare cases, a grade 13 must supervise other workers—and the more he supervises, the better for the job description. After an ambitious grade 12 convinces his supervisor that his particular project is important enough to merit a new section and that he should be promoted to grade 13 so he can head it, he goes out and gathers a group of grade 9s, 10s, and 11s to be promoted for assignment to the new section. Then new offices, clerical employees, equipment, and furniture must be requisitioned. As soon as the new section is in operation, everyone moves up the scale to fill the jobs vacated by its employees, so more grade 5s and 7s must be recruited from the outside.

Now our new grade 13 section chief must be constantly on the lookout for ways to bring more employees under his wing in order to position himself to make his ascent to grade 14. It would be hard to imagine a system that more effectively encouraged people's natural inclination toward empire building. Every person in the civil service system has a powerful financial interest in seeing the government get bigger.

Of course, in the struggle over bodies to supervise there are always losers, and some are shoved aside to work on nonexistent "special projects" alone—but they keep supervisor's salary as a badge of former glories. Nobody in the government ever gets a pay cut.

When Rep. Paul Simon was interviewed about the bureaucracy on CBS's "Sixty Minutes," he mentioned in passing that he had heard of a postal official who made $29,000 a year but did not work. Simon hastened to add that he was sure this was a rare situation indeed. After the program, to Simon's surprise, he received several phone calls and letters from highly paid bureaucrats who insisted that they too did no work. One official of the Postal Department called to say he was being paid $38,000 a year for doing nothing. Another government worker wrote:

"You are wrong when you say that the unoccupied $29,000-a-year bureaucrat is a rarity.... I have had no meaningful work to do since June 1965 and my present annual salary is $29,168. I share an office with another employee who is in the same salary and non-work category."

The cases of government workers who *actually* do nothing—who do crossword puzzles every morning and go to the track every afternoon —are, of course, extremely rare. What isn't rare at all, however, are the people who spend all day either in meetings and conferences or writing memos and conducting briefings about what went on in the meetings and conferences. Effectively, they do nothing, but for eight hours a day they at least maintain the appearance of activity.

A DIFFERENT WORLD

Although bureaucrats insist it isn't so, the world of government agencies is vastly different from the outside world. The idea of comparability, so reasonable on paper, not only is distorted in practice; it may also be intrinsically wrong in principle. Is it possible to compare a job in private industry, where performance is judged by widely recognized standards, with one in government where standards are fuzzy and unclear? Can you compare anything with a system in which people make $30,000 a year for jobs like Suggestions Award Administrator or Fringe Benefit Specialist or Manager of Creative Services? Is the comparison valid between a government worker whose job is totally protected and a worker in private industry who, despite his best efforts, may have his livelihood snatched away by such vagaries as the whims of consumers?

The government employee takes no risks. He faces no competition, unless he chooses to take part in in-fighting. And even if he loses out in office intrigue, his salary is not threatened and he cannot be fired.

To the outsider, the process by which government employees are promoted seems incredibly casual, despite the Civil Service Commission's stacks of printed procedures, standards, and regulations. No private industry would allow promotion to a $30,000-a-year job to be proposed at the middle-management level and then approved only by the department classifier, a $19,000-a-year administrative employee. The civil service is a system promoting random growth that may or may not fit in with the overall plans of management.

And it is an ingrown system without checks from the outside. From the Bureau of Labor Statistics auditors to the Civil Service Commission reviewers to the agency classifiers to the supervisors, everyone who determines salaries and promotions is an employee of government. Employees of the Office of Management and Budget and the General Accounting Office, the two efficient, no-nonsense government agencies, have put out studies and issued memos complaining that government jobs are over-graded, but since they are government employees themselves, their motivation to push for reform is not strong. While the integrity of the very best of government employees is of the highest caliber, many of their judgments are subjective—and in matters pertaining to one's own financial well-being, bias can often be so deeply ingrained as to be unconscious.

Firing a Federal Employee: The Impossible Dream

Leonard Reed

Among the more curious notions in contemporary America is that the way to dispose of an irksome charge is to label it a myth. Myth is the intellectual's substitute for "abracadabra," a mantra for driving out intrusive thoughts. So it is not surprising that at the United States Civil Service Commission the question of why it is so difficult to fire an incompetent government employee is greeted with an indulgent smile and the reply, "That's one of those myths."

Smile or not, the difficulty of dismissal for incompetence is an uneasy subject at the Commission. Officials would rather talk about what civil servants *can* be fired for. They call your attention to the Internal Revenue Service where, they say, people found guilty of wrongdoing are quickly dismissed. (Actually, they aren't dismissed. Faced with the alternative of jail, they resign. In 1976, of 71,000 tenured employees at the IRS, only six were dismissed for inefficiency.) If pressed on the problem of firing incompetents, the Commission's officials fall back on another formula: "Any unproductive employee can be fired if his supervisor has balls."

"That's where the problem is," Raymond Jacobson, executive director of the Commission, insists. "It's not the system."

But the statistics either belie Jacobson's contention or prove that federal managers are the world's largest collection of eunuchs. In 1976, out of two-and-one-half million federal employees, 21,710 were discharged, according to the Commission's method of bookkeeping (which includes in the total some strange categories, such as voluntary early retirements). Even at face value that amounts to an incredibly low discharge rate, slightly more than three fourths of one percent. (In the Washington headquarters of the Civil Service Commission, home of the Balls Theory and 3,300 employees, the discharge rate was less than half the federal average.) But closer examination of the books reveals that, if limited to tenured civil servants who were actually fired for inefficiency or "cause," the number is less than 3,500, for a discharge rate of one seventh of one percent—and, of those, a substantial number were reinstated in their jobs after appeal to the Commission. At that rate, a small business employing ten people would fire one person for inefficiency every 70 years.

The figures are so striking—it is so difficult to believe any work force could be so spectacularly efficient as to justify such a low dismissal rate —that one is led to suspect that what makes federal managers impotent is, in fact, the system itself.

The Civil Service Commission and the system over which it presides had their origins in the Pendleton Act of 1883. The system was conceived as a way of giving some stability to a career service and of freeing the President from the incessant pressure of office seekers by making competitive examinations the basis for hiring. The Act does not mention firing, and farthest from the minds of its sponsors was any idea of making it difficult to fire civil servants for poor performance. The only firings it meant to stop were mass *political* ones aimed at providing more jobs for loyalists.

Limitations on firing civil servants were first established in the Lloyd-LaFollette Act of 1912, and the Civil Service Commission has since then prescribed a maze of regulations regarding those limitations. The Commission has sole responsibility for amending firing procedures, and, in the words of a Commission attorney, "the amendments have almost invariably resulted in greater employee protection."

The movement away from the flexibility that any organization needs if it is to operate efficiently took on added impetus when the courts weighed in. Until the late 1950s the courts rejected attempts by dismissed civil servants to get judicial redress. Then a significant change took place: the Supreme Court held that under the Lloyd-LaFollette Act a federal employee's job was, in effect, property, and that he therefore could not be deprived of it without "due process of law." This interpretation has given the federal worker a special privilege granted to few other people in our society.

WONDERLAND

In one part of the Civil Service Commission's literature appears the sentence: "The Commission also established a Division of Efficiency to set up a system of uniform efficiency ratings for the departmental service, for use as a basis of promotions, demotions, and dismissals."

So much for Wonderland. In real life, efficiency ratings perform no such function, and as instruments in the firing process they are worse than worthless. Customarily the ratings of an incompetent worker consist of platitudes designed to make it easier for his supervisor to live with a situation he can't cure. Any criticism is veiled—instead of saying that Bledsoe has an infinite capacity for bollixing up schedules, one says, "As Mr. Bledsoe acquires managerial skills, his value to the agency will increase accordingly."

"Top management tells us to get tough in our efficiency ratings," one executive remarked. "But if you put in a critical sentence and the employee threatens a grievance action, they 'suggest' that you delete or tone down the offending sentence."

So year after year the unproductive employee accumulates ratings that make him out to be a Renaissance Man. When, indeed, matters reach the point of crying out for an employee's dismissal, the supervisor who contemplates the action is in a vulnerable position: the record shows a succession of satisfactory evaluations by previous supervisors, and he seems to be the only one who couldn't get any decent work out of the man or woman.

A LONG, LONG PROCESS

For other reasons having to do with the instinct for self-preservation, the federal manager is strongly motivated not to fire the incompetent. He knows, for one thing, that it will be a long, long process once he embarks upon it. S. John Byington, chairman of the Consumer Product Safety Commission, once wrote to Senator Charles Percy:

"A manager in the executive branch of the federal government who finds it necessary to terminate an unproductive or non-contributing employee—or even an obstructing employee—must be prepared to spend 25 to 50 percent of his time for a period that literally may run from six to 18 months."

One such manager related his frustration in trying to get rid of an incompetent who had been the despair of several supervisors before him: "When I came to the conclusion that he'd have to go, I went to the Agency Executive Officer, a man who was well aware of the problems this employee had been causing for years.

" 'Keep a book on him,' he told me. 'Keep a diary of when he comes in, when he leaves, how many times he is out of the office, how many times he goes to the john and for how long. Give him assignments and keep track of how many he flubs. Make sure you don't softpedal his failings when you write his performance ratings.' O.K., I kept a book. I felt like a fink. After several months of this I showed the Exec what I had.

" 'You can do better than that,' he said. 'I want an ironclad case.'

"This kind of thing went on for a while," said the executive, "and then I began to realize something: *I* was becoming the problem. This fellow had a lawyer. He was a member of the union. He had complained to his congressman that he wasn't being given fair consideration for *promotion!* And the agency just didn't want to get into a tangle. It was easier for them to adopt the attitude that I wasn't compiling a convincing case, that I was a lousy manager."

The executive shrugged. "There are lots of people around here who are misfits or incompetents," he said. "You get used to them and you learn to put up with it, like you learn to live with a toothache or a sore toe."

The federal manager who refuses to put up with it soon finds that his own reputation is beginning to suffer. He is creating friction, and at the higher levels of government, harmony is valued well above function. In writing *his* performance rating, *his* boss may well remark upon the unfortunate "personality conflict" with Bledsoe. Where the incompetent employee can "grieve" (personnel shorthand for filing a grievance claim) that he is being discriminated against—and it is an unimaginative clod who can't find *some* ground for so charging—the executive literally finds himself on trial; even if he is exonerated the charge becomes part of his own file.

Further weakening any determination to fire Bledsoe is the inflated condition of government agencies. Over the years most agencies have attained a degree of featherbedding that means underwork or make-work for substantial numbers of employees. But since anyone who suggests that his section or division is overstaffed is considered treasonable, tolerance for non-productive work becomes the ambient culture. In this laissez-faire atmosphere, Bledsoe's supervisor doesn't aspire to be the lone tilter against windmills. It makes more sense to work around Bledsoe than to fire him.

And, if patience is finally exhausted, Bledsoe can probably be transferred to another part of the agency. In a large agency there are many such "floaters"—people who live a nomadic existence, foisted on each successive supervisor when it is recognized that the previous one has suffered enough.

THE DEAN OF THE DEFENDERS

"Why do you want to fire anyone?" Donald Dalton asked, parrying my query about whether it has become virtually impossible to fire a federal employee.

Donald Dalton is the dean of a group of Washington lawyers who specialize in defending civil servants whose jobs are threatened. Chairman of the Civil Service Law Committee of the Bar Association of the District of Columbia, Dalton says he has taken "hundreds and hundreds of such cases."

He and the other lawyers who handle these cases are part of the system of job protection for federal employees, and, not surprisingly, Dalton sees the federal government as the oppressor of those employees who take their cases to him. Because under the law as now constituted his client always has a case, in Dalton's eyes the employee is always a victim of injustice—whether or not he is competent at his job.

"Government isn't like business," Dalton said. "People who work for the government have certain property rights in their job. There are laws you have to follow before you can fire somebody. The government wrote those laws, I didn't. The fellow who works for government has a right to see that they follow their own laws, and he comes to me for help to see that they do."

Dalton is undoubtedly right. If in the conflict between a federal employee's right to absolute job security and the public's need for a manageable bureaucracy, the Civil Service Commission, the Congress, and the courts continue to favor the former, the substandard federal employee can hardly be blamed for hanging in there.

HOW STURDY A BULWARK

Except for an office on the fifth floor occupied by its architect, a modern, seven-story building on Washington's Massachusetts Avenue is occupied exclusively by the national officers of the American Federation of Government Employees, who, from here, preside over the union's 1,500 locals.

As unions go, the AFGE, lacking for all practical purpose the ultimate weapon of the strike, is something of a marshmallow. Its bargaining power for higher wages is limited to lobbying Congress. This limitation hampers the union's ability to attract members from the federal work force. That it has succeeded so well (it has about 300,000 members) results from its having become another bulwark of the government worker's job security. Should a worker fail to receive a promotion he alone feels he is entitled to, the union takes up the cudgel for him. And if a worker's job is threatened, the union becomes a tiger, providing legal counsel. In 50 percent of the cases of dismissals that are appealed to the Civil Service Commission's Federal Employees Appeals Authority, the employee is represented by a labor union.

The AFGE is fortunate in having an unusually capable general counsel, in the person of Leo Pellerzi, a man who knows the working and non-working of government from inside and out. His inside experience came as general counsel for the U.S. Civil Service Commission from 1965 to 1968 and as the Department of Justice's Assistant Attorney General for Administration—the highest civil service level in government—during the next four years.

Like the Civil Service Commission itself, and like private lawyers who make their living by fighting dismissals of federal employees, Pellerzi sees as relatively inconsequential the unfireability of the incompetent civil servant. Like the Commission, whose philosophy he absorbed during his service there, Pellerzi takes the view that a dismissal action usually stems from the incompetence of the supervisor rather than the employee.

"Generally," he says, "you will find that a dismissal action is a failure of discipline, a result of falling out between the supervisor and the employee rather than any change in the employee's performance. And you can't just fire someone arbitrarily, I don't care what business you're in—as long as it's unionized."

Does the union concern itself at all with the question of incompetence when defending an employee against a dismissal action? That is a question that makes Pellerzi somewhat uncomfortable.

"The union," he says, "owes the duty of representation to *all* of its members."

BURDENING THE SYSTEM

The notion that dismissal actions are taken capriciously doesn't stand up under examination. The evidence all points in the opposite direction: that federal managers will put up with incompetence, laziness, and outrageous behavior far longer than the public has a right to expect. The Civil Service is weighed down with unproductive employees against whom no action is ever taken because of the frustrations involved in bucking the system of protection.

A federal executive, a woman, describes what is involved in trying to dismiss a typist who has become impossible to work with:

"She had been unsatisfactory for close to a year. . . . She was extremely moody and temperamental. Her attendance was terribly spotty. She did not take criticism of any sort. You never knew when she was going to blow. And during a long period when I took no notes—it was not yet even in my mind to start an adverse action—she would come into my office and ream me up one side and down the other. She would make the most outlandish accusations about my relations with other people in the division. It would happen, usually, when I called her in to discuss her attendance. She was hot-tempered, she had a foul mouth, and you could hear her all the way down the corridor when she laced off.

"The straw that broke the camel's back was her rather sudden refusal to carry out one clerical function which was a necessary part of her duties. She flatly refused. She just stopped doing it. When I realized that other people on the staff were having to do this girl's job I knew I had to take a hand. I went in and told her that I expected her to perform that function and complete it by four o'clock that afternoon. She was typing and she didn't reply. She went on typing and I asked her if she'd heard me. Without looking up, she said, 'I heard you.' And I said, 'Are you going to do it?' She said, 'We'll see.'

"She went home that day without having done it. I believe that was when I realized that drastic measures would have to be taken. I consulted with a great number of people in the administrative area of our agency. I got all the books and received verbal advice on how you initiate an adverse action. And I carried everything out to the letter. I spent a good part of the next two months documenting the girl's performance on the job. I wrote an extensive evaluation of her work, which I gave to her, and followed this with a memo to her requesting improvement in the deficient areas. She wrote a memo to me asking for 'specifics.' I asked her supervisor to reply by memo, giving more specifics. You would be astonished at the number of memos which flowed back and forth between me and various elements of the agency on this one case. Finally I was in a position to write the girl a formal letter telling her that I was initiating action to have her dismissed. I had the letter looked at by the people who know about this kind of thing and, on their instruction, gave it to her in the presence of a witness.

"The girl asked for a formal agency hearing on the charges, which is her right, and she got the union to represent her. The agency appointed a lawyer to represent me. More months went by and lots more paperwork. A hearing examiner was assigned. He wrote telling us the requirements for the hearings—you have to set the room up exactly the way they want it. The tables have to be set up in certain ways, you have to rent a tape recorder and hire two operators to take down the proceedings—that alone, and the subsequent transcriptions, ended up costing the agency something like $2,000.

"When the hearings finally did take place, six months had elapsed since I had decided to take action. The hearings lasted three days. By the rules of the game, the girl was there the whole time. I was only permitted in while actually giving my own testimony; I couldn't even be there when witnesses on my own side were testifying.

"Anyway, another month or so elapsed while the recordings of the proceedings were transcribed and relevant portions sent to all concerned parties for their comments or corrections. Then, after the transcripts were returned to the examiner and he was pondering his recommendation, the girl found another job and quit. Otherwise, it might still be going on.

"The system is actually geared, in my mind, to the incompetent. You really have to do something heinous for your supervisor to take any action because it's so damn much trouble. And it *is* a lot of trouble. I was warned it was a lot of trouble. And I found it occupying, and I'm not kidding, five eighths of my day toward the end. And 110 percent of my mind. The system and the rule book are geared to making you think 50 times before you start. The system assumes a supervisor has nothing else to do; the paperwork is unbelievable. My assistant, call her the office manager for this particular episode, and my secretary, the two of them were spending 50 percent of their time—that's one person, 100 percent—typing up reports with umpteen copies. A copy of everything, incidentally, had to go to the girl's representative. We couldn't hold a meeting to discuss the case and what we were going to do without either her or her representative being present. That's all the rules and regulations."

MISSIONARY ZEAL

There are a few agencies that perform finite, measurable tasks and that are small enough to offer strong motivation for firing incompetents. In a small agency the word gets around about the person who's deadweight, and it isn't so easy to palm him off. And budgetary limitations militate against hiring an additional person to do his work. Under these circumstances—which sometimes exist when an agency is young, still imbued with missionary zeal, and led by people not yet anesthetized by apathy—dismissal actions become somewhat more plausible. In the Edward Lafferty case, all of the above factors were present and the case was energetically and successfully prosecuted. Nevertheless, the task was a formidable one.

Lafferty, an economist who had been in the federal service since 1968, came to the agency in 1973. His job centered about plotting statistical charts in a very limited sphere, and it soon became apparent to his supervisor that Lafferty didn't measure up to even this relatively simple chore.

In light of Lafferty's having served in the government since 1968, the personnel people at the agency thought the problem might be less a question of competence than of a personality conflict with the supervisor. Adjustments were made in Lafferty's work arrangements and a series of specific assignments were given him. The results confirmed the supervisor's judgment that Lafferty had neither the economics background for the job nor any willingness to acquire it.

In March 1976 Lafferty's supervisor handed him a letter of intent to terminate his employment in 30 days. Signed by a top agency official, the letter cited incompetence, insubordination, and generally abusive conduct as the causes of dismissal. The charges were documented with specific instances, testified to by memoranda from a variety of people who had dealt with Lafferty, and by an account that his supervisor had kept over a period of several months detailing the results of assignments given to Lafferty. The letter plus the exhibits ran to 60 pages.

The accounts of the assignments were technical, but the descriptions of Lafferty's behavior are understandable to the layman. On one occasion, the letter said, his supervisor came to Lafferty's office to check on the status of the project Lafferty had been assigned. Lafferty became enraged, charged the supervisor with "harassment," and, threatening physical violence, ordered him out of the office. On another occasion, when the supervisor asked for additional data on work Lafferty had turned in, Lafferty told him, "You can take it the way it is or stuff it. . . ." On meeting the director of personnel in the cafeteria on one occasion, Lafferty said, "So you're the son of a bitch who's got it in for me. Maybe you'd like to step outside and settle it." The personnel director stared embarrassedly at his mashed potatoes as Lafferty let forth with a two-word description of him as the south end of a north-bound horse. That any one of these incidents could be tolerated without causing Lafferty's dismissal is itself a measure of how job security affects discipline in the federal service.

Lafferty had 15 days to reply to the charges and two days of official time off. On April 25 the agency's highest administrative officer wrote Lafferty that his reply had been considered and the decision made to terminate his employment on May 12. The letter told him he had 15 days to appeal the decision to the Federal Employees Appeals Authority.

Lafferty did appeal the case and hired a private lawyer to represent him. The agency then had to provide the Civil Service Commission with his entire file, now 103 pages long. The file, which contained a memorandum on every meeting at which the case had been discussed, was also available to Lafferty to help him prepare his defense. The appeal hearings, which took place in September 1976, lasted two days and resulted in two volumes of transcripts. The following month, the Appeals Authority issued a decision affirming the agency's dismissal action.

But more than two years had elapsed since Lafferty's incompetence had first been recognized. During most of that time he continued to receive his $20,000 salary. For about a year, various highly paid administrators at the agency had been spending a significant amount of their time on the case. And Lafferty still has recourse to the courts. How realistic is it to expect the people involved to continue to tackle such prosecutions? And this agency will one day become old, fat, tired, and cynical.

NOTHING OF VALUE

"Why do you want to fire anyone?" Lawyer Dalton asks.

There are two reasons.

The first is a coal miner in West Virginia who rarely sees the sun. He spends his days in a black hole, sometimes working in a tunnel too low to stand up in and breathing in dust that blackens his lungs and shortens his life. The money he earns from all this is taxed to pay for the upkeep of the federal establishment, and it is simply not fair to this man to make him contribute part of his wages to pay the salary of another man who is doing nothing of value.

The other reason is the need to make government perform better, a goal to which President Carter (like many of his predecessors) has pledged himself. For many fine and capable civil servants, the acceptance of the incompetent and the slacker affects their own attitudes and performance. For federal executives, the invulnerability of the unproductive worker makes a mockery of the whole concept of efficient management. While a general thinning out of the least productive people in government would be desirable, what is needed is not necessarily the mass exercise of fire power but rather the realistic capability. A great many of the marginally competent people would radically improve their performances if the safety of their jobs was not so absolute. The overprotection of the civil servant is not only destructive of an efficient government service; it encourages too many federal employees to make the least of themselves and ends by destroying them, too.

Exit, Voice, and Loyalty

Albert O. Hirschman

If you don't like the way things are going wherever you are, the chances are that you have two options open to you. You can either use "exit" or "voice."

Exit means: leaving under your own steam, quitting, switching, resigning, deserting, escaping from. It is comparatively neat and impersonal. It implies the end of your loyalty to whatever you are leaving.

Voice means: an attempt to change things through articulation—whether by addressing your dissatisfaction to those in a position to make the changes, or by grousing to anyone who will listen. It is far messier than exit, since it can range from faint grumbling to violent protest. And while exit is an either-or proposition—you either exit or you don't—voice is essentially an art, constantly evolving in creative new directions. In contrast to exit, voice implies a continuing (if strained) loyalty to the entity that is causing stress.

In some situations, of course, voice and exit can be successfully joined. Take the hippies. Their dissatisfaction with the surrounding social order led them to combine their exit from it with a demonstrative "otherness." By making their cop-out so spectacular—that is, by mixing deviance with defiance—they made their exit brim with voice.

In other situations, either voice or exit can become so unthinkable (or so attractive) that only one option is really open. Exit has often been unavailable to members of primordial human groups such as the tribe, the family, the church, and the state. Sometimes, again, exit is consciously rejected. Black Power, for example, refuses the traditional pattern of individual upward social mobility. Its open and exclusive reliance on the group process has had immense shock value because it spurns and castigates a supreme value of American society—success via exit from one's group.

The voice option, on the other hand, has played a very small role in competitive business enterprise. Here exit (on the part of the dissatisfied consumer) reigns supreme and is supposed to keep businessmen "on their toes." Occasionally an organization will make exit especially attractive in order to get rid of voice. In Latin America, for example, those holding power have long encouraged their political enemies and potential critics to remove themselves from the scene through voluntary exile. The right of asylum, so generously practiced by Latin American republics, could almost be considered a "conspiracy in restraint of voice." (A Colombian law once provided that former presidents would receive the same number of U.S. dollars in salary if they lived abroad as they would receive Colombian pesos if they remained in Colombia. With the U.S. dollar worth, at the time, between five and 10 pesos, the officially arranged incentive toward exit was tempting indeed.)

What is more powerful, exit or voice? Which one of these two options makes more of an impression on an organization? The answer is complex. Ordinarily it has been assumed that exit or the prospect of exit (of customers from a firm or of voters from a party) is all-powerful, but the evidence shows that voice, too, can influence decision-making in an organization. Look at the nomination of Barry Goldwater in 1964 by the Republican party. In that case, the most conservative elements of the party, who could not exit because they had nowhere else to go, were able to impose a candidate who was sure to lose the party many votes. Their voice was far more effective than the prospective exit of the middle-of-the-roaders.

The political power of those who have nowhere else to go in a two-party system (and who therefore use voice rather than exit) came to light in a different form with the Democratic defeat in 1968. The mobilization of the indifferent voters and the winning over of the undecided ones depended largely on the enthusiasm which each party could inspire among activist party workers and volunteers. Since activists are rarely middle-of-the-roaders, their enthusiasm can be dampened when a party moves to what the activists consider to be an excessively middle-of-the-road position. As the Democrats discovered in 1968, a platform designed to gain votes at the center can be counter-productive; it may damage rather than shore up the party's fortunes at the polls. The voice of those who have nowhere to go can impose negative returns on a move of the party to the center.

Clearly, the use of voice increases in situations where exit tends to be out of the question, and vice versa. In the intermediate cases—in which the choice between voice and exit is available—voice will often lose out because its effectiveness depends on creativity, or the discovery of new ways of exerting influence and pressure toward reform. However "easy" such a discovery may look in retrospect, creativity always comes as a surprise. Thus, there will be a strong bias in favor of exit unless loyalty helps to redress the balance by raising the cost of exit.

Loyalty is a key concept in the battle between exit and voice because it locks members into their organizations a little longer, thereby allowing more time for the use of voice. Members will exhaust all resources of influence at their command before resigning themselves to disloyalty-exit.

While loyalty may postpone exit, its very existence is predicated on the possibility of exit. Indeed, the availability of exit to even the most loyal member is often an important part of his bargaining power vis-à-vis the organization. The chances for voice to function effectively are appreciably strengthened if voice is backed up by the *threat of exit,* whether it is made openly or whether the possibility of exit is merely well understood by all concerned.

When a member has no feelings of loyalty, he probably has a low estimate of his influence on the organization. Therefore, his decision to exit will be easy and will probably be carried out in silence. But the *threat* of exit is something else again. It will typically be made by the loyalist—that is, by the member who cares, who leaves no stone unturned before he resigns himself to the painful decision to leave.

Suppose an organization heads in the "wrong" direction from the point of view of a group of members. Such members will begin—at some point—to use their influence to correct and reverse the process. These attempts will become stronger as disagreement widens. There soon comes a point in this process at which exit would take place if there were no feelings of loyalty.

But loyalty now acts as a brake on the decision to exit. The *loyal* member does not exit, but something happens to him: he begins to be acutely unhappy about staying on. He contracts qualms or, in the phrase used by German Communist party members dissatisfied with the party line, he has *Bauchschmerzen* (belly aches). At this point he usually will make stronger attempts to change things; he will intensify the use of voice for this purpose. Then, assuming that disagreement widens still further, he will consider exit and threaten it, if he thinks that such a threat can be expected to enhance the effectiveness of voice. Finally, loyalty may reach its breaking point and exit ensues.

But here a word about two other elements—"unconscious loyalty" and self-deception—is in order. Let us start with a situation that has been described by psychologists:

When the likeness of a cat is made to change gradually into that of a dog through a succession of images which are shown to a subject, and, if later the same series is shown in reverse order, the eye behaves as though it were "loyal" to whatever figure it started with. When the sequence is shown in the cat-dog direction, a majority of images will be labeled "cat" and vice versa. In much the same way, the general difficulties of recognizing change are a breeding ground for unconscious loyalist behavior when an organization begins to deteriorate. Since unconscious loyalist behavior keeps qualms from developing, it will also forestall the intensification of voice.

And since it also postpones exit, it will be prized by organizations whose management wants its members to refrain from both exit and voice. Such organizations, moreover, will be looking for devices to convert conscious loyalist behavior into unconscious loyalist behavior.

Yet there often is no clear dividing line between these two types of behavior, because the member of the organization may have a considerable stake in self-deception, i.e., in fighting the realization that the organization he belongs to is going downhill. He will try to repress this awareness as long as possible, particularly if he has reached his position in the organization the hard way. The more severe the cost of his initiation into the organization, the greater his self-deception will be.

Assuming that there is a limit to self-deception, however, it is likely that the severe-initiation members will eventually display more initiative than others in righting the situation—after having at first been more complacent and passive. It is also possible, of course, that by the time the member is no longer able to close his eyes to what is going on, deterioration will have reached the point where exit becomes the only sensible reaction to the sudden revelation of rottenness. Hence severe initiation may eventually activate both voice and exit.

A different kind of loyalist behavior occurs when an organization is able to exact a high cost for exit. Such costs can range downward from loss of life, as with the Mafia, to loss of lifelong associations formed through years of work in one place. Along the way are such intermediate penalties as excommunication, defamation, and deprivation of livelihood. Organizations able to exert these high penalties for exit are usually the traditional human groups already mentioned, such as the family, the tribe, the religious community, and the nation. Because such organizations exact a high price for exit, they also have a built-in defense against what is normally one of the member's most potent weapons: the *threat* of exit. If exit is going to be followed by severe sanctions, the very idea of exit will be repressed; hence the threat will not be uttered for fear that the sanction will apply to the threat as well as to the act itself.

What happens to *voice* in organizations where the price of exit is high? Some tentative suggestions can be advanced by distinguishing between those organizations where the price of entry is zero (because, as in the case of the family or nation, one enters them as a result of one's birth) and those where the price of entry and the price of exit are both high. Since the high price of exit does away with the threat of exit as an effective instrument of voice, these organizations (which include such modern inventions as gangs and totalitarian parties) will often be able to repress both voice and exit. In the process, they will largely deprive themselves of both of these mechanisms for reform.

When a member is trying to decide whether or not the time has come to leave an organization, he will sometimes be held back by a conviction that the organization would go from bad to worse if he left. This is especially true if he is a member of an organization involved in an important aspect of public policy.

For example: if I participate in the making of a foreign policy of which I have increasingly come to disapprove, I can resign my policy-making position. But if I leave, I cannot stop being unhappy as a citizen of a country which carries on what seems to me an increasingly disastrous foreign policy. In such a case, I am both producer and consumer when I am on the job. But when I quit, I remain a consumer of foreign policy, even though I no longer have a hand in producing it.

In considering exit under such circumstances, I must weigh, on the one hand, the disutility, discomfort, and shame of remaining a member. But on the other hand, I must also measure the degree of my influence as a member, as well as the extent to which additional deterioration of the organization would occur if I were to get out. The ultimate in unhappiness (and in paradoxical loyalist behavior) occurs when such a member expects the public evil produced by the organization to reach an intolerable level as deterioration proceeds. The decision to exit will then become more and more difficult the longer he fails to leave, for the conviction that he must stay on to prevent the worst will grow stronger all the time.

Loyalist behavior of this type—"the worse it gets the less I can afford to leave"—can serve an all-important purpose when an organization is capable of dispensing public evils of truly ultimate proportions, as is true today of the world's more powerful states. The more wrongheaded and dangerous the course of these states, the more we need a measure of "spinelessness" among the more enlightened policymakers, so that some of them will still be inside and influential when a potentially disastrous crisis breaks out. It will later be argued that in such situations we are likely to suffer from too much spinelessness, rather than too little. But it is worth noting that the magnitude of public evils now available to the centers of world power has given a new social usefulness to protracted spinelessness (failure to exit)—so long as it turns into spine (voice) at the decisive moment.

Organizations dealing in vital matters of public policy thus have an environment peculiarly suited to loyalist behavior (i.e., postponement of exit in spite of dissatisfaction and qualms). It is almost as if "my country, right or wrong" transforms into the seemingly perverse variation, "my country, the wronger the myer." But if and when exit does occur, its nature can theoretically be expected to differ from the I-couldn't-care-less exit that usually occurs when one switches from one brand of toothpaste to another. The departing member will presumably be interested in making his exit contribute to improvement of the organization he is leaving—an improvement which he may think impossible without radical changes in the way the organization is run. To exit will now mean to resign under protest and, in general, to denounce and fight the organization from without instead of working for change from within. For the alternative is now not so much a choice between voice and exit as between voice-from-within and voice-from-without (after exit).

Unfortunately, it does not always work out that way in practice. Recent history shows that high officials who decide to resign because they disagree with public policies do not blast those policies when they resign. Instead they present the decision to leave as purely private—one leaves because "an irresistible offer" has come his way, or "in fairness to my family." Clearly, these officials confuse exit from a private good, such as toothpaste, with proper exit from "public goods" that are produced by public policies. Such confusion is deeply frustrating and demoralizing to the citizenry. Imagine the relief that *would* have been felt if at least one of the public officials who "dropped out" of the Johnson Administration in disagreement over Vietnam had thereupon publicly fought official war policies. Or consider the relief that was so widely felt when the McCarthy campaign made it possible for many Americans to do just that, instead of merely copping out.

While exit from Europe or from the settled portions of the national territory has played a most prominent role in United States history, exiting seems to have become a lost art. In certain important areas of American public life, the inability to resign in protest applies to men on opposite sides of the political spectrum who were known to disagree strongly with official policies; they range from a General MacArthur to an Adlai Stevenson. In 1966, Barbara Garson satirized Stevenson's predicament in *MacBird!*, when the "Egg of Head" weighed exit and voice and found exit wanting in attractiveness:

In speaking out one loses influence.
The chance for change by pleas and prayer is gone.
The chance to modify the devil's deeds
As critic from within is still my hope.
To quit the club! Be outside looking in!
This outsideness, this unfamiliar land,
From which few travellers ever get back in. . . .
I fear to break; I'll work within for change.

Two agonizing war years later, the continued reluctance of high officials with "qualms" to break with the Johnson Administration was searchingly analyzed, together with other bureaucratic aspects of the conflict, in an April, 1968, *Atlantic* article called "How Could Vietnam Happen?" by a former insider, James C. Thomson, Jr. One of his principal points of explanation was what he calls the *domestication of dissenters*, which is achieved through "assigning" the role of "official dissenter" or devil's advocate to the doubters within the government. In the process, the doubter's conscience is assuaged, but at the same time his position is made explicit *and predictable*; this predictability means a fatal loss of power for him; his position becomes discountable. As Thomson put it:

> Once [Undersecretary of State George] Ball began to express doubts, he was warmly institutionalized: he was encouraged to become the in-house devil's advocate on Vietnam. The upshot was inevitable: the process of escalation allowed for periodic requests to Mr. Ball to speak his piece; Ball felt good, I assume (he had fought for righteousness); the others felt good (they had given a full hearing to the dovish option); and there was a minimal unpleasantness. The club remained intact; and it is of course possible that matters would have gotten worse faster if Mr. Ball had kept silent, or left before his final departure in the fall of 1966. There was also, of course, the case of the last institutionalized doubter, Bill Moyers. The President is said to have greeted his arrival at meetings with an affectionate, "Well, here comes Mr. Stop-the-Bombing. . . ."

Thus the dissenter is allowed to recite his piece on condition that he engages in "role-playing" as "a member of the team." In this way, he is made to give up in advance one of his strongest weapons: the threat to resign under protest.

Obviously the bargain is a poor one for the dissenter. So the question arises: why would he stand for it? Partly, at least, because the final policy decision can always be made to look like a middle course between the opposing "hawk" and "dove" points of view; members of both groups can be made to feel that "if it had not been for me, an even more sinister decision would have been taken."

The "dove" in particular will argue that it is his duty to remain at his post, however much he may "suffer." Considering the enormous power for good and particularly for evil that he constantly sees displayed around him, even the tiniest influence seems to him worth exerting. But opportunism can in this situation be rationalized as public-serving rather than self-serving; it can even masquerade as secret martyrdom. Given so delicious a mixture of motives, a member can indulge in opportunistic behavior with an intensity, persistence, and abandon out of all proportion to its justification. The "dove" will vastly overestimate his influence as well as the damaging effect his exit would have upon the course of events. Hence, Lord Acton's famous dictum can be updated to: "Power corrupts; and even a very little influence in a country with huge power corrupts hugely."

This is one reason why the decision to exit in protest from the government of this most powerful country is particularly and deplorably infrequent.

Why "deplorably"? Because exit has an essential role to play in restoring quality performance in government, just as it does in any organization. It will operate either by making the government reform or by bringing it down, but, in any event, the jolt provoked by clamorous exit of a respected member can be an indispensable complement to voice. A case in point was Senator Eugene McCarthy's decision to run for President, which turned out to have a powerful influence on events. This was an exit from the club of top Democratic politicians, a breaking of the rules of the game as traditionally played within the governing party (the rule being that one does not oppose the President's bid for reelection). But there was no similarly clamorous exit from the President's "official family," even though several members of that family had serious misgivings, and some even left. Having been satirized by Barbara Garson and analyzed by James C. Thomson, Jr., this reluctance to exit loudly has been recognized more and more as a national problem and even scandal. James Reston wrote in a post-mortem on the Johnson Administration:

> One thing that is fairly clear from the record is that the art of resigning on principle from positions close to the top of the American government has almost disappeared. Nobody quits now, as Anthony Eden and Duff Cooper left Neville Chamberlain's Cabinet, with a clear and detailed explanation of why they couldn't be identified with the policy any longer. . . . Most of those who stayed on at the critical period of escalation gave to the President the loyalty they owed to the country. Some . . . are now wondering in private life whether this was in the national interest.

Mr. Reston might have added that exit is powerful not only because of its direct effect on public opinion, and thereby on public policy; it also has a subtle, unsettling effect on those who stay behind. He who exits renders his arguments unanswerable. The remarkable influence wielded by martyrs throughout history can be understood in those terms, for the martyr's death is exit at its most irreversible, and argument at its most irrefutable.

In conclusion, no argument is made here for the use of exit rather than voice or of voice rather than exit. What is needed, however, is a wider exploration of the hidden potential of both options, of the obstacles in their way, and of institutions that might foster either voice or exit when one or the other is unduly neglected.

Courage without Esteem: Profiles in Whistle-Blowing

Taylor Branch

"Whose bread I eat, his song I sing."

—Middle High German Saying

In 1956, William H. Whyte wrote *The Organization Man* and warned that the independent American yeoman was being snuffed out forever by the "team player"—that an increasingly intertwined mesh of large institutions was closing off opportunities for the individualist like a zipper across the lips. The ambitious man would henceforth labor to build a broad network of esteem, good will, and obligation within the organization by emphasizing the amiable side of conformity and the flexible side of enthusiastic intelligence. This network would become the playing field upon which he would massage egos, put things together, innovate at the margins, and otherwise strive to become a captain of the team. When a nostalgic modern man tried to "stand on his own two feet," he would find them helplessly dangling in the air because the organization provided both his security and his advancement. When he tried to take a stand on principles and ideals, he would learn how to give and take.

Reverence for established organizations was so diminished in the 1960s, however, that a truly new breed arose—the whistle-blower. This fresh creature unexpectedly threw off the deepest impulses of the organization man—loyalty to the "team" and self-promotion as a team player—to publicly expose the crimes and inadequacies of his own institutions for a higher cause, generally the "public interest." There is scant encouragement, if any, for such a role in our literature or mythology. In fact, whistle-blowing is severely hampered by the image of its most famous historical model, Judas Iscariot—and by the judgment of Tacitus, who wrote about A.D. 100 that "traitors are disliked even by those they favor." Getting loyally along is so vital a social command that a child's flesh learns to crawl early at the thought of a tattle-tale or turncoat, however noble his purpose. And an adult knows instinctively that he who slays his institutional home will wear the mark of Cain.

Despite these obstacles, whistle-blowers have achieved a measure of public legitimacy—so much so that Ralph Nader sponsored a conference in their honor. Nine members of the new breed ascended the podium and presented the sunny, inspirational side of their deeds. It was clear that their employers—chiefly government agencies—were villains against the public, but it was also clear that these employing organizations had struck back harshly against them. Some of the speakers were obviously martyrs to their whistles, with only a clear conscience and a bit of media attention to make up for broken careers. Since the press will make news of the whistle-blower only while he is unusual, and since martyrdom seldom catches on, there is reason to believe that internal muckraking is a profession with an extremely limited future—regardless of its usefulness. A few case studies will reveal the kind of people who have exposed from within, what happens to them and to their charges, and the enormous psychological pressure upon them to keep differences inside the family. Then people can guess whether the whistle-blower will spawn a generation of non-organizational men for the public interest—or is merely a late whimper on William Whyte's relentless organizational tide.

CHARLES PETTIS

In February of 1966, Charles Pettis headed for Lima, Peru, to his new job as resident engineer on Peru's long-standing dream—to build a highway across the Andes. A 44-year-old engineer and geologist, Pettis was to play a crucial role in the 146-mile, $46-million project that was designed to open up trade for the first time between Peru's coastal cities on one side of the mountains and the isolated interior regions on the other.

The highway would not only bolster the hopes and incomes of most Peruvians, but it would also refurbish the image of American foreign assistance. It was an aid project through and through, with $12 million from the Agency for International Development and $23 million from the Export-Import Bank—the balance from Peru. There were the usual minor irritants for the recipient country, such as AID contracting regulations that effectively eliminated all firms except American ones from the bidding, but such things were overlooked in general enthusiasm for the road.

Pettis was under contract to Brown & Root Overseas, Inc.—an international engineering firm based in Houston, whose foreign aid business had prospered mightily since Lyndon Johnson entered the White House. Brown & Root was hired to protect the interests of the Peruvian government by overseeing the construction efforts of the main contractor, Morrison-Knudsen of Boise, Idaho. As resident engineer, Pettis went to work for his client, the Peruvian government; and his signature was required on the payroll to signify that Peru's interests were being protected and that the contract specifications were being enforced.

His misgivings about the project began when he surveyed the design and found that it called for cutting channels up to 300 feet deep through the notoriously unstable Andes mountains—with almost sheer cliffs to be left on the sides of the road. He was further disturbed that the design team had taken inadequate geological borings to determine the mountains' susceptibility to slides, which is considerable. These faults and many others led him to conclude: 1) that the road could not be built as designed, and 2) that large overruns would result. Nevertheless, Morrison-Knudsen commenced work.

Open conflict set in at the construction site when Morrison-Knudsen demanded that the monthly payroll be amended to include charges for slide removal. (The slides were so bad that 31 men were killed on the road.) Pettis refused on the grounds that such payments were not called for by the contract and that the Peruvian government would lose a great deal of money by such actions. "At first, Brown & Root supported me," says Pettis, "but they had a big meeting in February of 1968 and the tables began to turn. Bert Perkins of Morrison-Knudsen said he bid the job low because of prior association with Brown & Root all over the world—and because they expected to get a break. I'm sort of hot-tempered and old-fashioned in things like that, and I said I wouldn't be a party to such a thing."

Brown & Root soon ordered Pettis to begin boosting the payroll—out of fear that Morrison-Knudsen might otherwise attack the flimsy design, or perhaps out of corporate fraternal understanding. When Pettis would not go along, he was replaced by a more pliable man named B. W. Donelson—who promptly began authorizing supplementary payments to the contractor. Donelson brought an element of the old Yankee *bandido* to the plot by obtaining a subcontract from Morrison-Knudsen to feed the workers. By cutting food costs, he was able to harvest a profit of some $250,000 from the very contract that he was overseeing. He also managed to divert about 25 Peruvian laborers from the road to work on the construction of his private home.

In December of 1968, Brown & Root fired Pettis after he refused to reassure the Peruvian government in exchange for "any other job in Latin America." Peru had stopped payment on the road largely because Pettis would not tell the transportation ministry that the road was being constructed properly or the payroll figured honestly. Enormous psychological pressure was mounted against Pettis by the Americans to get him to recant. "There were a lot of little things that really add up to make you feel isolated," he says. "For example, the contractor people's kids threw eggs at my kids and would have nothing to do with them. And the American Consul in Lima gave me a temporary passport and said it was a bureaucratic error."

Pettis has been without salary since December of 1968, and more than a half dozen job offers have been "suddenly cancelled," he says. "Every firm in the business considers me a 'rat.'" When he asked his lawyer to talk with Brown & Root about a possible breach of contract suit, the attorney wrote back that the company's position "seems to be that your first duty was to the Brown & Root 'team' rather than to the Peruvian government, and that by your actions you violated this duty."

Pettis and his wife are in the process of moving to Spain, where they hope to set up a small school. He is rather bitter about the whole conflict in Peru: "This is the kind of thing that's ruining the United States all over the world. We look like a bunch of crooks, and anyone who tells the truth about it is considered crazy. I feel that when an engineer takes a job like that highway, he has to protect his client. I hate this thing of costs being $8 or $10 million above the contract. You've got to stand up against the pressures on that kind of thing to live with yourself. You sure won't make much money that way—I mean what the hell did I have to gain out of this?—but you have to do it. Looking back on it, I believe that I would do the same thing again. You really have no choice."

JAMES BOYD

The shrillest, most piercing whistle of the 1960s was blown by James Boyd and three associates in the office of Senator Thomas J. Dodd. Boyd had been the Senator's closest aide over a 12-year career when he began noticing financial wheeling between Dodd and large contributors during the 1964 reelection campaign.

As a result, Boyd and a secretary named Marjorie Carpenter (whom he later married) resolved to leave after the campaign. The two had planned to exit quietly and loyally, but when they discovered more details of Dodd's unethical election dealings, they began to consider going public.

After detecting their disenchantment and signs of snooping in the records, Dodd fired both plotters before they had firmly seized the whistle. Then, the Senator flexed his political muscles by denying his aide employment elsewhere in Washington and exercised his personal power by playing with Boyd, alternately offering him his old job back and chastising him for disloyalty. The way Dodd treated Boyd was the final act required for his public exposure.

"We didn't want to fight him," recalls Boyd. "I had been very close to him personally over a period of years, and the loyalty thing is one of the strongest of the Hill's ties. Also, being an Administrative Assistant is a nice life in many ways. I mean he did what I asked him to 90 per cent of the time, and that makes you feel significant. You *are* significant. The campaign fund diversion in 1964 was bad, but it took Dodd's malevolence to make his actions real, not abstract. I felt small and like I was being toyed with for the first time since I was in the Marine Corps. He was really hurting people and then abusing his power over me to cover up his abuses of the public. Still, there was nothing ennobling in the decision to sink my teeth into Dodd and hold on until one of us lost. It was one of those times when you think you are right but you still feel horrible."

For a full seven months after they were fired, Jim Boyd and Marjorie Carpenter agonized and vacillated over whether to expose Dodd and, if so, how. "We shifted from day to day," he says, "overwhelmed by the unlikelihood of it all. We kept wondering 'who are we to take him on?' And there was always a fear of looking naive—of summoning up a burst of moralism and then having everyone laugh and say that's just the way things are done."

Finally, the conspirators decided to go public. In a Topkapi-style caper, the Boyd-Carpenter team removed about 7,000 documents from Dodd's office for Xeroxing, documents that formed the basis for 23 Pearson-Anderson columns. The whistle was formally blown, although

The Washington Post got off to a late start by suppressing the first two columns and then running edited versions of the others only after Drew Pearson pressured the editors into lifting their news embargo.

The impact of the exposure took a long time to really hit Senator Dodd. At first, congressional cohesion was remarkable. Liberal Senator Birch Bayh wrote Dodd: "We're all with you on this yellow attack by Pearson." And conservative Russell Long remarked, "I'll support you all the way on this, Tom, even if you're guilty." Congressmen and senators united around their community of interest—that is, around their universal fear of having facts about them exposed by rebellious staff members—to focus their scorn on the "stool pigeon" question and on the probable chromosome mutations of traitors to the Congress. But finally, the pressure was too much, and Dodd was censured by the Senate on June 23, 1967.

The backlash against the whistle-blowers, however, was much swifter. Marjorie Carpenter received support from her new employers, the Lawyers' Committee for Civil Rights Under Law, but she resigned when her new fame produced strain and apprehension within the organization. And Boyd quickly lost his job as a parttime speechwriter for a House subcommittee under Congressman John Blatnick. Blatnick, while sympathetic, explained that he had no choice because committee Chairman George Fallon had cut his staff budget by one position's salary—reportedly at the behest of Speaker John McCormack, who may have been moved by the treachery against his good friend, Tom Dodd. Boyd wrote a book, *Above the Law,* in 1967, and did some ghost-writing, but he did not receive full-time employment until maverick foundation man Philip Stern hired him in September, 1968—almost four years after he left Dodd and almost three years after the first Pearson column.

While the case against Senator Dodd was being methodically de-tailed, official Washington promptly demonstrated how much it matters who you are in a conflict of the whistle. Boyd offered 7,000 documents to the FBI for a possible investigation of a variety of charges against Dodd. The august Bureau declined an investigation and launched a probe of *Boyd,* not excluding his private life. The supply of rumors was ample, complete with stories that the conspirators were sex offenders and that they had been paid by Pearson (or Dodd's political enemies) to unearth their volumes of dirt.

The Dodd episode was certainly not remunerative for Jim Boyd and his colleagues, nor did it win them great public appreciation. And their exposure did not provoke a general reform movement in the Senate. Dodd's honor was thoroughly soiled, but he retained his committee posts, his seniority, served three more years in the Senate, and ran for a third term in 1970. (It was not out of the question for him to have won.) In short, Boyd and his friends paid a high price and the public really gained little. Nevertheless, Boyd is not sorry. "It was the greatest liberating experience of my life," he observes. "It cut away all sorts of restrictions and taboos that kept me from saying what I think honestly. What a Senate aide does is to promote the image of a politician, selling out little by little in rational, absolutely essential steps. I didn't realize what 12 years like that can do to you, even after we decided to expose Senator Dodd. It was the fight itself that opened my eyes to all this."

These are strange feelings for a man of modest origins in Connecticut —a non-ideologue and non-movement person who seized an opportunity to work up through the grime of politics in the 50s after starting as a stamp-licker and errand boy. He made only a minor dent in the ethic and power of the organization man, but he escaped the syndrome himself.

LIEUTENANT LOUIS FONT

Perhaps the most delicately skillful whistle-blowing in recent years has been performed by Army Lieutenant Louis P. Font. A middle-American Eagle Scout from Kansas City, he achieved a life-long ambition by winning a place at West Point—where he graduated in the top five per cent of his class in 1968. He won a two-year scholarship to Harvard's John F. Kennedy School of Politics, and commingled there with people concerned about the war (including Henry Kissinger). "My views against the war hardened at Harvard," remembers Font, "but they had already begun to change in my last year at the Academy. For three years I had ranked in the top quarter of my class in 'military aptitude,' which is essentially a peer-group conformity rating. But by the end of my senior year, I was in the bottom quarter because I started reading about the politics of the war instead of its tactics. The key word at West Point is 'attitude,' and when you start thinking too much—or want to go to graduate school—the social chemistry goes bad and you become an outcast. I supported Robert Kennedy, and people told me he was a traitor."

On February 27, 1970, the Harvard Lieutenant became the first West Point graduate in history to apply for discharge as a conscientious objector. Two weeks later the Army ordered him to leave Harvard and report to First Army Headquarters at Fort Meade, Maryland. The Army rejected his application in June, stating that he failed because he lacked sincerity and because he objected to the Vietnam war in particular and not to all war. "It really disturbed me that they ruled I lacked sincerity," says Font. So he went to court seeking an order for his discharge. The judge turned him down on the grounds that selective objection was not legally established, but he did find the Lieutenant sincere and ordered the Army to give him a "meaningful job" at Ford Meade pending the outcome of his appeal. Then the real battle began.

"The Army thought that I would go back to my old West Point self at Fort Meade—away from all those hippies at Harvard," says Font. "And if that didn't work, they wanted me to wait quietly through my appeal so that they could order me to 'Nam if it failed. That would force me to stand a rough court martial, and I would be an example that would discourage dissent. But I want no part of this war or this Army. The war is immoral, and the Army is fat and corrupt. And when you're dealing with the Armed Forces, it's all or nothing. If you just do half-way stuff—sitting around, not screaming—they'll win every time. They'll transfer you or wear you down and break you somehow."

So Lieutenant Font began his counterattack. One of his jobs was to help new officers find off-base housing. After two or three reports on racial discrimination produced no action, he leaked the evidence to the press and the story produced a sizable stink. "They really freak out around here when stuff like that hits the papers," he said. "They know it's right, and it flies right into the face of the volunteer army campaign to make things sound rosy." The Fort Meade command then switched Font to another job and ordered him not to speak to the press. Soon he found himself inspecting the enlisted men's barracks, and he began collecting affidavits about rats, roaches, the absence of hot water, faulty sewage, broken windows and walls, and general dilapidation. He secured a medical opinion that some of the barracks were "unfit for human habitation." After several of his reports were routinely filed away, he sent copies of one to several senators and congressmen in January (a serviceman is guaranteed the right to communicate with members of Congress). They then turned the information over to the press, and the Fort Meade brass got burned again—looking rather foolish to the Pentagon, where generals no doubt wondered why the First Army couldn't control its officers and prohibit such embarrassment.

This proved too much for Major General R. G. Ciccolella, the First Army Chief of Staff. When Font arrived at headquarters to deliver a copy of his report to the top three generals ("Always go as high as you can with complaints. That way they can't deny knowing about the problems."), Ciccolella ordered him arrested. Font was charged with five ludicrous offenses (example: failing to secure the permission of a building's "commander" before entering), each of which could earn him five years in the stockade. The Lieutenant countered by charging Ciccolella with assault and battery during the headquarters incident.

Ciccolella, by the way, has a reputation for impetuous outbursts. A fiery stump of a man, he was assigned to Fort Meade after his public utterances as Chief of the U.S. Military Assistance Advisory Group on Taiwan made people somewhat nervous lest he unleash himself on the mainland. Fort Meade, in fact, is something of a haven for such generals, who must, of course, be assigned somewhere. The Fort also houses Major General Samuel W. Koster, the commander of the American Division at the time of Mylai, and Lt. General Jonathan Seaman, who cleared Koster of Mylai charges. Font further muddied the legal waters by charging the latter two generals with war crimes. For good measure he charged Post Commander Colonel A. W. Alexander with dereliction of duty because of the barracks conditions.

"The whole discipline of the Army is based on placing each man in a Catch-22 situation so that no matter what he does, he's screwed," reasoned Font. "When that helplessness is driven home, he becomes docile and manageable. I have the Army in a kind of reverse Catch-22. They don't want to get rid of me and yet they do. If they give me a job, they lose, because there's so much corruption everywhere that I'll find something wrong. If they don't give me a job, I'll hit them with the court order.

"You have two main advantages in fighting the Army as compared with a civilian bureaucracy," he continued. "First, Army officers react sharply and often foolishly to exposure. If General Ciccolella had taken my barracks report and said, 'Well done, Lieutenant Font, I'm placing you in charge of a 12-man committee to study this problem and design programs for solving it,' he would have had me, especially in the press. Instead, he reacted like an officer—instinctively covering up because he knew he was responsible—and he made a mistake. The second advantage is that the Army wants desperately to keep people in, whereas other bureaucracies want to keep themselves pure and don't mind firing dissidents. The first desire of an organization is to get rid of someone like me. But that's exactly what I want—out."

Lieutenant Font's own psychological watershed is long past, having occurred over the decision to apply for conscientious objector status. The prelude to whistle-blowing is often like the agony of facing the draft or a service commitment—with similar fears and social pressures upon dissenters. Font really avoided the problem of strong loyalty to the traditions and associations of West Point by building new ties at Harvard. "My real loyalties are to my conscience and my friends at Cambridge," he says, "not to the Academy or to the Army. As far as I am concerned, I am still a civilian." Once he made the choice to make the stockade a higher priority than going to Vietnam, it became progressively easier to fight the Army with everything he had learned at West Point. "But I don't know what would have happened if I hadn't had those two years at Harvard," he mused. "I might have gone crazy."

JACQUELINE VERRETT

Unlike Lieutenant Font, the vast majority of potential whistle-blowers are most emphatically not seeking discharge from their livelihood. In fact, the inhibitions of the purse have probably caused more whistles to be swallowed than any other single factor, with a specially crushing effect on those having families and obligations. The question of survival against reprisals therefore assumes critical importance, and the most successful public clarion in this regard has been Dr. Jacqueline Verrett of Health, Education and Welfare's Food and Drug Administration.

For a dozen years, Dr. Verrett has been pumping chicken eggs full of the molecular polyglots that are added to American food to make it look better, last longer, and—above all—cost less. A pioneer in the chick embryo testing method for food additives, biochemist Verrett became disturbed when her tests showed that cyclamates caused substantial, grotesque deformities inside the eggs. She began reporting these findings through FDA channels on March 7, 1968, and continued to bring them up in meetings, memos, and her semi-annual reports.

By the fall of 1969, the cyclamate findings were being talked about in scientific circles—based on Dr. Verrett's research and parallel findings elsewhere. So she was not terribly surprised when NBC's Paul Friedman asked for an interview in late September (having seen a column on cyclamate research by Jean Carper). "The cyclamate publicity had been going on for some time," says Dr. Verrett, "and I didn't think the NBC interview was any big deal. I kind of backed into this controversy."

When she sought routine clearance for the interview, Dr. Verrett's office was suddenly besieged with about a dozen lab-coated and administrative officials of FDA—an unprecedented gathering. They earnestly remonstrated with her to forego the interview because of the "undue public alarm" that would no doubt arise if her deformed embryos were to appear on the TV screens of the cyclamate-consuming masses. This concern appeared to spring from a double-standard in FDA on both test results and media policy. In the summer of 1969, for example, Dr. Verrett had produced a preliminary study of another suspect additive, monosodium glutamate (MSG), using only 180 eggs. Although she found no harmful effects, she emphasized that the test was in no way conclusive. Nevertheless, FDA Commissioner Herbert Ley rushed to Congress and hailed the "exquisite, sensitive, new toxicological approach" that found MSG as safe as (old-fashioned) apple pie. The cyclamate data, by contrast, came from a thorough investigation which used about 13,000 eggs and established a definite causal relationship between the chemical and embryo deformities. Yet cyclamates remained officially safe and no one rushed to Congress—only to Dr. Verrett's office to head off public panic.

Dr. Verrett withstood the pressure and proceeded with the NBC interview. "It's taxpayers' money and taxpayers' research here," says the biochemist, "so I believe that the public is entitled to know about the results—especially if you are careful not to overstate the conclusions. I give the American public credit for taking information for what it's worth. As far as I know, there was no great public alarm about cyclamates. The only great alarm took place in the Secretary's office."

Indeed, there was some commotion in Secretary Finch's office. He was soon visited by Donald Kendall, president of the Pepsi-Cola Company and friend to President Nixon. Having no doubt consumed large quantities of his own cyclamate-laden soft drink, Kendall was perhaps concerned about his health and in any case sought assurances from higher authorities than Dr. Verrett that the additive was as safe as MSG. Finch was also contacted by representatives of Abbott Laboratories, the major producer of cyclamates and a regular participant in health disasters.

The upshot of the cyclamate revelations was that the additive was removed from general use on October 18, 1969—not on the basis of FDA data, but because of a wondrously coincidental discovery of bladder cancer effects by Abbott. The effect upon Dr. Verrett was that she was twice censured by Secretary Finch for unethical conduct. Also, during the period between her NBC appearance and the announcement of the cyclamate ban, she was prohibited from granting interviews or even answering her office telephone.

Such direct criticism from a Cabinet officer is normally more than enough to focus agency enzymes on a low-level bureaucratic bacillus— and drive him from the government. Yet Dr. Verrett has survived. "I'm still kind of a leper around here, though, if you want to know the truth," she said. "I'm called to some meetings if it's absolutely necessary, but that's about it."

Her bureaucratic afterlife probably stems from an odd combination of circumstances. For one thing, at present her skills are almost indispensable to FDA because a great many additives are to be tested in the near future as a result of consumer pressure; and, ironically, her chick embryo method has been determined to be the best for rapid screen-testing. Also, her testing unit is unusually independent, which means that she can work effectively even in bureaucratic isolation. Most other government employees at her level would become helpless and frustrated without the active cooperation of many associates working toward group solutions. Finally, she has some support from the Congress, including Senator Warren Magnuson. None of this means that Dr. Verrett is guaranteed eternal life at FDA, of course.

In the meantime, Dr. Verrett is cheerfully injecting additives into chicken eggs, although her overall outlook does not inspire much chemical confidence in the American diet. "I can't say that I'm very optimistic about our effect here," she said. "There is a kind of tightening up and restriction that is pro-industry and anti-consumer. In some ways, we are worse off than we were a year and a half ago."

"And one sad thing is that you have to get really dramatic test results to have any hope of making an impact. If thalidomide had caused mental retardation, for example, I think we would still be using it," she lamented while lighting up another cigarette. "I'm not too worried about smoking these things. The additives may get me first."

ERNEST FITZGERALD

Ernest Fitzgerald, whose exposure of a $2 billion overrun on the Air Force C-5A contract earned him the most expensive whistle yet recorded, is more typical than Dr. Verrett of the organizational maverick's life expectancy. Immediately after his testimony before Senator Proxmire's Joint Subcommittee on Economy in Government in November, 1968, Fitzgerald was removed from his tasks of overseeing costs on major weapons programs and reassigned to audit functions on bowling alleys. His civil service tenure was rescinded, and the Pentagon's Office of Special Investigations began a probe into his background. This investigation, under Brigadier General Joseph Capucci, resulted in a thick file of unfavorable comment from informers identified only as T1, T2, T3, and T4. (One of these said that Fitzgerald's old Rambler marked him as a "penny-pincher.") Jack Anderson ran a special report attacking the Capucci file in December, 1969, but it was not widely seen in Washington because *The Washington Post* refused to print it. Meanwhile, Fitzgerald contracted a normal case of foul organizational halitosis, with the result that his fellow employees talked a lot about him but not to him. "I just wasn't invited to meetings anymore," he says. "Isolation is the standard treatment. I can't think of anything that was invented just for me. Maybe a half dozen of my close friends kept up contact, but their careers haven't gone anywhere either. Everything changed very quickly."

About a year after his first testimony on the C-5A, Fitzgerald's office underwent a reorganization and his job was abolished. Air Force officials defended this severance as an "economy move" before the Congress—with straight faces—and they withstood the questioning of incredulous Congressmen who criticized them for focusing their budgetary scissors on Fitzgerald rather than on his disclosures regarding the C-5A. The flap over the dismissal was rough, but the Air Force survived and those who handled the affair were promoted.

While not surprised that the majority of the uniformed Air Force and Lockheed personnel despised his deeds, Fitzgerald was a bit chagrined at the response of the "defense liberals" and leftover whiz kids.

"The liberal people in the Pentagon said that excess costs came from a deliberate policy of achieving goals other than efficiency," continued Fitzgerald. "They said it was all a welfare push based on humanism and reordered national priorities and that such things had to be sold to Congress disguised as weapons systems. Those goals are all right with me, but I don't think social reform should be accomplished by constructing a vast middle-class WPA through the Pentagon. Nor should you do it with concealment and lying before Congress."

One former high Air Force official reflected the disenchantment with Fitzgerald's methods. "I think the sense of annoyance with Fitzgerald really came from the complexity of the C-5A issue. His charges were so blunt that his motives were called into question. I'm not suggesting that he was wrong, but I do think you should make every effort to work things out internally before you blow the sides out of an organization."

Like Dr. Verrett, Fitzgerald's initial decision to speak before Congress was not preceded by lengthy soul-searching. Perhaps he did not foresee the vitality of the Air Force reaction, but the major reason for his relative nonchalance about the decision seems to be his straightforward, somewhat homespun nature. A dedicated wastehater, he told them what he knew when they asked. The tactics of Air Force retaliation—especially the Capucci gumshoes act—hardened his resolve not to back down from the correct figures.

JOHN McGEE

Most whistle-blowers receive treatment in the Fitzgerald mold, but without the notoriety. Take John M. McGee, for example. A middle-level engineer, he went to Bangkok in May, 1967, to monitor the delivery of petroleum, oil, and lubricants (POL) to Thailand and South Vietnam for the Navy Fuel Supply Office. He immediately began complaining to his supervisor, Arlie Rankin, that huge quantities of petroleum were being stolen for a well-organized black market because of a lax and corrupt system of invoice controls. "He told me that every-thing had gone smoothly before I arrived, and that he would have me fired if I caused any trouble," said McGee. "That's when we began to develop personality differences, because I wanted to get an investiga-tion into the whole mess. The delivery system is so big and confusing that even the officials don't really know who's responsible."

Things deteriorated rapidly after McGee wrote the Navy Fuel Supply Office in Washington and requested (without success) that headquarters look into the monitoring system. Supervisor Rankin finally took the highly unorthodox step of ordering McGee to stay out of his office (where the records were kept) and to communicate only in postmarked letters. "It's kind of funny, looking back on it," says McGee, "but at the time I didn't think so. I mean, here were two grown men working closely together on a multi-million dollar operation and playing like little kids. We saw each other every day but business had to be con-ducted by mail, with big postal delays. One week he wrote me 17 letters and I had to reply. Pretty soon I got fed up and complained to him, in a letter, that our communications system was 'gobbledy-gook.' Then he cited me for disrespect in an official letter of reprimand, on the grounds that I had called his correspondence system 'gobbledy-gook.' "

This document, known as the "gobbledy-gook reprimand," was ap-pealed up through the NFSO personnel command, but the appeal was not acted upon. McGee appealed through grievance channels to the Commanding Officer of the NFSO, Captain Richard Jones, for an inves-tigation of the POL system and was turned down. He then asked for an investigation by the Air Force Office of Special Investigations, which did probe the matter but classified its report and filed it away. He then wrote for help from the Civil Service Commission, which declined and termed the matter a "personality disagreement" after consulting—in standard procedure—McGee's supervisor. Finally, McGee received a personal visit from an authorized representative of the NFSO Com-manding Officer who delivered a "resign or be fired" ultimatum.

"That was the real turning point," recalls McGee. "Resigning would have meant breach of contract, and I would have been required to pay for transporting my family and belongings back to the States—and to reimburse the Navy for sending me over. Getting fired would have meant that I couldn't expect to get another job. I would have had to buckle under and do what they wanted, except that I tape recorded the ultimatum conversation, and the guy really hit the ceiling when I told him because he knew the ultimatum was illegal."

In March, 1968, John McGee, disabled war veteran with a soft coun-try accent, who "just wanted to get to the bottom of this"—blew the whistle by writing a letter to Senator William Proxmire. The Senator demanded an investigation by the General Accounting Office, and a preliminary report showed that 52 per cent of all petroleum deliveries to Thailand (about 5.5 million gallons) had been stolen over a 10-month period in 1967. The situation looked worse in South Vietnam. The GAO released a more complete report on July 28, 1970, which detailed the techniques of theft and the weaknesses of control. Although both the oil companies and the government agencies are required to keep records for inspection, the GAO study was limited and contained no precise estimates of the problem "because of the nonavailability of knowledgeable personnel and of pertinent records pertaining to POL activities in Southeast Asia. . . ." The petroleum thefts were carried on by organized rings of truck drivers and others, who sold the goods on the black market. They did very well. So did the American oil companies, because the government was forced to step up its POL orders to make up for the stolen quantities. Everyone was getting along nicely except the public, a critical but distant party to the arrangement. And the public didn't seem to mind, which is why McGee looked so foolish when he rocked the boat on the taxpayers' behalf.

Having exposed a major scandal against the public interest, John McGee received the whistle-blower's reward and was transferred to Washington, where he was filed away in the bureaucracy. "I didn't have any job or any duties," he said. "I just occupied a desk. I read the *Post* in the morning and the *Daily News* in the afternoon." After more than six months of these tasks, he was again transferred in June, 1969, to a bureaucratic Siberia substitute at Pensacola, Florida. This took place on the direct order of Secretary of the Navy John Chafee, reacting to severe pressure from Senators Proxmire and Montoya. McGee arrived in Pensacola and was assigned to a nonexistent program, which required him only to keep up with correspondence regarding its proposed birth.

"I am still radioactive around here," says McGee. "I have been for more than three years. Once you go outside with criticism, that happens to you. The people down here are afraid that I'll find some small skeletons in their closet. No matter how much I try to explain the circumstances of the petroleum incident, they still think I'm a risk. And most of the people resent me, too. They know that Secretary Chafee put me down here, and they believe that I got my job because of political pull with Senators—that I'm a privileged character. It's no fun, but your skin gets pretty thick after awhile."

John McGee plans to stick it out with the government because he has so many years invested toward retirement and because he can't get a good job recommendation. He is discouraged that his actions and the

GAO reports have not really cleaned up the POL delivery system in Southeast Asia.

Of course, McGee's controversy concerned a relatively major scandal, though small compared to the C-5A, and the GAO reports actually took it to the back pages of some newspapers. Nothing at all is heard about more puny fish. "There is no telling the number of people who get quick medical discharges after they make waves or speak out," says B. B. Bray, staff director and federal employee ombudsman for a House subcommittee. "They get sent to a psychiatrist and then out, or they get reorganized. The personnel people say well he's got a file this thick, which indicates that he has a poor personality, a bad disposition, and that nobody can get along with him.

"Things haven't gotten a bit better in the last 10 years, and maybe worse," he continued. "The system is such that responsibility never gets pinned down to those people who hurt the public. Not only do they fire the complainants, but they get promoted. There is a cancerous element in these things: the agencies are more interested in finding out who complained than in the substance of the complaint. The Pentagon will spend a thousand dollars to cover up a nickel error, and the other departments aren't much better. I've talked to an awful lot of employees who are afraid of becoming another Fitzgerald."

YOU CAN'T GO HOME TO MONTICELLO

Job vulnerability is obviously a critical psychological factor in the mind of a potential whistle-blower, and it will probably become more so as large organizations come to dominate an increasing portion of the nation's employment. The modern jilted employee can no longer return to Monticello or become a self-made husbandman with ease. If he becomes a damaged good, tainted by a reputation as an organizational squealer, he may find so many doors locked that a drop in station or a change in profession will be required for grocery money.

And the organization's position makes some sense, too. The bosses don't really like to be lectured by a middle-level technocrat, for it wounds their pride and jars their sense of place on the great chain of being. Also, a certain amount of cohesion does seem necessary to operate a large organization. But most important, the disloyal employee can hurt the collective interest of the organization by damaging its *image*, the public face on which an appropriation usually depends.

There is little doubt that organizations will continue to react hostilely to blowers of the whistle—or that the employee will continue to have difficulty finding alternative work. The legal rights of the jobholder are meager in this regard, since the courts generally hold that employees are not protected for public utterances which impair the "special relationship" in the office or which promote "disharmony and inefficiency." Basically this means that the employee may not make remarks which injure the atmosphere at work. This is a broad area of course, but the courts have interpreted it to mean that employee's criticism becomes less protected as it concerns matters closer to his job responsibilities. The whistle-blower will be the last to be afforded license on this scale, because he flies right into the eye of the storm.

Beyond the question of vulnerability is the question of *effectiveness,* an idea which is especially inhibitive upon people on the rise in an organization. It is no accident that most whistle-blowers have reached a career plateau—a point at which they can no longer stifle their whistle in the honest hope of attaining a pinnacle some day from which they can *really* clean things up. One of the truly seductive capacities of an organization follows from the young person's conviction that he can do more tomorrow and tomorrow—by which time, of course, he has so much invested and is so dependent that principled impulses are forgotten or dismissed with a sigh. In a fundamental sense, whistle-blowing takes you out of the stream and closes off options.

And the effectiveness trap is woven together with the instinct of group loyalty to produce a powerful psychological block against the whistle. Something deep in the character of decent people revolts at the thought of exposing an employer's failure. It is unseemly. It smacks of muckraking, looking on the negative side, and grandstanding. It is associated with scandal sheets, zealots, and people who oversimplify the world into good and evil without room for the murky truth. All these attitudes are epitomized in the organization man, but they are real. They are so powerful, in fact, that many government employees have fought to the wall and bitten back their consciences without even giving a thought to going public. They are best illustrated by people who have rejected the whistle.

SWALLOWING THE WHISTLE

After the invasion of Cambodia in 1970, word slowly got out around Washington that Anthony Lake, Roger Morris, and William Watts— three top members of Henry Kissinger's National Security Council staff —were leaving the Administration because of basic policy disagreements. There were no press conferences, statements, background conversations, or letters of conscience leaked to the press. The only publicity consisted of a few isolated, "insider" columns—praising the courage of the men for leaving and marveling at the decorum, mutual amicability, and lack of embarrassment with which the separation was accomplished. It was, in short, the way one should resign.

The whistle was spurned for various reasons. William Watts—who, as staff secretary to the Council, sat in on most top-level policy meetings regarding the war—emphasizes the protection of the President's capacity to govern as a reason for reticence. "I have an enormous respect for the office of the President," he said recently, "and I just think that man has got to have enough confidence in his staff so that he doesn't have to worry that they will betray confidences or attack him in the press. Presidents are paranoid enough already. All the problems of running the country converge in that Oval Office, and I believe you should make every effort not to make those problems more difficult. The whole country was about to fall apart after Cambodia anyway, so all we really had was an irresponsible potential to create greater discord. We could have built up some public brownie points with self-serving publicity— and made a lot of money, too. But we would have been playing God with some of the very basics of how the society runs itself.

"Besides, the possibility of our influencing the policy was absolutely minimal," he continued. "If we had been Cabinet members or even sub-Cabinet members, our resignations might have had some impact— but not staff members, no matter how important we like to think we are. Sure, we may have made a slight dent in the public belief that the President is right by virtue of his superior information. We could have said that we had seen almost the same intelligence and could not in conscience support the policy, but that came out in the stories anyway. I never gave more than a passing thought to really going public, having made up my mind about publicity before I took the job."

Watts also spoke of personal loyalty to Henry Kissinger, but this factor was dwelled upon much more by another member of the trio, Roger Morris. "The main reason I did not want to go public was that I have intense admiration and sympathy for Henry," he said. "I think he is head and shoulders above anyone else at that level. He had been kind to us and very open about things. When you've lived with the complications and personalities of a policy, it's hard enough to totally disagree with it—much less make a personal break with friends you disagree with. We were in the anomalous position of being inside the Administration writing statements for Richard Nixon while our wives and friends were out on the Ellipse demonstrating against his policy. And I guess if you can't resign from the Nixon Administration, you can't resign from anything. But making a personal attack out of it is different, because you've seen the reasons and agonizing behind a man's public stance. We were in a position of trust, and I really didn't want to make life harder for Kissinger.

"My main motive in leaving was not to change the policy anyway. If I had wanted to do that, I would have stayed on and fought inside because the chances are that I would have been more effective there. But the price was too high personally to retain that effectiveness, and I really wanted to dissociate myself from the Cambodia decisions."

Watts and Morris are slightly ambivalent about whether whistle-blowing is a selfish act of pure gratification or a principled sacrifice of one's career. On one hand, they tend to see public exposure as a self-serving play for the quick headline, and yet they also recognize that it generally means professional disaster. "If we had gone public, we would have lost our credibility," said Morris, "and that's most of what you have. The foreign policy establishment punishes people whom they consider disloyal. It's more clubby than most others, and the members shun controversial outspoken people almost as if they were Charles Manson."

"I'd look very closely at a guy who walked out of there and shot his mouth off," agreed Watts. "If he did it once, he could do it again. It's really not a good thing to do in the long run."

Going public is taboo for the organization man because it appears self-seeking—far too openly so for a time when aggressive self-effacement is the key to success. This is an increasing dilemma for the whistle-blower, for an effective siren must be sounded so *loudly* to get attention that the ego will appear to have taken over and gone wild. This makes one appear almost like a vote-getting politician, and they are notoriously poor bureaucratic strategists.

Personal loyalties present one of the most genuine, perplexing problems of the whistle-blower. A friend who provides someone with a job and a personal confidence is not easy to denounce in public discourse, where you must be crudely for or against him. These complex human strings kept Jim Boyd paralyzed for seven months between his break with Senator Dodd and his pilfering of the records. And Boyd acknowledges that Dodd could still evoke almost a campaign spirit in him with tales of past experiences. When you understand someone (as Dostoyevsky understood Raskolnikov), with his foibles and weaknesses and jumbled motives for every decision, it's difficult to classify him as a public enemy and act accordingly. Boyd was helped over this threshold by Dodd's malevolence toward him. Kissinger's staff members were not.

The personal loyalty tie may help explain why high-level employees provide so few exposures. The average whistle-blower comes from the middle levels of the bureaucracy—high enough to have an overall picture of some pillage against the public interest (as opposed to the highly specialized or clerical workers below), and yet low enough to escape personal ties with those responsible for policy.

There is yet another unique factor in the decision of the Kissinger staff members: however violent their disagreement with Administration war policy, they did not believe it a *crime* like Dodd's corruption, McGee's petroleum theft, or Pettis' Latin American fraud. "Nixon wasn't getting any kickbacks in Cambodia," said Morris, "and Kissinger certainly wasn't in anybody's pay. It was a disagreement." Whistle-blowing is essentially a conservative action in the sense that you are bringing facts to light which on their face should provoke an adverse public reaction. John McGee was not trying to change people's minds about theft—he was merely exposing a situation that he found self-evidently wrong and harmful to the public. The Kissinger staff members would have played a true political role had they gone public, seeking to persuade people rather than to simply provide evidence.

THE FOG OF RESPONSIBILITY

Actually, this distinction bodes ill for the future of whistle-blowing, because there is scarcely any public folly which more than 50 percent of the citizenry will agree is a crime. Even the cover-up of the C-5A overrun was presented as a policy disagreement, and everything tends to slide on the disagreement side of the scale as relativism prevails. Furthermore, the responsibility question is becoming so diffuse and cloudy that many exposures die a natural death for lack of a clear target. This is true of every case discussed above except for the Boyd whistle, which is clearly off trend. The petroleum scandal, which hung in confusion until the outrage faded away, seems more typical. The resulting lack of effectiveness will no doubt be discouraging to potential followers of John McGee, who will mark both his plight and his lack of impact. The only advantage obtained by this diffusion of responsibility is that private fiefdoms of information tend to break down. Since Ralph Nader exposed the societal effects of corporate decisions, for example, people feel they have more of a right to know what corporations do—and the corporate whistle-blower is no longer a foreign idea. We are all involved, so we all have a right to know.

These complexities explain why the very term "whistle-blower" causes people to blanch in a room of Ivy Leaguers or other sophisticated people. It suggests that facts still explain themselves without needing the interpretive services of a professional task force. It suggests a clear division between right and wrong, with no hedged bets. In short, it seems like a throwback to simpler, bygone days.

This is partly a failure of the language. "Whistle-blowing" was impressed into service when no other phrase could be found that avoided the overtone of treason. The term suffers from the flippant image of its origin: the caricature of the bulbous-cheeked English Bobby wheezing away on his whistle when the maiden cries "stop thief." Daniel Berrigan once complained that the phrase "non-violence" fails to capture the sheer power of the peace philosophy. Similarly, "whistle-blowing" fails to capture the anguish and higher loyalties of the act.

Liberalism appears to be the real villain in this onslaught against the whistle-blower. It invented relativism and the concept of broad social responsibility to soften moralism and harsh individual accountability. And it invented the team player and the group ethic to take some of the evil sting out of social Darwinism. But bedrock conservatism played an equally villainous role by sanctifying the vested interest. All organizations mix these two brews. Businesses are increasingly run by team players—although the leaders do not like this compromise of the self-made man. And more liberal organizations like universities, foundations, and magazines are vested interests by their dependence on dividends, advertising, and taxes—although they like to consider these materialist sources even less than the businessmen enjoy contemplating their friendly cooperative management. So the rise of the organization transcends ideology. As a vested interest, the organization man dislikes the whistle-blower only when the whistle strikes home. As a team player, he dislikes Judas all the time.

This confusion and diffusion and failure certainly promises a hostile environment for the turncoats of the future, and yet there are some hopeful signs. For one thing, whistle-blowers have a good record—not of effectiveness, but of being right. And the situation has not deteriorated so much that people cannot recognize a gross injustice when the loyalists get rewarded for corruption while the mavericks get exiled for being honest. As long as people can read the Boyd story and recognize the potential for sloth in the establishment, there will be support for his courage. Looking at things negatively, there are more opportunities for the whistle because organizations are probably getting worse.

There is also a shifting of values underway—involving a poorer image of the vested interest and a broader loyalty to the public. The 1960s loosened the bonds of the Organization Man and more people are now willing to dissent openly from the policies of their employers. Acting on this broader loyalty usually doesn't pay well (which is why it's a value change), but it can and has produced at least a grunt of response from the government and from corporations.

There are promising variations on the theme—such as the "secret patriot" approach, in which employees plot with public interest groups or with members of the press, who then provide a substitute exposure. And growing numbers of people are first cousins to the whistle-blower

—people who let it be known that their loyalty is to what the organization should be and who are constantly prepared to quit or be fired to uphold that loyalty.

The full-fledged exposure from within, however, will continue to be rare. It will probably still spring from a combination of raw scandal, courage, and odd circumstance like the McGee tape and Font trip to Harvard. And, ultimately, the whistle-blower will still be a very extraordinary person. In the era of team players, that is both his virtue and his curse.

The Revolving Door between Government And the Law Firms

John A. Jenkins

Federal Trade Commissioner Stephen A. Nye was in the job market. A San Francisco antitrust lawyer, Nye was cleaning out his desk at the FTC without any assurance, he told me, that a law firm would take him on. Had there been overtures from other firms? Not yet. It would be wrong to discuss employment with firms that had cases before the Commission. Nye would take a West Coast vacation, then start looking around.

Shortly before Nye left the FTC in 1976, I examined his phone and appointment logs, as well as those of his fellow commissioners. Of the outsiders who were listed as having visited Nye to discuss Commission matters (a perfectly legal practice), the name of Wallace Adair stood out. Adair, an attorney with the Washington law firm of Howrey, Simon, Baker & Murchison, represented Kennecott Copper Corporation, which was under an FTC order to sell off its $1.2-billion Peabody Coal subsidiary. Kennecott had been dragging its feet. It wanted the FTC to reopen the case and amend its divestiture order, and had retained Adair in an effort to achieve that result. Nye sympathized, but the other Commissioners wouldn't budge. Adair had made frequent visits to Nye's office while the case was before the Commission, in order "to make sure my vote was still a sure vote," Nye said at the time. He insisted that Adair had received no special treatment.

Weeks later, after Nye left the FTC, I phoned him at home. "He's not here," said the voice at the other end of the line. "You can reach him at Howrey & Simon. He started there yesterday."

"He's probably in Mr. Adair's office," the law firm's receptionist added cheerfully when I called.

It would be unfair to suggest that Nye's partnership in Howrey, Simon was a quid pro quo for prior favors Nye may have granted the firm; there is no evidence to support that contention. But Nye's is not an isolated case. It happens in almost every government agency. Washington lawyers—be they in government or private practice—are a close-knit group. They are advocates for hire, and their frequent shuttles between public and private practice attest to that fact.

Consider the case of William Ruckelshaus, who was the first director of the Environmental Protection Agency from 1970 to 1973. In 1974, shortly after leaving the government, Ruckelshaus set up his own law firm. "Well over half the firm's initial partners were former EPA officials," said a *New York Times* article, "and at least in the beginning, a substantial number of its clients were those who had problems with the agency." Ruckelshaus' firm (he resigned his practice last year) quietly contacted his old agency 178 times in 1974 and 1975 on behalf of 20 different clients. The *Times* said the largest number of contacts, 37, were made for the Society of the Plastics Industry, a trade association vitally interested in air pollution controls that EPA is considering placing on manufacturers of polyvinyl chloride. The pollution controls that are ultimately imposed on polyvinyl chloride—which is believed to cause cancer at some stages of production—could cost the industry millions of dollars. Weaker controls would be cheaper.

The *Times* account about Ruckelshaus alleged no wrongdoing on his part, or on that of his law firm. It was just another demonstration of the way Washington lawyers gain power from government service, and then use it to their clients' advantage. The very corporations Ruckelshaus regulated when he headed EPA were paying him handsomely to use his considerable influence at the agency on their behalf. For a Washington lawyer, this is simply business as usual. Agency alumni who become Washington lawyers continue to be part of the agency's inner circle, enjoying easy access to their successors in government. Sometimes, it's as if they had never left.

"There is at least one palpable benefit to Washington lawyers who were government officials," writes Mark Green in *The Other Government.* "As a Securities and Exchange Commission lawyer said of a phone call from Manuel ('Manny') Cohen, once SEC Chairman and now a Wilmer, Cutler & Pickering partner: 'You know, I still jump when he calls.'"

"The story is told of the lawyer who enjoyed a three-martini lunch during a hearing before the Interstate Commerce Commission," author Joseph Goulden says in *The Superlawyers.* "When time came for the proceedings to resume, he instinctively sat down in the hearing examiner's chair and gaveled for order. Someone had to remind the poor fellow he had resigned two years previously and belonged at the counsel table on behalf of a trucking firm."

Newton Minow is perhaps best remembered for the "vast wasteland" comment he made about television while serving as Federal Communications Commission chairman. During his 1961 FCC confirmation hearing, a senator asked Minow why he was qualified to become the commission's chairman.

"Two things," he replied. "First, I'm not looking for a job in the communications business; and second, I don't want to be reappointed." Minow later became a Chicago lawyer. He represented ATT.

There is something unsettling about the ease with which lawyers can slip in and out of government. Cynics wonder whether the implicit promise of a lucrative law partnership later on is incentive enough for a government lawyer to do favors for the defense. The United States has more lawyers per capita than any other nation, and as their numbers increase, our trust in them declines. Public mistrust of lawyers breeds mistrust of the regulatory agencies they deal with, and, ultimately, mistrust of the government itself.

Even the lawyers themselves don't trust one another. Washington's hottest legal battle these days isn't taking place in a courtroom. It is being waged within the District of Columbia Bar's Legal Ethics Committee—a group of lawyers whose job is to regulate other lawyers.

Although Congress, the American Bar Association, and the federal agencies have long recognized that conflicts of interest can occur when lawyers switch sides, it is only now, perhaps due in part to a twinge of post-Watergate morality, that the issue is being seriously addressed. The D.C. Bar's ethics committee has been considering adoption of a new conflict-of-interest rule that would prohibit an entire law firm from handling a case if one of the firm's partners worked on it while he was in government. Washington law firms claim they hire so many ex-government types that the blanket disqualification rule would make this city a legal ghost town. Federal agencies, in turn, contend that the

rule would make it impossible to recruit bright new legal talent, because top law school graduates would sign up immediately with private
law firms to avoid the disqualification problem altogether. Together,
law firms and federal agencies have reacted to the D.C. Bar's proposal
like matrons confronting a cockroach. They are flailing away, doing all
they can to kill it.

At the center of this controversy are the means by which the conflicts
of interest that arise when a government attorney departs federal service and joins the other side can be avoided. A lawyer could take with
him a wealth of knowledge about the government cases he's been
prosecuting and use that knowledge against the government, to the
advantage of his clients in private industry. The 1962 federal conflict-of-
interest law clearly prohibits this—it says that a former government
attorney is disqualified from representing anyone else in matters that
he "personally and substantially" worked on while with the government.

But if one lawyer is disqualified, what about the other members of his
firm? The disqualified lawyer could skirt the law by sharing his knowledge with others in the firm still working on the case. Agencies have
sidestepped this sensitive issue by permitting others in the firm to
continue handling a case as long as the disqualified attorney is
"screened" from participation. This means he may not discuss the matter with his colleagues, and he may not share in fees his firm receives
from the case.

It is this screening process that the D.C. Bar's ethics committee is
calling into question. The panel's draft opinion says, essentially, that the
process is a sham—an unenforceable scheme cooked up by lawyers who
want their economic pipelines to the agencies to remain open regardless of the potential for abuse.

"There have been abuses of the screening process, I don't think there
has been any question of that," says Hofstra University Law School
Dean Monroe Freedman, prime mover of the proposal and until recently the ethics committee's chairman. "There isn't a single lawyer in
Washington who will tell you there are not abuses. The abuses are not
of low visibility, they're absolutely invisible. That's the problem. All you
have to do is walk into the next office and close the door, or chat over
lunch, or at somebody's house at dinner time."

Traditionally, lawyers have recognized that when one member of a
law firm is disqualified from working on a case, his other partners are
also disqualified *unless* the opposing party "waives" disqualification
and permits the firm to screen out only the disqualified lawyer. Waivers
are routinely granted in private litigation, and even though the federal
conflict-of-interest law says nothing about the government's preroga-

tive to waive disqualification, agencies regularly do so. But these agencies almost never disclose the standards they apply in deciding whether to permit participation by a former agency attorney or his law firm; only now, in the wake of the D.C. Bar's action, are some beginning to do so. Only a few agencies, like the Federal Trade Commission and the Federal Maritime Commission, have written their clearance regulations into the federal code.

The Justice Department, which handles federal conflict-of-interest prosecutions, lacks published clearance standards. The conflict-of-interest law underlying the agency rules is so loosely administered that Justice has sought to prosecute only six individuals in the past ten years for violating it. Agencies made 40 recommendations for such prosecutions during that period.

Several years ago, a reporter who wanted access to the FTC's clearance records was forced to file a Freedom of Information Act request, wait six months, and then pay hundreds of dollars in "search fees" before the Commission finally produced the records. Once obtained, they showed haphazard and inconsistent application of the clearance rules; in no cases were reasons given for clearance decisions. The resulting series of articles pressured the Commission into making all future clearance decisions public—an action without bureaucratic precedent. Then, as now, the Commission was giving its former employees every benefit of the doubt; rarely were they disqualified from participation in agency proceedings.

A former FTC executive director had asked permission to represent some auto dealers being sued by the Commission, and the Commission had given its approval—even though that same official had responsibility for the lawsuits while at the FTC, and "probably" had seen three confidential memoranda discussing the cases. Commission chairman Lewis Engman wanted the lawyer disqualified. "The Commission has a duty to the public not only to *assure* it of absolute scrupulousness, but to *convince* it of that fact," he wrote. "In effect, the majority is asking the public to believe the Commission on blind faith. They are saying in essence, 'Although the memoranda sent to the official's office are nonpublic, take it from us, those memoranda really are not sensitive.' This is not very convincing to me."

Still later, in a similar case, Engman castigated his colleagues for again siding with a former employee on a close clearance question. "We must put aside our personal beliefs about his actual inside knowledge and view the case instead from the public's perspective. The public has no access to the particular facts of these clearance cases. Unable to read the documents or investigate the employee, the citizen on the outside can look only to the kind of position the employee occupied, and the kind of inside information he was likely to be exposed to in that position, when drawing a conclusion about the propriety of clearance. To prevent that conclusion from being a cynical one, I would adopt a stringent standard. I would deny clearance whenever a former employee acquired, or was in a position where he typically would have acquired, non-public information which either is in fact sensitive or belongs to a class which typically is sensitive." Engman said his standard "may disappoint ten worthy lawyers for every scoundrel it deters," but "the sweep of this basic rule is sensible, if, as I suggest, apparent impropriety is related to the broad issue of government accountability."

Engman's minority view would have relatively few lawyer adherents inside government (and none outside), because officials realize that the clearance decisions they make now will be applied to them later. It's as if the officials had a vested interest in keeping clearance actions secret, and clearance standards purposely vague.

"The screening device, itself, involves a serious conflict of interest," says Monroe Freedman. "It compounds the conflict of interest. Take the situation at the Federal Communications Commission, where Dean Burch's law firm was challenged. He was a former chairman of the FCC. Five commissioners ruled that Dean Burch's law firm should not be disqualified. They simply said Burch should be screened. Every one of those commissioners, for practical purposes, was deciding his own case for next year. And that's the conflict of interest in the screening device. The conflict is compounded by having it decided in the very agency where you're worried there is a conflict."

There is a certain irony to Nicholas Katzenbach's postgovernment employment record. Katzenbach was attorney general during 1965 and 1966, when the Justice Department commenced a major antitrust investigation of IBM. The government filed its lawsuit against the giant corporation in 1969—about the same time Katzenbach became IBM's general counsel. Before he joined IBM, officials of Justice's Antitrust Division, which had developed the lawsuit, provided their former superior with a memorandum stating that a search of the division's files had not disclosed evidence of "any direct decision-making involvement" by Katzenbach in the IBM case. The division's "comfort letter" was unusual, a recent study by the Washington-based Center for Law and Social Policy pointed out, because the expression "direct decision-making involvement" is narrower in scope than the statutory standard for attorney disqualification. The 1962 federal conflict-of-interest law says former government officials are disqualified from cases in which they participated "personally and substantially ... through decision, approval, disapproval, recommendation, the rendering of advice, investigation, or otherwise."

Without having any "direct decision-making involvement" at Justice with regard to the IBM antitrust investigation, Katzenbach could have been advised of it, could have discussed or rendered advice on the case, or could have been completely familiar with it.

A promising attorney actually might pass through the revolving door several times during his career. At the outset, there would be a post-graduate indenture at, say, the Securities and Exchange Commission or the FTC; then a term as a law firm associate. At mid-career, he might move back into the commission as a general counsel or a senior official, later to grab the brass ring—a partnership in a major law firm, with an accompanying six-figure income.

At the Food and Drug Administration, Washington's regulatory Sisyphus, the revolving door turned smoothly for Peter B. Hutt, who was the agency's general counsel from 1971 to 1975. Hutt, a specialist in food and drug law, came to the FDA from Covington & Burling, a law firm generally regarded as among Washington's most prestigious, and one that represents many food and drug companies regulated by the FDA. The appointment raised eyebrows on Capitol Hill. Rep. Benjamin Rosenthal said Hutt "should not be appointed to a job of supervising his former clients. Every decision he makes is under a cloud. It is time that we in Washington say that the in-and-out incestuousness between industry and the regulatory agencies has to end." No one disputed Hutt's expertise in the field; nor has anyone alleged that Hutt carried out his FDA duties with anything less than complete dedication and diligence. The issue was, and continues to be, one of improper appearances. Would C & B clients unfairly benefit from Hutt's FDA work?

In any event, the agency received the value of Hutt's considerable legal expertise in the food and drug field, and Hutt got an insider's perspective on how the FDA operates. Hutt recently returned to C & B, and that has been the cause of still more controversy. His predecessor as FDA general counsel became president of the Institute of Shortening and Edible Oils, and his successor, Richard Merrill, was a University of Virginia professor who also served a stint at C & B. At least one other FDA lawyer recently jumped directly to C & B. ("They have a Divine right," Rep. Robert Drinan said of Covington's special relationship with the FDA.)

A perusal of the richly bound volumes of the *Martindale-Hubbell Law Directory* can tell us a great deal about the Washington lawyers who switch sides. One of the most successful was Mortimer Caplin, Commissoner of Internal Revenue in the Kennedy Administration. The government's number-one tax man set up his own law firm (Caplin and Drysdale) in 1964 to counsel corporate clients on the intricacies of avoiding Uncle Sam's tax bite, and today his firm is the country's most prestigious for tax work. *Martindale-Hubbell* says five of the firm's seven other senior partners left government with, or shortly after, Caplin. In fact, the general counsel's offices at Treasury and IRS must have been severely depleted by the time Caplin got through combing them for law partners.

"Caplin essentially founded a law firm on the basis of his service as a commissioner," said a colleague who didn't want to be identified.

"His is the leading tax firm in the country, and he is their business getter," said another lawyer. "You might as well call the firm 'Former Commissioner of the IRS and Drysdale.' On the other hand, they are *very good.* He set up the firm, so it was hardly a situation where he was looking for a job [while commissioner] among law firms who were practicing before him."

Caplin's successor at IRS was Sheldon S. Cohen. He too set up his own tax law firm when he left IRS in 1969. Three of the firm's four other partners were government tax lawyers who left IRS or Treasury with Cohen, according to *Martindale-Hubbell.*

"It's almost expected" that government tax lawyers will use federal service as a stepping stone to a lucrative private practice," says an experienced tax lawyer who did that himself. "You can't get these people to take the job otherwise. The typical tax attorney is knocking down $100,000 a year in private practice. The way we manage to compensate them [for lower government salaries] is by enabling them to use these jobs as a useful step in their upward mobility. Treasury can offer useful inducements to upward mobility. Tax attorneys are there only to advance their own personal careers. And that's disastrous from the government's point of view."

This frequent turnover can be murderous for the agencies, killing continuity, stalling important programs, and generally making it more difficult for them to fulfill their missions. The turnover problem is so acute at the FTC that a Connecticut consulting firm was called in to recommend a solution. More than 18 per cent of the FTC's 600 attorneys leave the commission each year—and two thirds of them for private law firms. Two thirds of those who leave have been there less than three years. At that rate, the agency must hire 100 extra lawyers each year just to keep fully staffed.

The bold language drafted by the D.C. Bar ethics committee—language imputing a lawyer's disqualification to his entire firm—could bring this interchange to a halt. But proponents of such a broad disqualification standard suffered a serious setback in late 1976, when the committee fell two votes short of the ten needed for the rule's approval.

A tough disqualification rule would also be disastrous for any Washington law firm with a substantial practice before one federal agency. If a firm hired away even one of an agency's lawyers, its partners would risk disqualification, and that would mean a loss of clients. If a firm didn't hire ex-agency lawyers, it might lack anyone with the necessary expertise—or clout—to handle cases before that agency. Again, no clients.

Big firms detected this Catch-22 early, and they have been applying relentless pressure—in a lawyer's gentlemanly way, of course—to scuttle the proposed ethics opinions. "I've never seen anything like it," says Freedman. "It's been astonishing. There has been intensive lobbying on a personal level." Freedman says he knows of two ethics committee members who supported the disqualification rule but who were "feeling so much heat" they were inclined to vote against it. "They acknowledged that they couldn't justify a switch intellectually, but were reacting to the pressure they were getting" from Washington lawyers.

Because those in government and the private bar feel equally threatened by the committee's proposal, they have sometimes joined forces to lobby against it. "A very interesting thing happened," Freedman says. "I had a conversation with Lloyd Cutler [a highly respected Washington lawyer who adamantly opposes the disqualification proposal]. He was trying to persuade me to change my mind, and he said, 'Look, you have a meeting coming up. Could I send a representative to be heard on the issue at that meeting?' I said, 'Okay.'

"So at the next meeting, not one but two representatives of Lloyd Cutler showed up—both from the Justice Department, and one was an assistant attorney general of the United States! *When Lloyd Cutler sends a representative, he sends someone from the Justice Department!* That, it seems to me, illustrates the unwholesome relationship—or interrelationship—between the law firms that represent those who are regulated, and the government agencies that do the regulating."

Cutler, who wields as much power as any Washington lawyer, doesn't dispute the essential elements of Freedman's story, although he denies there was anything improper in what he did (Freedman doesn't allege impropriety). Rex Lee, the assistant attorney general (in charge of Justice's Civil Division) that Freedman spoke of, insisted "the views I hold are mine—I have no personal interest in this thing." And the Justice official who accompanied Lee that day called Freedman a "self-appointed vigilante. . . . Who the hell does he think he is?"

What will happen if the ethics committee's disqualification gambit fails? Freedman says, "If the legal ethics committee does not take some responsible position on this—if, for example, the committee were to wash its hands and not meet objections that groups like Common Cause have—the most important next battle is going to be before a committee of Congress. I have had calls from several different committee staff members, expressing concern about the action. Congressional action would trump everything else, and might be the last thing that the opponents want, because that likely would be phrased in criminal terms."

part 5
MAKING BUREAUCRACY RESPONSIVE: PITFALLS AND PRESCRIPTIONS

The old saying that "the road to hell is paved with good intentions" may or may not be true in a theological sense, but it is certainly an occasional fact of political life. As we have seen already, the efforts of reformers to ingrain merit into the federal executive branch have ended up protecting incompetency as well; several programs whose purpose is to distribute benefits to individuals and local governments have engendered bitterness rather than satisfaction; agencies that were created to regulate the activities of private interest groups have promoted and defended their interests instead; and laws that were meant to serve the public interest have quickly infuriated the public. The twin political disasters of our time—Vietnam and Watergate—were fostered in part by people who thought they were serving some higher purpose.

The probability that future political reforms *will* fail is a direct function of our neglect of the reasons why past political reforms *have* failed. One chronic problem is that new laws are often passed hastily, with inadequate consideration of their consequences. As a result, observes one commentator, "the unanticipated consequences of social action are always more important, and usually less agreeable, than the intended consequences." Thomas Redburn's "Open Files: Letting Exxon In" provides a case in point.

Another rueful lesson for reformers is that politics cannot be taken out of government. As Paul Dickson shows in "Delivering the Mail: We Did It Once and We Can Do It Again," the idea that the United States Postal Service can be run like a business—a philosophy now embodied in law—makes more sense in theory than in practice. For one thing, says Dickson, it ignores our history: "One of the complaints the colonists had against the King was a postal service that emphasized profits over service."

Experiences like these make any thoughtful reformer cautious. Nevertheless, one thing seems clear: ours is a political system in which the people, through their elected representatives, are meant to govern— to make their own mistakes and to try to correct them. To the extent that unelected bureaucrats become a privileged and powerful class, the possibility of democratic government is foreclosed. Thus, efforts to reduce "New Class" privileges and trim bureaucratic power would seem to be among the first items on any reform agenda.*

Ironically, just as yesterday's reform can become today's problem, yesterday's problem can become today's solution. Charles Peters, for example, offers "A Kind Word for the Spoils System," that old bugaboo of high school civics classes everywhere. Though Peters does not urge abolition of the civil service method of staffing the federal government (he authored a civil service bill of his own in the West Virginia legislature), he argues that a blend of turnover and tenure would help to make the executive branch both more responsive and more effective. Similarly, Peters maintains in "Why Jimmy Carter Doesn't Hire Jimmy Carters" that new administrations should broaden their talent pool by looking outside the "Northeast Network" as well as in it. These proposals would infuse added doses of both politics and merit into bureaucracy.

In "Impact Aid: Another Fleecing," Howie Kurtz argues that bureaucratic power goes hand in hand with bureaucratic privilege. Thirty years ago, the federal government began giving money for education to school districts that had a high concentration of federal employees. Today those districts tend to be among the richest in the country. But because Congressmen fear alienating the bureaucrats in their constituencies, the program lives on. This should alert reformers to the fact that to change bureaucracy will require changes in Congress, perhaps in the manner suggested by Michael Nelson in "How To Break the Ties that Bind Congress to the Lobbies and Agencies."

*By now, readers will have noticed that many of the articles in earlier sections contain reform proposals as well. In particular, see Michael Nelson's "Bureaucracy: The Biggest Crisis of All" and Jack Gonzales' and John Rothchild's "The Shriver Prescription."

Open Files:
Letting Exxon In

Thomas Redburn

No piece of legislation has ever reached the altar with a richer dowry of good-government approbation than the Freedom of Information Act, known in government circles as the FOIA. It was embraced publicly by nearly every politician with a fervor previously reserved (in the days before population explosion) for celebrations of motherhood. The struggle was long, beginning way back in the late 1950s, when the issue was first raised, to 1966, when John Moss of California forced the first information act through Congress, up to 1974, when a fearless legislative branch overrode President Ford's veto to add new teeth to the FOIA; and at every stage the air was thick with praise. A typical example comes from Ralph Nader's Freedom of Information Clearinghouse: "Information is necessary to determine whether the government is protecting the public interest. Access to such information is the lifeblood of a democracy, and if it does not flow to the citizenry, democracy withers."

If the results of the Freedom of Information Act have not completely lived up to these high sentiments, they have, at least, opened a few little cracks in the edifice of government operations. Nader and his own associates have used the Act repeatedly to pry documents and data out of recalcitrant agencies and have brought lawsuits which have set precedents in interpreting the law. A handful of newspapers, theoretically among the principal beneficiaries of the law, have bestirred themselves to file requests for information their reporters were denied. Most recently, private citizens have sent their cards and letters streaming into Washington demanding to find out what the FBI and the CIA may be hiding from them in the files.

Yet despite all the good it has done, the Freedom of Information Act has also had consequences rather different from those advertised by its sponsors. Just as freedom of the press is, in Liebling's phrase, guaranteed only to those who own one, freedom of information has been guaranteed mainly to those who can hire high-powered lawyers to Indian-wrestle the government into submission. The mixed results of this well-intentioned act add another small chapter to the majestic saga of the American law. They also suggest that Congress could take a second look at the fine-sounding reform bills it periodically deigns to pass.

After the more restricted, original act was passed in 1966, comparatively few people tried to take advantage of it. Even so, moans went up from bureaucracies all over Washington, as civil servants complained about the crushing burden of the Act. The burden most often mentioned was that imposed by over-curious Nader's Raiders and other public-interest zealots, who were bogging down the government with limitless requests for secret information. Thousands of man-hours were invested in the fight to determine whether the most innocuous government memo should be classified confidential or not. Agencies resorted to a variety of backhanded methods in an attempt to keep the public-interest people away from the government's hoards of data. They grew ever more creative in interpreting the several categories of "exemptions" which, under the provisions of the 1966 Act, permitted certain kinds of information to remain secret. The bureaucrats' intransigence on this point was part of the reason the 1974 amendments, which greatly limited the exemptions, sailed through the Congress.

But as soon as these new amendments went into effect, the moans arose anew, this time primarily for a different reason. The tales of terrible burdens were there again; it seemed that hundreds of overworked civil servants were nailed to their desks as they coped with the FOIA crisis. This time, however, the burden was imposed not by the insatiable Naderites but by Washington's large law firms and the corporations they represent. Fairly trampling down the few public-interest representatives, the hand-maidens of the nation's concentrations of economic power rushed to take advantage of a new twist in the government-business game.

There are several types of requests, with different effects. One category of requests comes from corporations trying to discover the trade secrets of their competitors. These have been especially prevalent at the Food and Drug Administration, which, because it must approve applications for new drugs and food additives, has enormous amounts of secret commercial information in its possession. The chairman of the FDA, Alexander Schmidt, announced in June that eight out of ten requests coming into his agency were from corporations—and a great number of these, apparently, from companies trying to find out what their competitors were up to. Theoretically they will not find out, for the Act contains a provision exempting trade secrets and confidential financial data from public disclosure. But this provision has not kept companies from trying. One reason they consider the effort worthwhile is that a new provision of the law requires the government to decide within ten days after a request is made whether it will release the information or withhold it. Hopeful that, in the rush to answer a complicated information request within a limited time, a secret will slip out by mistake, the corporations have inundated the courts with lawsuits. "What's wrong with that?" asks Mark Green of the Corporate Accountability Research Group. "We think that if companies are going after each other's secrets, it can only enhance competition."

It is in another of its effects that the Act has more profoundly backfired, and that has happened when the corporations take on the government rather than squabble among themselves. The most dramatic illustration has occurred at the Federal Trade Commission, which, like the FDA, is uniquely susceptible to this kind of suit. Under its recently invigorated management, the FTC has become one of the tougher regulatory agencies (considering the competition, this, of course, is modest praise). It spends most of its time conducting investigations of various industries, and many of these investigations lead to lawsuits and complaints.

Soon after the new provisions went into effect in February 1975, officials at the FTC began to realize that they were receiving an unusual number of requests for information under the FOIA. Moreover, the requests were not at all what was expected. In 1968, the FTC itself had been the target of the original Nader's Raiders project and was constantly coping with public interest requests. Now the flood came not from the FTC's critics, but from the corporations.

In the old days, the FTC would conduct its investigations in secret; then if it did file a suit against a company, the company's lawyers were required to use the time-consuming and elaborate legal process of "discovery" to find out what goods the FTC had on them. Within the corporate world, someone quickly figured out that the FOIA could serve as a shortcut to discovery, and many companies filed requests in an effort to find out how far the government investigators had gone. Exxon, for example, filed a FOIA case to learn about the FTC's study of vertical integration in the oil industry. The Washington law firm of Covington and Burling made sure to cover every base by filing a blanket FOIA request on all the cases its corporate clients had pending before the FTC. Several other lawyers who were interviewed said that they had not yet used this quickie discovery method, but would not hesitate to if the circumstances were right.

RELIEF FROM THE COURT

The overall results haven't exactly turned upside down the history of the government's relationship to its supplicants. Of the 91 cases in early 1975 in which the FTC decided to turn over the requested information, ten came from public interest groups, reporters, newspapers, and the like. All the rest were from corporations and their legal counsel. To name just a few: Kirkland and Ellis asking for documents concerning their client, Polaroid; the American Association of Advertising Agencies requesting a 1971 study on the relationship between advertising and drug abuse; a request from a number of law firms for the files on an investigation of the plastics industry.

In 1975, the Supreme Court stepped into the arena to offer a bit of relief for the FTC. On April 28 the Court ruled that government officials faced with FOIA requests can exercise a degree of discretion that might thwart the "discovery" ruse. In *NLRB v. Sears, Roebuck,* the Court said that agencies henceforth could distinguish between "pre-decision" material, the sort of evidence on which a lawsuit might later be based, and "post-decision" material, the files illuminating why the government chose a certain course of action. Under the law, the "post-decision" documents must generally be made public; but the agencies may use the "pre-decision" classification to prevent the targets of an investigation from sabotaging it. That, at least, is the feeling of people now working with the law, most of whom admit that the effect of the FOIA will not be clear until the substantial amount of litigation now under way is decided one way or another.

FRAUDULENT FAIRNESS

Like the campaign reform laws, which were supposed to make politics clean but in many cases made it harder to knock off incumbents, the well-intentioned Freedom of Information Act illustrates some of the difficulties of proposing simple answers to the more complicated questions about the balance of power between industry and government, and citizen and state. In the short run, the one clear beneficiary of the system is the legal profession, which has a whole new category of litigation opened up to it. With the law schools producing thousands of extra lawyers each year, the profession may well be greeting the muddled language of many reform laws with the same sense of relief and pleasure medieval scholars must have felt toward the ambiguities of the Bible.

In the longer run, the Freedom of Information Act illustrates the difficulty of trying to redress the balance of legal power without altering the spurious "fairness" of the adversary system of justice. It is, of course, only "fair" that Exxon and its brothers should be able to take advantage of the Act, just as it is "fair" that John Connally should have been able to hire Edward Bennett Williams to get him off the hook. This is the glorious impartiality of the American legal system, which says that any man who can afford to hire Edward Bennett Williams will get a good defense—and that a few lucky indigents, who happen to have one of the good public defenders assigned to them, will have a chance, too. So it is with the Freedom of Information Act: anyone who can afford to have his Washington powerhouse law firm breathing down the FTC's neck, or who happens to work for Ralph Nader, will have a wonderful chance of having his "freedom of information" recognized. As for the rest of us . ... well, it often does not seem worth the bother.

Laws like the Freedom of Information Act are undoubtedly steps in the right direction; the fact that large economic powers benefit by them should not necessarily reduce their value to the people who originally sponsored them. But the recent experience with the Act suggests that the next time we're ready to "open up the government" or "give some power to the little guy," the first priority might be to find an escape route from the trap of adversary justice.

Delivering the Mail: We Did It Once and We Can Do It Again

Paul Dickson

The major precedent for our sad and ever so unpopular Postal Service is one that dates back before 1776. At that time one of the complaints the colonists had against the King was a postal system that emphasized profits over service. Dissatisfaction with that business-like operation was, as many historians have stated, just the kind of thing that led to independence. "Instinctively, [the colonists] believed in postal service," one of these historians has remarked, "not postal profits."

This is not the beginning of a "Bicentennial Minute," but a recollection of the policy of a service-first post office which lasted five years short of a full 200. The policy ended in 1971 when a "business-like" postal corporation was created to make the system pay for itself.

At this moment, nostalgia for the old pre-1971 system is widespread; even the leaders of the tarnished Postal Service admit that things were better a generation ago. The nostalgia has many strains, ranging from those who fondly recall the single-digit first-class stamp, the less-than-a-nickel penny postcard, and the postmark that told you where your letter actually came from (not PA 217, which is postal newspeak for Upper Black Eddy, Pennsylvania) to the business patron who only has to think back a few months to the good old days before once-a-day delivery. But perhaps the most poignant bit of nostalgia is shared by liberals over 35 who recall cherished moments like this:

Conservative: How can you possibly call for the government to get involved in *(fill in the blank)*? You know what'll happen, don't you? They'll screw it up and the only people who'll be served by it are those who run it.

Liberal: But what about the. . . .

Conservative: Besides they'll run out of things to do and start issuing oppressive guidelines and make our lives miserable.

Liberal: OK, but. . . .

Conservative: I know. I know. You're going to tell me about the TVA.

Liberal: Actually all I wanted to do was mention the Post Office.

Conservative: (Loud gulp.)

At this point our liberal went into a devastating discourse about innovation (the first group to put the airplane to practical use, to string telegraph lines between cities, etc.), service, and the growth of commerce, culture, and education fostered by the beloved system which ties the nation together. Above all he praised the efficiency of the postal system as the ultimate proof that government could work.

As Wayne Fuller points out in his book, *The American Mail: Enlarger of the Common Life,* "Those who saw the abuses of unbridled capitalism . . . pointed with pride to the Post Office as an example of the benefits a government-owned business might bring to the people."

Now, both the Liberal and the Conservative huddle together in awe of a quasi-governmental disaster that disproves both the former's notion of effective government ownership and the latter's urge toward business-like self-sufficiency. Both of them seem quite capable of telling and retelling horror stories to underscore how bad it is, but neither is certain about its meaning or solution.

There is more to their mutual unease than simply keeping the first-class letter rate below a quarter or testing different philosophies of government. Postal service is the one thing government provides that comes closest to being universally received and universally useful, the only outward and visible sign of the federal government that the average American comes in contact with every day. It is also one of the most easily comprehendable elements of government, in that it is all but impossible to gloss over or cover up deteriorating service.

For all these reasons, there is clearly more to the past triumphs and present failures of the U.S. Mail than the U.S. Mail. One needs no commission report or poll to conclude that most people's perception of the quality and efficiency of government is directly tied to postal services. This was cause for rejoicing in Washington not that many years ago. Typical were these lines from a 1931 book on postal policy by Rep. Clyde Kelly: "Those who see this institution as a great service enterprise may be sure that it has been one of the mightiest factors in American progress, paying dividends in enlightenment and mutual understanding beyond the power of money to express. It has been the nation's most profitable institution, inspiring fraternity of feeling and community of interest, and furnishing the surest guarantee of the stability and security of the Republic. . . ."

Despite factions in Congress which occasionally toyed with the notion of putting all or part of the system in private hands, the formula of "service first, worry about deficits later" was never significantly challenged, for the simple reason that it was working. By the 1920s there was ample evidence that the policy had worked to the extent that the nation was in proud possession of a system complete with all the postal services that a modern industrialized nation could ask for. Postage was cheap; rural free delivery was bringing service to every corner of the nation; and all the extras—postal savings, money order service, parcel post, airmail, special delivery, and more—were in place.

PATRONAGE AND POSTMASTERS

Here are some of the reasons why it worked: For one thing, the politics that were taken out of the Post Office in the name of reform in 1971 had their dark side, but they were also a major strength of the old system. For instance, even though local postmasterships were assigned by political patronage, they were generally demanding, highly visible jobs which not only spotlighted the person in the job, but also the elected and party officials who got that person the job. Occasionally, the doltish brother-in-law of a congressman or party leader was given the local mail and postal service dukedom, but not often.

Another advantage of the political system was that it virtually guaranteed that management was local and therefore responsive to local needs and especially attuned to take pride in their work. As the old Post Office was being dismembered in favor of the new, old-timers fretted that reform would mean assigning big-city hotshots to run things for a large rural county (or vice versa); these doubters were looked on as unprogressive types harboring outdated notions about "outside" managers.

Ironically, it was the politicians who turned against the political Post Office while others had a higher respect for it. In *The American Mail*, Wayne Fuller wrote, "Politics in the Post Office, like leaven, was the ferment that forced changes in the postal system, made the service responsive to the will of the people, and made the Post Office a mechanism for developing the nation's political system." (By the way, this is not nostalgia speaking. Professor Fuller wrote this in 1972, when hopes for the new corporation were still high.) One clue to why politicians were so willing to jettison politics in this realm may be in the way votes are obtained. Old-style postal patronage gathered few votes and a lot of complaints—compared to well-executed, 30-second spots. For the modern politician, the burden of responsibility for local appointments outweighed the potential benefit.

A more obvious ingredient in the successful recipe was the aforementioned policy of service first, accompanied by a wary eye, but not a phobia, for the postal deficit which has been with us for all but a few of the last 100 years. Save for the few who argued for breaking even, most modern legislators, Postmasters General, and Presidents were quite content with an agency of government which pleased the people and paid back the lion's share—85 per cent to 90 per cent—of its costs in revenues (In 1976, under the new setup it recovered only 78 per cent). Think about that for a while. You as a taxpayer subsidized ten to fifteen per cent when it was a service. Now that it's supposed to be a profit-maker, you pay 22 per cent.

What a lesson for us! As we go forward to take on the task of bureaucratic reform—which is now inescapably necessary, not just for for the Postal Service but for the government as a whole—here are the simple truths we must remember:

1) Government should *serve* the people. This, not profit or anything else, is its primary purpose.

2) That the government will serve the people well is best assured by making it *politically* accountable to the people.

The era of civil service has produced a bureaucracy that is practically immune to the concerns of the public. The postmaster in Cedar Rapids need not fear the wrath of the local citizens if he is a career civil servant. But a congressman who was responsible for the appointment of the inept Cedar Rapids postmaster could have lost the next election

A RACE WITH CATASTROPHE

How did we become so confused that we forgot that what we wanted from the postal system was not profit but service? We wanted the mail delivered. What we're getting is reduced mail delivery, which is producing not profit but more deficit, because poorer service means lower volume.

This is not to say that putting politics and service back into the postal system will necessarily solve all its problems. Obviously the postal system was having difficulties before it became a corporation. But it is important to emphasize that many of those difficulties were unique to the period 1945–70. During those boom years the volume of mail leaped from 37,917,000 pieces to 84,881,000, while a major element of the postal system, the railway mail service, was collapsing along with its sister, passenger service.

By 1966, problems began surfacing. Reports were reaching Washington of snafus all along the line, the most dramatic of which took place in October, when the main post office in Chicago gagged on 10 million pieces of mail and stopped functioning for almost three weeks. Meanwhile, on the fiscal front this was the first year in which the postal deficit reached the billion-dollar mark. This took place during the watch of Lyndon Johnson's Postmaster General Lawrence O'Brien, who took a look at things, made his famous remark about the Post Office being in "a race with catastrophe," and told Johnson that a major reorganization was in order. Johnson, in turn, created the blue-ribbon Commission on Postal Organization under the direction of Frederick Kappel.

The Kappel report was delivered in June 1968 and was clearly negative. The American Post Office was mismanaged, too political, technologically backward, inefficient, and in dire need of new equipment, buildings, and ideas. The report also projected a postal deficit of $15 billion by 1978 unless something was done. Its prime remedial suggestion was that the Post Office was a business and as such should be reorganized as a government corporation which in time would have no deficit.

WINDOW DRESSING

The new corporation took flight on July 1, 1971 when the anachronistic Pony Express symbol gave way to the stylized eagle. For the first 18 months, there was great optimism about the new Postal Service, a mood abetted by the encouraging statistics and announcements of innovations coming from the office of Postmaster General and Board Chairman Winton M. Blount. The press, which had almost universally supported the idea of a new organization during the debate, was primed to listen uncritically as the litany of new departures was presented: a new, fast, and damage-free parcel post service would be in place by 1975 ... routine 24-hour air mail service to Great Britain was just around the corner ... an ombudsman was now in his office ready to accept and rectify patrons' complaints ... top-flight Madison Avenue ad agencies were being signed up to promote the use of air mail and other special services ... all sorts of snazzy consulting firms and think tanks were being brought aboard to help tackle the most vexing problems inherited from the old Post Office.

All this hoopla was followed by a broad series of rate increases, with more to come; and then there was the death of *Look* magazine replete with a post-mortem that in part blamed new rates for the demise. Rep. H. R. Gross and several allies uncovered some cases of flagrant overspending and waste.

The Christmas 1972 mailing was a disaster. Congressmen, who had relinquished most of their power over the Service, were stunned. About all the individual legislator could do was stuff the Congressional *Record* with horror stories. When, for instance, the eight train carloads of mail which contained an emergency mass appeal from CARE for the relief of victims of Nicaragua's Christmas earthquake were lost for nine days, CARE officials maintained that great damage had been done to their urgent campaign. Within a few months no less than a half-dozen separate bills were calling for the abolition of the new organization and a return to the old.

The horror stories have continued to pile up, and what was called the "postal mess" in the late 1960s is now the "postal nightmare" of the 1970s. The only vindicated factions are those who feared the loss of rural post offices and the few who were convinced that creating a break-even postal corporation did not add up to true reform.

The situation is now bleak: a steadily rising deficit, talk of bankruptcy, almost certain cutback to five-days-a-week delivery, the prospect of a 17-cent first-class letter rate by year's end. If anything, most of the touted solutions of the early days of the postal corporation have added to the problem. A few examples tell the tale:

Early retirement schemes cut the payroll to some extent but also weeded out some of the system's best and most experienced hands when they were needed most.

Not long after launching a major ad campaign to sell domestic air mail service, the Service itself discovered that first class was just as quick.

An expensive electronic system designed to monitor the comings and goings of mail delivery trucks has replaced a simple, index-card system that worked.

Postal workers have reported that mail is allowed to stack up for as long as 24 hours in order to get "uniform flow" for new cancelling machines.

A new generation of machines has learned to eat packages and letters.

As *The Washington Post's* Ronald Kessler concluded after a stinging series of reports on the excesses and failures of the new Service, ". . . postal management has shown remarkable consistency. When faced with major decisions, it invariably chooses the wrong course."

BACK TO POLITICS

The big question is where do we take it from here?

The beginnings of the answer are simple enough. Back to politics and service. Not to a system that is solely political. There should be a balance between the continuity of expertise provided by a tenured civil service and the accountability of the political appointee. But the balance has shifted way too far in favor of the former.

Ronald Kessler, in his *Washington Post* series, pointed out a simple but dramatic saving the post office could make:

Many of the Postal Service's problems would be solved if it offered standard-size envelopes with preprinted boxes where mail users would write zip codes, according to Dr. James C. Armstrong, a former postal official who left to become corporate planning manager of American Telephone and Telegraph Co. Armstrong said the Postal Service could encourage the public to use these envelopes by charging lower postage if they are used. The standard-size envelopes and uniform zip codes could easily be read by relatively inexpensive machines, Armstrong said.

There is no reason to believe the public would not accept the use of such envelopes, particularly as an alternative to further deterioration of postal service, as readily as it accepted direct long distance dialing using area codes.

So politics will help, standardization will help, but nothing will help more than a return to service as the primary aim of the post office. When government forgets that its object is to "deliver the mail"— whether it is in the form of an efficient military, an excellent national park system, or a letter on your desk the next day—it's time to remind our elected representatives that *they* at least *are* accountable.

A Kind Word for the Spoils System

Charles Peters

Anyone who has had a reasonable amount of contact with the federal government has encountered people who should be fired. There are, of course, some superb civil servants—maybe ten per cent of the total —who have every right to become indignant at blanket criticism of government workers. There are another 50 to 60 per cent who range from adequate to good. Unfortunately, that leaves 30 or 40 per cent in the range downward from marginal to outright incompetent.

Yet fewer than one per cent are fired each year. This is because 93 per cent are under some form of civil service and are therefore virtually impossible to fire. We once reported, for example, the story of an employee of the Internal Revenue Service whose discharge was overturned even though he had repeatedly reported for work dead drunk. His union successfully contended that the IRS should have established programs to detect and treat alcoholism among its employees. With that kind of thing the likely product of a series of hearings and appeals that could last for years, it is the rare administrator who will attempt to fire anyone.

Imagine yourself a supervisor with an employee who does nothing all day but read the paper and take coffee breaks. Thinking of firing him, you might turn to Title 5 of the U.S. Code and peruse parts 752.101 through 752.402 and 772.101 through 772.404, which describe one hearing and appeal right after another. By the time you reached the end of 772.404, you'd say the hell with it and toss him the sports section.

Something has to be done. You can't reform the government without having the power to choose the people who work within it.

UP FROM CIVIL SERVICE

I came to this position after a long journey through government that I began on the other side of the civil service question.

In the late 1950s, while working on the staff of the West Virginia legislature, I drafted a bill designed to transform a patronage-ridden personnel system into a civil service based on merit and offering genuine career protection for state employees. Wanting to get that bill enacted into law was one of the reasons I ran for the legislature in the next election, and it was a proud day in my life when the bill, bearing my name, was passed in the following session.

Then I came to Washington. Having seen the evils of too much political patronage, I was now exposed to the evils of too much civil service. The terrible disruption of continuity that came from massive personnel changes following each election in West Virginia was offset in Washington by the excessive defensiveness and caution of civil servants primarily devoted to the protection of the institution for which they worked. If you can be fired only if your job is abolished—as is practically the case with a civil servant—then your only fear is that your agency will be diminished in size in a way that might threaten your job. Furthermore, the civil servant is not accountable to the public he is supposed to be serving. If an Elizabeth Ray is found on Capitol Hill, the Congress, which has no civil service, can fire her and the electorate can unseat Wayne Hays. But what can we do if they both work at HUD or HEW? Finally, the civil service takes two million people out of what it is fashionable to call the political process. (It used to be called just plain "politics," and the fact that, when we want it to sound good, we have to dress it up as "political process" is a sign of the depths of regard to which politics has sunk, about which more later.) Whatever you call it, it's quite a loss. Remember, 200,000 of them are superb people, and the Hatch Act forbids their making their political views known to us.*

It is widely assumed, on the other hand, that a political patronage system will result in unqualified people, not selected on merit, making decisions for partisan political reasons. Let's take a look at this assumption.

Why do political employees have to be unqualified? You can require by law that a politically appointed secretary be able to type 50 words a minute, just like the civil service appointee. As for selection on pure merit from all the applicants, that is not done now in the civil service. As Ann Pincus pointed out in "How to Get A Government Job," the

---

*We could eliminate the Hatch Act, of course, but that would give the civil servants the political power to make their jobs even more invulnerable to politics.

present civil service is a patronage machine that instead of being run on a political basis is run on the basis of friendship. You can get a civil service job by knowing someone who is in the agency where you want to work. He gives you an advance tip on the opening, writes a job description tailored to fit your experience, and then requests your name from the Civil Service Commission. Isn't it possible that a job might be filled better by politicians who are interested in putting together an administration that will do a good enough job to get them reelected? The same principle applies to most other decisions. Why shouldn't they be made on a partisan basis if the motive behind them is doing a good enough job to be reelected?

The only real advantage I have seen to the career civil servant is continuity. When I worked at the Peace Corps in the 1960s, we had a five-year limit on employment. The result was the stimulation offered by a steady infusion of new blood and a much more adventurous group of employees than are attracted by the security of the civil service tenure. There was, however, the same lack of continuity I had seen in West Virginia. By the time I left, staff meetings had taken on the character of a series of broken records, as I heard problems discussed again and again as if they were brand new and the agency had no experience to suggest their solutions.

There is one other reason for not doing away with civil service tenure completely. It's that, occasionally, unwise or corrupt political decisions may threaten institutions like federal agencies, thus making it in the self-preservative interest of the civil servants who work in them to blow the whistle on whatever wrongdoing is going on. The role of the FBI and the CIA during the Watergate scandals shows how crucially important the loyalty of the civil servant to his institution can be. When people in the White House wanted to contain the investigation, it was the civil servants who rebelled, who blew the whistle, who leaked to the press. Indeed, the Watergate stories of the FBI and the CIA illustrate both the good and bad sides of the civil servant's institutional loyalty: an essential if only occasional and self-preservative willingness to stand up to political authority gone wrong, coupled with a mindless and equally self-preservative dedication to covering up his institution's own sins.

So instead of abolishing the civil service, I would urge cutting it by 50 per cent, and filling the remaining half with political appointees who can be fired at any time.

Being able to fire people is important for two reasons: 1) to permit you to hire the people you want and to get rid of those you don't want, and 2) to make it possible for you to attract the kind of risk-takers who are repelled by the safe civil service and the political emasculation it entails.

The problem with achieving all this is that for years Americans have been brainwashed by textbooks that make politics sound bad and civil service sound shiny clean. I suspect it all began when the Italian and Irish immigrants took over the elective offices in Boston and the Wasps had to figure out how to salvage something for themselves. "Politicians are inept, partisan, crooked; we are able, objective and virtuous," was their refrain, and it sounded good to their friends across the Charles at Harvard, who then put it into their textbooks from whence the doctrine spread across the land. Whatever its origin, the idea that politics and politicians are bad is now ingrained in many Americans. Not long ago a governor of my state, trying to appeal to this feeling, said of himself, "I am not a politician, I am a statesman."

We have an idiotic regard for people who are "above" politics. James Forrestal, then Secretary of Defense and one of countless possible examples, was praised by *The New York Times* for being above politics when he didn't support Truman in 1948. He and the *Times* were astounded when Truman fired him. Forrestal was a Coriolanus. For him being above politics really meant being above the mob.

We have too many Forrestals now, and what they don't understand is that being above the mob means being above the practice of democratic politics. They, and a good many of the rest of us, have forgotten that democratic politics is supposed to be the way we determine who governs this country. My colleague James Fallows recently wrote in the *Texas Monthly* that we need "the politicians, whose job is openly to ask other people for support. They can't be shy or coy or proud about it: they have to try to persuade. . . . You can't last long in such a calling if you close your ears to those who disagree; in order to persuade, you must first understand.

"On the other extreme, we have those who never have to persuade anyone of anything—or at least not very often. The exalted physician is the classic example. However kind he may be, people come to him only as supplicants, and he speaks to them with the voice of resonant authority. Professors, writers, and others of the ilk are in the same boat. They don't have to *listen* to the other side because they can pronounce rather than persuade. There are 'politics' in these professions, no doubt —but the politics is usually such a seamy, backstairs business that no one can treat it respectably. In-house politics is a dirty little game in most professional worlds; consequently anyone who actually makes his living this way can hardly merit respect. If you are really good, the thinking goes, you won't have to scramble; people will come to you with offers. This is why the intellectual community was so delighted by Walter

Mondale's withdrawal from the presidential race. By pulling out he said, in effect, that anyone who is willing to run for President doesn't deserve the job. Oh joyous confirmation of all existing prejudice! We happy, enlightened few deserve to run the country—but of course we won't demean ourselves to try."

There is no better illustration of this attitude and its currency among conservatives and liberals alike than the recent Supreme Court case of *Elrod v. Burns,* in which Justices Brennan, Marshall, White, Stewart, and Blackmun joined in ruling that a newly elected Democratic sheriff could not fire Republican political appointees from the previous administration. Firing the appointees would violate their First Amendment rights, the Court ruled, because dismissal would punish them for having exercised those rights when they supported the losing Republican candidate for sheriff.

This is outrageous reasoning. Are the learned judges going to contend that my First Amendment rights are threatened when I run for office and am defeated? Of course not.

But is my freedom of political belief any less threatened if I run for election and lose my elected job when I'm defeated than if I support a candidate and lose my appointed job when he's defeated?

Political freedom is the freedom to run for office, to support others who run for office, and to win or lose as the electorate may decide. But the *Elrod* case says that everyone who had a political job on the day it was decided will now keep it for life. There is now no freedom for those who want to gain office by supporting other candidatees who might convince the electorate they could do a better job—and who would do a better job if they could take their own team into office with them.

The Court excluded policy-making jobs from its ruling, arguing that that omission alone would be sufficient to keep the system responsive to the electorate.

What the Court forgets is that, if the government is to work, policy implementation is just as important as policy making. No matter how wise the chief, he has to have the right Indians to transform his ideas into action, to get the job done.

Why Jimmy Carter Doesn't Hire Jimmy Carters

Charles Peters

An important point was missed in the criticism of Jimmy Carter's cabinet and sub-cabinet choices. It is that Carter failed to take advantage of his unique knowledge of the able people out there in the part of America that is beyond the Northeast Network—the people from Iowa and Florida and Ohio who worked for him in his long campaign. He had spent almost two years traveling all over the country, getting to know his supporters by spending the night in their homes. I had thought this meant we might at last have a government that took advantage of the vast supply of talented people out in the provinces—the decent, intelligent, imaginative people who did not go to the right schools and had not become part of the Network. I had hoped Carter would realize that there were lots of people out there just like Jimmy Carter and Jody Powell, people who could hope to gain responsible positions in the national government only by participating in politics. They weren't going to be recommended by their fellow IBM or Rockefeller Foundation directors because the only boards they were on were Boise Cement's and Cedar Rapids Electric's.

The trouble with the Network is that most people in it, be they Republican or Democrat, conservative or liberal, don't really believe in democracy. They simply haven't had the experience to support such a belief. If you've gone to private schools and either been an officer or avoided military service, your actual experience with the people is rather slim. When distinguished columnists want to tell us what the people think, they talk to cab drivers, since they are the only ordinary people columnists come in contact with. Network people are elitists. If they can accept the idea that kids as bright as Huck and Tom are born in Hannibal, Missouri every day, they assume those kids will naturally go for a scholarship at Harvard or Yale, go on to live in places like Washington or New York, and become certified Network members.

One of the few sizable Network groups that has some idea of the talent out there is lawyers. A fair number of Washington and New York and Boston lawyers have to get out of the Corridor at one time or another to try a case in the boondocks. Assuming an easy victory is in the offing, they decide to relax and enjoy the trip, only to find—not always, but surprisingly often—some hayseed running rings around them. The truth behind this phenomenon is that while a Harvard Law School class, taken as a whole, is a good cut above a similar class at Ohio State, there will be very little difference between the top ten students at either school. But, while most of the Harvard ten will go to Network cities, most of the Ohio ten will stay in Ohio. They were the kind of people I had hoped Jimmy Carter would identify, but when I asked transition people if they had ever seen a talent search file with a note in it reading "Jimmy met this guy in Dayton and thought he was first-rate, let's find a place for him," the answer was no.

It's really a loss, and not only because there are a lot of people in the rest of America who are just as talented as those in the Network. The people out there also tend to be considerably saner than their Network counterparts. People who stayed in their home town with their family and friends have tempered their ambition with other, countervailing drives, and that tempering process gives them a stability and a range of human contact that are lacking in the people who left home to take a Harvard scholarship and then went on to Washington or New York. It's odd that Carter and his wife seem to see the virtue of having roots for themselves but not in others.

The excuse that is always given for not venturing outside the Network is that even if there are fine people out there, they just lack expertise.

But that concern didn't stop Carter from announcing the appointment of Patricia Roberts Harris as Secretary of Housing and Urban Development.

Expertise. There's absolutely nothing in Patricia Roberts Harris' background to suggest she knows anything about housing or urban development. Her most often cited credentials—ambassador to Luxemburg and dean of the Howard Law School—don't qualify her to do anything. The demands of the first job are such that it was filled satisfactorily by the late Perle Mesta, who achieved recognition as the hostess with the mostest. The Howard job was held by Mrs. Harris for only one month. Usually such short-term employment is not even listed on resumes.

If there is nothing in her background to suggest the expertise that is supposed to be lacking in people from the hinterlands, there is something in that background that demonstrates why it's such a terrible shame not to see fresh faces in Washington.

In January 1971, Mrs. Harris accepted an appointment as a member of the board of directors of the National Bank of Washington. At the time she accepted, she knew the bank was being used to defraud mine workers. Here's how the fraud worked:

The miners' union, the United Mine Workers of America, owned the bank. Income from the bank's dividends paid for the salaries and the expense accounts and the Cadillacs of the union's officials. Much of the bank's income, from which the dividends were paid, came from the miners' pension fund, which was deposited in a non-interest-bearing account. In other words, the pension fund, instead of earning income to pay pensions to aged and disabled miners, was being used to take care of union officials in the style to which they were accustomed.

Fourteen months before Mrs. Harris joined Tony Boyle on the board, Boyle had defeated Jock Yablonski for the presidency of the UMW in an election that was later overturned because of fraud. Ample evidence of that fraud had appeared in newspapers and magazines before Mrs. Harris joined Mr. Boyle at the board table. Mr. Boyle was, of course, later convicted of Yablonski's murder and is now in prison. At the time Mrs. Harris joined the bank board all that was known about the murder was that one of the gunmen was the son-in-law of a union leader who had strong connections with Tony Boyle, and that there was enough evidence on father and son-in-law to indict both of them. But as Edward Bennett Williams always says, as he is pocketing his $100,000 fee, every citizen is entitled to be presumed innocent. So forget about the murder, forget about the fraudulent elections. Just remember the interest-free pension account.

How do we know Mrs. Harris knew about it? We know because we wrote her a letter, pointing out the pension fraud, and asked why she was joining the board. She didn't answer.

Mrs. Harris didn't resign from the board then, and she didn't resign three months later when a federal court found the bank liable to the pensioners for $11,000,000. She finally left the board in December 1971, not because she thought there was anything wrong with the bank but because she had been asked to join the board of Chase Manhattan.

Mrs. Harris was not alone on the National Bank's board during 1971. Here are some of the other directors: Clark Clifford, former Secretary of Defense; True Davis, president of the bank and former ambassador to Switzerland; Crosby Boyd, board chairman of *The Washington Star;* Liz Carpenter, former press secretary to Ladybird Johnson; Elwood R. Quesada, former director of the Federal Aviation Agency.

Now these are typical Washingtonians. Able—remember the job Mrs. Harris did on the Credentials Committee for the 1972 Democratic Convention? Charming—have you ever talked to Mr. Clifford or Mrs. Carpenter? They aren't consciously evil. They don't sit around wondering how best to exploit the masses. But they don't know the masses. They don't get upset at the theft of miners' pensions because they don't know any miners.

What we need in Washington is people who do know miners—miners and farmers and factory workers and small businessmen. We need people who couldn't bear to ignore the problems of their friends or to betray their interests.

This is not to say that there are no scoundrels in the non-Network world. There are plenty. But there are also plenty of good people who know their communities, who lead healthy, involved lives that bring them into contact with all classes, and who, simply because they aren't isolated like Network people, have some chance of caring about ordinary people and their problems.

Impact Aid: Another Fleecing

Howie Kurtz

Washington is full of programs that serve little purpose, and President Carter is constantly proclaiming his deep antipathy for government waste. So it would seem, logically, that this would be a time when the useless activities of the federal government were rapidly falling by the wayside.

That isn't the case, of course. Reforming government is extremely difficult because even the worst program helps somebody, albeit perhaps somebody undeserving. When the beneficiaries of misguided government largesse are politically strong, which they often are, they can usually make sure that the program that helps them stays alive regardless of its merits. Defense contractors keep needless weapons programs going; social workers keep welfare programs a mess; federal employees remain impervious to firing even for gross incompetence.

A classic case in point is a program known formally as School Assistance to Federally Affected Areas, and informally as impact aid. Impact aid was designed to serve a real purpose more than 30 years ago, but now it's largely a form of welfare for the rich. The Carter administration has tried to do away with the program's most unfair aspects, but so far to no avail—the people it helps may be undeserving, but they're very powerful and very reluctant to give up their special little deal. Because impact aid has a constituency, in other words, its survival doesn't depend on whether or not it's a good program.

Impact aid was created with the best of intentions during World War II, to solve a small crisis the war had brought on at home. Hundreds of thousands of military personnel and other government employees were being moved around the country according to the dictates of the war planners in Washington. Communities might have huge influxes of troops taking up temporary residence.

One thing these influxes of people would upset in communities was public school systems. Public schools are usually financed through property taxes; if a military base is built in a school district all of its personnel will send their children to the public schools there, but they won't be paying property taxes. Therefore the school district is saddled with a huge increase in students without any offsetting increase in revenues. No federal government building has to pay property taxes (as private buildings do), and military personnel who live on bases don't own houses and so don't pay property taxes either. This problem is especially severe for the military in wartime, but it's also evident today—for example, in the District of Columbia, where the vast amount of space taken up by tax-free buildings means the schools are woefully underfinanced.

Impact aid is money the government pays to the "impacted" school districts, to make up for this imbalance between students and revenues and to bring the affected schools up to normal financing levels. But there's one catch in the program that makes it almost completely nonsensical today: the aid is parceled out to school districts according to how many government employees live in them, regardless of whether the school districts are being deprived of property tax money. Thus a school district full of federal employees who own homes and pay property taxes still gets impact aid.

So the school districts with the most federal employees get the most impact aid, even though these districts are often among the richest in the country already. Fairfax County, Virginia, a Washington suburb with a median family income of about $28,000, gets more than $13 million a year in impact aid. Prince George's County and Montgomery County, Maryland, both also well-off Washington suburbs, get $10 million and $6 million respectively (1978 figures).

On the other hand, the entire state of Wisconsin, with a median income of about $10,000, gets only $3 million a year. Cleveland collects just $828,000; Milwaukee, $398,000; Buffalo, $350,000; and Jersey City, $263,000.

Every President since Harry Truman has tried to scrap the program, and every year Congress has dug in its heels and refused to go along. This is because impact aid's sponsors, in their wisdom, have seen to it that 400 of the 435 congressional districts receive at least some money from the program. Even in areas that are short-changed, any congressman who dares oppose the program is virtually certain to hear from angry school officials who are counting on their share of the federal money.

The latest effort to reform impact aid is the brainchild of Health, Education and Welfare Secretary Joseph Califano, who has proposed to stop paying impact money to districts where federal employees live but don't work. His reasoning is that a county like Fairfax has many federal employees living in it, but almost all of them pay property taxes. They are likely to work in the District of Columbia, so there aren't many tax-exempt government office buildings in Fairfax either. In short, the number of federal employees living there has no real impact on the local tax money available for Fairfax's public schools, but the schools get a tremendous amount of impact money.

Congress made a half-hearted attempt to deal with this situation in 1974, deciding to phase out aid to the home districts of federal commuters but also to guarantee that each district would receive at least 90 per cent of the money it got the year before. The second provision effectively de-fanged the first. Califano wanted to move much more quickly on taking the commuters out of the program, knocking out a major portion of next year's estimated $823 million in impact aid. With the savings, he said, the government could "meet other educational needs such as those of the handicapped and disadvantaged."

The White House approved Califano's plan, but its opponents were already hard at work trying to kill it. Somebody leaked a copy of the plan to *The Washington Star,* which ran a story that triggered a predictable outcry. Worried school officials started calling their congressmen. Military lobbies like the Retired Officers Association began firing salvos. Within three days, Rep. Herbert Harris, a second-term liberal Democrat from Fairfax County (and, like the other Washington-area congressmen, a skillful saboteur of any bill that might hurt federal employees) got 75 of his colleagues to sign a letter condemning the proposal. The letter warned the administration against "shirking its responsibility for the impact of the federal presence on our local public schools."

As the pressure continued to rise, any congressman who was leaning toward voting with Califano probably decided it was more trouble that it was worth. There is no political benefit in opposing a program that most people have never heard of and much risk of incurring the wrath of its beneficiaries. As Harris says, "the program has a lot of support, because it does reach into so many school districts."

But Califano, who doesn't have to run for reelection this year, didn't buckle under the pressure. He went ahead and proposed a $76 million cut in 1979's impact aid by phasing out the money for federal employees who live in one school district but work in another. The Maryland and Virginia suburbs alone would have lost about $5 million. Califano did try to soften the blow by promising that every district would get 75 per cent of the aid it received in 1978, thus delaying the inevitable for a few years.

Some congressmen are hard pressed to justify the program now that a Democratic administration is calling it unfair. Under the Republicans, they could argue that they were just trying to save some badly needed aid to education from the conservative budget ax. But now that Califano is calling for those funds to help the disadvantaged, liberals have shed the cloak of principle and are fighting for more bucks for the folks back home.

That's unlikely to help Califano much, though. Unless the White House makes a concerted push to cut back impact aid, which seems unlikely, the program will probably stay intact as a simple giveaway to federal employees.

There are suburban counties like Montgomery and Fairfax surrounding every major city in the country. These suburbs have, for the most part, modern, efficient school systems financed by local property taxes and populated largely by white middle-class students. Many of their parents commute to jobs in large cities that have deteriorating schools where discipline takes precedence over education.

Any policy based on reason would have to recognize that schools in Cleveland and Detroit are in far more desperate shape than those in the suburbs of Washington. Why should a steelworker in Buffalo, for instance, pay part of his hard-earned salary for a federal program that hands out $13 million to Fairfax County, Virginia, but only $350,000 to the decaying schools that his own children attend? As Senator William

Proxmire, one of the few politicans who has fought against impact aid in Congress, says, "This simply can't be justified as national policy."

The impact aid system is also unbelievably complex: there are 23 different ways a school district can qualify for various kinds of payments. The computerized printout of how the aid is distributed runs over 300 pages. "It's an incredible morass," says one insider. "It's a ridiculous way to run a program." Perhaps the nicest thing that can be said about impact aid is that it keeps a growing number of bureaucrats off the jobless rolls.

Few would argue that the federal rug should be suddenly pulled out from under school districts that have relied on impact aid for many years. The aid could be phased out over a couple of years while the schools looked for ways to make up the difference. Several studies have shown that most school districts could replace their impact aid with only a slight increase in property taxes; Fairfax County's $13-million grant, for instance, is only five per cent of its total school budget.

The reason Califano and Carter seem unable to get rid of impact aid is, simply, self-interest politics. It's very hard to push anything through Congress that will mean less money for a lot of members' districts—and it's much easier to pass a new program if it offers a little something to a majority of congressmen. A solid bloc of intransigent congressmen can be a bigger obstacle to reform than the most vehement unions and special interest lobbies.

PLAY TO THEIR SELF-INTEREST

One way around this problem is to build enough pressure to overcome it. If the President really pushes a worthy cause like abolishing impact aid, if politicians who remain intransigent are made to look simply greedy, if the press, and in turn the public, overcomes its indifference and becomes aroused, then it's possible to achieve change undiluted by political buyoffs. The survival of a program like impact aid is a testament to congressmen's inclination to vote only in the narrow self-interest of their districts, but with more effort they might be persuaded to do otherwise this time. If Jimmy Carter doesn't make an issue out of impact aid, however, the congressmen will go about their business as usual, the program will survive, and nobody outside of the Washington area will know the difference.

How To Break
the Ties That Bind
Congress to the
Lobbies and Agencies

Michael Nelson

One of the familiar facts of Washington life is the cozy relationship between a lobby and the executive agencies and congressional committees that affect its interests. The Department of Agriculture, the agriculture related committees and subcommittees, and the agribusiness lobby are perhaps the best known such seamless web. Lobbyists give parties where high department officials (both political appointees and civil servants), congressmen, and key members of the congressional staff mingle. They become close friends who help one another stay in Washington in positions of reasonable power, which is the main life goal of most of them. They seldom see any wrong in the relationship: it takes care of them. Unfortunately, it does not take care of the public.

I have a suggestion that will break up these relationships. My point of attack is the congressional committee.

Congressmen generally obtain committee assignments by asking their party leaders for them, and with a little patience, tact and apple-polishing, they can pretty much get the ones they want. Therein lies the rub, for as you might expect, the ones they want are usually those that will put them in the best position to advance the special interests of their particular districts and thus get them reelected. Representatives from union districts shoot for Education and Labor, westerners for Interior, farmers for Agriculture, and so on.

The result is a committee system—and thus a Congress—that operates on the premise that good national policy on agriculture, education, energy, etc., is best made by those who owe their careers to farmers, teachers, oilmen, and other narrow interests. Fortunately, it is a problem that can be solved, and with surprising simplicity.

To begin with, in order to prevent committees from being dominated by those with particular axes to grind, congressmen should be assigned committees not by choice, but literally by chance. Let each party simply place the names of its members of Congress into one hat, the party's committee vacancies into another, and then draw names from hats until everybody has his assignment.

Then, to keep both committees and congressmen from ossification, legislators—including committee chairmen—should be reassigned no less than once every four years. This would dissolve the closed alliances between committees, agencies, and lobbies. Randomly assigned members would less likely be predisposed by personal desire or political interest to support the private pressure groups and government bureaucrats in their committees' policy areas. And the cost of "buying" congressional support with favors or donations would be prohibitive, given the rapid turnover in membership.

Other advantages would follow. Getting reeducated to face new challenges every four years would help cure tired blood in congressmen and Congress alike. With the constraints of seniority gone, new members would have an incentive to develop and introduce fresh ideas. It was, after all, in the 19th century, when the average Congress contained more new members than veterans, that the legislative branch was in fact the "first branch" of government.

The insufferable egotism of committee chairmen would be another unmourned casualty of a system that would turn them out frequently and without prejudice. With seniority no longer a factor, committees could simply elect their chairmen. And the petty jurisdictional jealousies that keep, for example, energy and intelligence policy scattered among a dozen or so committees would disappear if congressmen had no permanent stake in promoting one committee over another.

An important side effect of this change might be that it would make far easier the kind of executive branch reorganization that Jimmy Carter envisions. The hidebound committee structure is now one of the greatest barriers to that reorganization, since committee members' own status and power is so dependent on the continued size, wealth, and power of the agencies they are supposed to be overseeing. Instead of tough regulators of the agencies, the committees often become cheerleaders and salesmen for them.

The main arguments I can foresee against my proposal are that the random selection would deny congressmen the chance to use the expertise they have when they enter Congress and that the four-year limit would deny them the chance to develop any expertise while they're there.

It seems to me that the expertise we need in congressmen has to do with their ability to discover the facts they need to know—the ability to question the experts and draw from them the information they need —and to draft wise laws based on those facts. To the extent that special knowledge is relevant, it can be supplied by a committee staff, half of whom should have long, fixed terms so they can provide for a continuity of expertise and half of whom should have no tenure at all, and provide for periodic injections of new experts with new ideas about the subject involved.

With the present system, there are no tenured members of the committee staffs. Expertise comes from the senior congressmen and those members of the staffs who have been able to keep themselves in good with the senior congressmen. They are almost always willing servants of the affected lobby.

If Jimmy Carter is serious about bringing under control the power of "the political and economic elite" he talked about in his acceptance speech at the Democratic convention, encouraging this simple procedural reform would help him more than anything I can think of.